THE MISSING LINKS IN TEACHER EDUCATION DESIGN

Self Study of Teaching and Teacher Education Practices

Volume 1

THE MISSING LINKS IN TEACHER EDUCATION DESIGN

Developing a Multi-linked Conceptual Framework

Edited by

Garry F. Hoban

University of Wollongong,
NSW, Australia

A C.I.P. Catalogue record for this book is available from the Library of Congress.

ISBN-10 1-4020-3338-9 (HB)
ISBN-10 1-4020-3346-X (e-book)
ISBN-13 978-1-4020-3338-4 (HB)
ISBN-13 978-1-4020-3346-9 (e-book)

Published by Springer,
P.O. Box 17, 3300 AA Dordrecht, The Netherlands.

www.springeronline.com

Cover image by Karl Mutimer from EmLab at the University of Wollongong.

Printed on acid-free paper

Printed in the Netherlands.

DEDICATION

To my mother, Olive, who has always been my inspiration and comfort

Contents

Conclusion

List of Figures and Tables

FIGURES

TABLES

List of Contributors

Peter Aubusson is Associate Professor in Science Teacher Education at University of Technology Sydney where he belongs to the Teacher Learning and Development Research Group (TLD). He was a school science teacher for over ten years during which time he researched his own practice. His current research interests include analogical thinking, teacher professional learning, and investigations with teachers to try 'new' strategies and approaches. His research interest in teacher education began in the early 1990s and his studies include initial and post initial teacher education. Peter proposed using chain links for the cover.

Clive Beck is Professor in the Centre for Teacher Development and the Department of Curriculum, Teaching and Learning at OISE/University of Toronto. He is past-president of the Philosophy of Education Society. He teaches graduate courses on teacher research, teacher development, and school renewal. In the Mid-Town elementary preservice program he teaches social foundations and supervises practice teaching and action research. His books include Educational Philosophy and Theory and Better Schools. His main areas of research are preservice teacher education and social constructivism in teaching and teacher education.

Amanda Berry is a Senior Lecturer in Education at Monash University where she works mainly in the areas of preservice and inservice science teacher education. Amanda's research focus is the self-study of teaching practice, an interest that began during her career as a high school science teacher, before joining Monash University. She has a keen interest in the collaborative learning about teaching that can take place between teacher education colleagues and in the power of modelling in teaching about teaching.

Robert V. Bullough, Jr. is Professor of Teacher Education in the McKay School of Education and Associate Director for Teacher Education Research, Center for the Improvement of Teacher Education and Schooling (CITES), Brigham Young University. He is Emeritus Professor of Educational Studies, University of Utah. His most recent book is *Uncertain Lives: Children of Promise, Teachers of Hope* (New York: Teachers College Press).

Brian Cambourne is an Associate Professor at the University of Wollongong. He has an interest in promoting quality teaching within the Faculty of Education at the university and using alternative approaches to teacher education.

Anthony Clarke is an Associate Professor in the Department of Curriculum Studies at the University of British Columbia where he holds a position as a 'teacher educator' with research interests in self-study, the practicum, and supervision.

Gaalen Erickson is a Professor at the University of British Columbia and Director of the Centre for the Study of Teacher Education.

Linda Farr Darling is an Associate Professor at the University of British Columbia and a key person in their Community of Inquiry in Teacher Education program.

Brian Ferry is Associate Dean Graduate at the University of Wollongong. His research interests are information technology in education and alternative approaches to initial teacher education.

Anne R. Freese is a Professor in the Department of Curriculum Studies at the University of Hawaii. She served as Director of the Master of Education in Teaching (MET) Program and taught in the program for eight years. Her research interests include self-study of teacher education practices, teacher research, reflective practice, and school-university partnerships.

Pam Green is a Ph.D. candidate at the University of Kansas in the Department of Teaching & Leadership, with a concentration in the area of Curriculum & Instruction. She previously taught home economics, and also served as a Child Nutrition Programs Consultant at the Oklahoma State Department of Education.

Mary Lynn Hamilton is an Associate Professor in the Department of Teaching and Leadership at the University of Kansas where her research focuses on teachers' professional knowledge and issues of social justice.

James K. Hampton is the Assistant Professor of Youth Ministry at Asbury Theological Seminary in Wilmore, KY. He is a Ph.D. candidate at the University of Kansas, where his studies have centered on the foundations of education.

Garry F. Hoban is a Senior Lecturer and director in the Faculty of Education at the University of Wollongong, NSW Australia. His research interests include technology enhanced professional learning for inservice teachers and reflective practice for preservice teachers. He is the author of *Teacher Learning for Educational Change: A Systems Thinking Approach* (Open University Press, 2002) and is the editor of this book.

Lisa Hunter is a researcher in the areas of young people, middle years of schooling, embodiment and physical culture, and health and physical education. She holds a joint appointment in the School of Education and School of Human Movement Studies at the University of Queensland, lecturing in the Middle Years of Schooling Teacher Education program.

Fred Korthagen is a Professor of Education at the IVLOS Institute at Utrecht University, the Netherlands. He specializes in the relation between the professional and the personal aspects of teaching. More information about Fred Korthagen and his publications is available on http://www.ivlos.uu.nl/deorganisatie/wiewatwaar/medewerkers/korthagen/6795main.html

Julie Kiggins is a Lecturer in the Faculty of Education at the University of Wollongong. She coordinates an alternative teacher education program called the KBC (Knowledge Building Community-Mentor Program)

Clare Kosnik is Executive Director of the Teachers for a New Era project at Stanford University. Previously, she was Associate Professor in the Department of Curriculum, Teaching and Learning at the Ontario Institute for Studies in Education, University of Toronto, and Director of the Elementary Preservice Program at OISE/UT. Professor Kosnik is currently Chair-Elect of the Self-Study of Teacher Education Practices Special Interest Group of the American Education Research Association. She is co-editing the upcoming Kluwer text: *Making a difference in teacher education through self-study: Studies of personal, professional, and program renewal.*

Vicki Vubler LaBoskey is a Professor of Education at Mills College in Oakland, CA where she co-directs the Teachers for Tomorrow's Schools Credential Program. She received her Ph.D. from Stanford University in Curriculum and Teacher Education. She is President of the California Council on Teacher Education and also Chair of the American Education Research Association's Special Interest Group, Self-Study of Teacher Education Practices. She is one of the four editors of the *International Handbook of Self-Study of Teaching Practice* published by Kluwer in April of 2004.

John Loughran is the Foundation Chair of Curriculum and Professional Practice in the Faculty of Education at Monash University. His research interests include science teacher education, teacher-as-researcher and reflective practice. He is the Past-President of the Self-study of Teacher Education Practices SIG of AERA and is co-editor of the International Handbook of Teaching and Teacher Education Practices (Kluwer).

Diane Mayer's research interests include teacher education, teachers' work, teacher professional learning, and professional standards for teachers. She provided leadership in teacher education in at the University of Queensland and the University of Southern Queensland for fifteen years prior to moving to the University of California at Berkeley in 2004.

Jane Mitchell is a Senior Lecturer in the Faculty of Education at Monash University having previously held positions at the University of Queensland and Charles Sturt University. Her research interests focus on pedagogy and curriculum in teacher education.

Anne M. Phelan is an Associate Professor in the Faculty of Education at the University of British Columbia. Her research interests are teacher education and curriculum studies. She has published in a variety of journals including Teaching and Teacher Education, Studies in Philsophy and Education and Curriculum Inquiry. She is currently leading a study of the initial education of teachers, nurses, physicians and social workers entitled "Discourses of Conflict: A Multidisciplinary Study of Professional Education."

Stefinee Pinnegar is an Associate Professor of teacher education at Brigham Young University. Her work focuses on self-study and teacher education. Her interest in teacher education is the development of practical memory for teaching. In self-study she works on the methodology of self-study and uses it to improve her own practice as a teacher educator.

Margie Ridgeway teaches English, Spanish, ESL, and Special Education at Bert Nash School, at the Atchison Juvenile Correctional Facility in Atchison, KS. She is a Ph.D. candidate at the University of Kansas, with a major in TESOL (teaching English to speakers of other languages) and a minor in Indigenous Nations Studies.

Tom Russell is a Professor in the Faculty of Education of Queen's University, Kingston, Ontario, Canada. His teaching includes secondary science methods, action research and reflective practice, and pre-service practicum supervision, while his research focuses on how individuals learn to teach. He is a co-editor of the *International Handbook of Self-Study of Teaching and Teacher Education Practices* and *Improving Teacher Education Practices through Self-Study.*

Lisa Patel Stevens is a lecturer in the Middle Years of Schooling Teacher Education program at the University of Queensland. Her research interests include digital literacies, the cultural construction of adolescence, and the intersections of language, literacy and culture.

Elizabeth Tudball is a SOSE (Studies of Society and Environment) lecturer in the Faculty of Education, Monash University. Her research interests include Civics and Citizenship, Professional Learning Communities and Teaching and Learning in Social Studies. She is currently working on a 3-year project with the Australia Japan Foundation with Japanese Social Studies teachers.

Series Editor's Foreword

This series in Teacher Education: *Self-study of Teacher Education Practices (S-STEP)* sets out to illustrate a range of approaches to self-study of teaching and teacher education practices and to highlight the importance of teachers and teacher educators taking the lead in reframing and responding to their practice in order to foster genuine educational change. The series will complement the International Handbook of Self-study of Teaching and Teacher Education practices (Loughran, Hamilton, LaBoskey, & Russell, 2004) and create strong examples of self-study that will further define this important field of teaching and research.

As self-study is generally initiated by, and focused on, teachers, teacher educators and the relation to their students (Bullough & Pinnegar, 2001), there is an inevitable necessity to determine whether or not practice is consistent with the evolving ideals and theoretical perspectives espoused by participants. The research is improvement-aimed; participants wish to transform themselves first so that they might be better situated to help transform their students and the institutional and social contexts that surround and constrain them. Hence, self-studies of teacher education practices commonly demonstrate strong links between teaching, learning and program organization (and structure) as a search for enhanced teaching and learning about teaching is pursued. Not surprisingly then, Hoban's notion of *The Missing Links* makes an excellent beginning point to launch the series. In this book, Hoban offers a conceptualization crucial to the "what", "how" and "why" of teacher education programming.

THE MISSING LINKS

As Hoban makes clear in chapter one, the need to develop quality teachers in order to enhance the teaching and learning of students inevitably requires a close scrutiny of the ways in which teachers are educated about teaching and learning. Hoban does not suggest that his conceptualization is the one and only true way to consider the nature of teacher education programs. But, what he does do is draw particular attention to the purpose of teacher education and to remind us of the importance of responding to the complex nature of teaching and learning about teaching.

Hoban illustrates how research consistently concludes that a "conventional" approach to teacher education programming has little influence on the way that student teachers come to view teaching; much less impact their practice. Rather, what he suggests is that instead of focusing on the individual elements of a teacher education program that there is a need to pay much more attention to design. In so doing, he begins to articulate his multi-linked approach to teacher education design argued on the basis of teaching as a complex profession that can be neither taught, nor learnt, simplistically.

The way in which the book is structured then examines in detail each of the four nominated links that together comprise a coherent conceptual framework for teacher education program design. The four links are:

- conceptual links across the university curriculum;
- theory-practice links between school and university settings;
- social-cultural links amongst participants in the program;
- personal links that shape the identity of teacher educators.

Each of the links is illustrated through exemplars derived from studies in "real" teacher education programs where the issues under consideration are analyzed and portrayed in such a way as to build a solid understanding of the link itself. At the end of each section, the studies that have been used to illuminate important aspects of the particular link are then distilled into a coherent whole to more fully display the nature of that link for the reader.

The four links then frame the book as they help to bring to life the separate design features that, when combined, promote coherence in a teacher education program. Importantly, Hoban argues that by focusing on the links rather than the independent elements (that are so often the main area of attention in teacher education programs), that the dynamics of teaching can best be learned. Hence, through his conceptualization, the complexity of teaching and learning about teaching is more fully realized and the value of the knowledge of teacher education practices begins to stand out as crucial to the valuing of teacher education itself.

Although the book is set out in a logical and progressive fashion, this is not to suggest that it needs to be read from cover to cover in a linear fashion. Clearly, an interest in any of the four links is not negated by the need to read all that precedes, or follows, that link. In fact, the studies that combine to instantiate each of the links are, of themselves, interesting and insightful examinations of particular approaches, ideas and practices in teacher education. Thus, each of the chapters can indeed be read as stand alone studies in their own right just as the four links also stand alone as coherent and meaningful on their own. Yet, it is in combination that teacher education design is fully realized and able to be appropriately responded to in a manner commensurate with Hoban's aspirations for the book as a whole.

Because Hoban maintains a strong focus on the individuals within a teacher education program (students, teachers and teacher educators), he (and his chapter authors) constantly remind us of the importance of the "self" and how it is that in educating the "self" that real insights into the complexity of teaching might emerge. Just as Berry (2004) draws attention to the notion of tensions in teaching and learning about teaching that are derived from understanding teaching as problematic, so too Hoban continually draws us back to the complexity of teaching to remind us of the difficulties created when applying simple solutions to intricate problems. And, it is on this basis that perhaps many of the "conventional" teacher education program structures and practices falter and why conceptualizing teacher education through a multi-linked approach is so important.

Hoban is not inherently critical of the good work and fine efforts of so many involved in, and concerned for, the world of teacher education. Rather, what he attempts to do through this book is to create an agenda for meaningful change so that the hopes and aspirations of all involved might be more fully realized.

Currently, it could well be argued, that teacher education reform is hampered by the predominance of a structural approach predicated on making the most of that which already exists; despite the obvious inadequacies. Hoban invites us to see the problem from a different perspective, to reframe (Schön, 1983) the situation and to approach it as one in which dynamic, as opposed to disconnected learning is pre-eminent.

There can be little doubt that by concentrating on Hoban's four main links that genuine program coherence might be achieved. Yet, importantly, it is the social and cultural connections that he is personally drawn to highlight. In binding the links so that a teacher education program coherently holds together, the connections between participants (teacher educators, student teachers and teachers) matters because of the ongoing influence of identity formation. Because social interaction between participants so dramatically impacts on relationships and practice, and if program design is to be dynamic and responsive to the complexity of the profession of teaching, then this link is one that can not be overlooked, or worse, avoided, in program design. Moreso, what Hoban would argue, is that the social and cultural connections need to be strengthened—for if this link is sufficiently tempered, program coherence will more likely be achieved.

In this book Hoban has forged the links that comprise his approach to designing teacher education programs. The scholars he has assembled and charged with explicating particular aspects of his links help to demonstrate the extent to which research in teacher education is advancing. Such advancement is in response to the growing concern of participants for enhanced learning outcomes in teaching and learning about teaching; and is becoming increasingly evident internationally. Not surprisingly then, many of Hoban's chapter authors are themselves leaders in the field of self-study of teacher education practices (*S-STEP*) as their personal involvement in, and concern for, teacher education drives their own research and practice; and the emerging research agenda for teacher education itself.

It seems obvious then that this book, with so much to offer the world of teaching and learning about teaching, is most appropriate to launch a series that is designed to positively challenge the work of teacher education. I have great pleasure in commending this book to you and trust you find it not only interesting and thought provoking but that it becomes a catalyst for the development of coherent teacher education program *re*design in your setting.

Research that influences practice and practice that influences research; that is an agenda worth pursuing. Hoban has offered the invitation, how do you choose to respond?

J. John Loughran

REFERENCES

Berry, A. (2004). Self-study in Teaching about Teaching. In John Loughran, Mary Lynn Hamilton, Vicki LaBoskey & Tom Russell (Eds.), *International Handbook of Self-study of Teaching and Teacher Education Practices.* (pp. 1295–1332). Dordrecht: Kluwer Academic Publishers.

Bullough, R.V. Jr., & Pinnegar, S. (2001). Guidelines for quality in autobiographical forms of self-study research, *Educational Researcher, 30* (3), 13–21.

Feiman-Nemser, S., and Floden, R. (1986). The Cultures of Teaching. In M.C. Wittrock (Ed.), *Handbook of Research on Teaching* (3rd ed., pp. 505–526). New York: Macmillan.

Loughran, J.J., Hamilton, M.L., LaBoskey, V.K., & Russell, T.L. (Eds.) (2004). *The International Handbook of Self-Study of Teaching and Teacher Education Practices (Volumes 1 & 2).* Dordrecht: Kluwer Academic Publishers.

Schön, D.A. (1983). *The reflective practitioner: How professionals think in action.* New York: Basic Books.

Zeichner, K. (1999). The new scholarship in teacher education. *Educational Researcher, 28*(9), 4–15.

Chapter 1

Developing a Multi-linked Conceptual Framework for Teacher Education Design*

Garry F. Hoban
University of Wollongong, Australia

> We teacher educators do need to change, but change is also needed in our work settings, in the way that schools and universities are linked, and in a variety of other arenas. Change in teacher education programming will continue to be superficial and tenuous until the multiple sources of the "problem" of teacher education are recognised and explicitly addressed.
>
> (Tom, 1997, pp. 2–3)

We need quality teachers like no other time in history. At the beginning of the 21st Century, the information technology revolution is well under way, schools are dealing with increasing political, cultural and social diversity, and knowledge is growing exponentially. Teaching is more complex than it has ever been before. We need teachers who are reflective, flexible, technology literate, knowledgeable, imaginative, resourceful, enthusiastic, team players and who are conscious of student differences and ways of learning. In short, we need dynamic teachers who understand the complexity of the profession and can think on multiple levels. Such a teacher is more likely to be produced by a program that portrays this dynamism.

In this book, I do not nominate 'the one best way of educating teachers' for that would be nonsensical. Teacher preparation programs vary according to the goals, course content, beliefs of the teacher educators, students and teachers, as well as the social-cultural contexts of schools involved. However, I do argue that a quality teacher education program needs to be guided by a coherent conceptual framework with interlinked elements. Such a program would help preservice students[1] to build their own knowledge about teaching and to understand its complex nature. The purpose of this book, therefore, is

* This chapter is an adapted version of an article by G. F. Hoban entitled *Seeking Quality in Teacher Education Design: A four dimensional approach* that was published in the Australian Journal of Education (2004), 48(2) (pp. 117–133) and edited by J. J. Loughran. Reproduced by permission of the Australian Council for Educational Research Ltd.

[1] The terms "preservice teachers", "student teachers", "teacher candidates" and "trainee teachers" are used interchangeably throughout this book.

G. Hoban (ed.), The Missing Links in Teacher Education Design, 1–17.

to develop a multi-linked conceptual framework to promote coherence in the design of a teacher education program. However, this book does not promote one particular teacher education design, but rather *how to think* about teacher education design. Many of the ideas have been distilled from educational literature as well as from exemplary teacher education programs in three different countries—Australia, mainland USA, Hawaii, and Canada.

Typically, design usually starts by specifying the elements of a teacher education program and then sometimes moves to considering the links after most of the planning is done. For example, a conventional design process starts with nominating the courses to be taught, puts them in an order and then places the practicum in such a place as to cause minimal disruption. Last of all, the course instructors are selected often based on who is available and they tend to work separately and in isolation to each other. Also, there is often little consideration concerning which teachers will be involved in supervising the preservice teachers on practicum. This thinking is mechanistic—it puts different elements in place first and then perhaps considers the links between them *after* the structure has been designed. The common result is that courses run in isolation with little relationship between the school and university settings. Few structures are provided to support instructors, preservice teachers and teachers who are supposed to be working as a community of practice to share ideas. Such a mechanistic approach is fragmented and promotes an incoherent teacher education program notable for the absence of *links*; it is left to students to make their own connections. It is no wonder that 25% of teachers leave in the first five years of their employment because they cannot cope with the complexity of the profession.

This book flips this conventional approach around. It starts with the links arguing that more thought needs to be put into the initial design of a teacher education program. A design is a plan based on purpose for function. It is common in industry to put a lot of time into the design of a product or process before implementation so why not for teacher education? I believe that a teacher education program should be designed for two purposes:

(i) to help preservice teachers to learn about teaching because a connected program enables them to engage in building their own knowledge; and
(ii) to promote a point of view that teaching is a complex profession influenced by many interconnected factors.

Using a program design to address both of these purposes will be brought together in the last chapter of the book. It therefore seems reasonable to pose the question, "If a coherent teacher education program helps students to make links between the elements why not use the links in the initial planning? This thinking places a priority on establishing multiple links amongst the elements rather than identifying independent elements.

The rest of this chapter is presented in three sections. First, I provide a brief global view of change in teacher education design as a context for the book. Second, different views about the nature of teaching and learning to teach are examined. This includes a discussion about assumptions that underpin conventional teacher education programs as opposed to programs that promote teaching as a complex profession. Third, a multi-linked conceptual framework is proposed to guide the design of a coherent teacher education program. A feature of such a program is the connections between the elements which are the *missing links* and are often not a priority, but an afterthought when designing teacher education programs.

TEACHER EDUCATION: A BRIEF GLOBAL OVERVIEW

As we begin the 21st century, there are many diverse views about the quality of teacher education and what to do about it. Some teachers brand teacher education as "out of touch" (Leef, 2001), some teacher educators view teaching in schools as "bad practice" (Goodlad, 1993), some preservice teachers call their teacher education experiences "inadequate" (Wideen, Mayer-Smith, & Moon, 1998), whilst some researchers (Kennedy, 1991; Scannell, 2002) praise the quality of some programs[2]. Coupled with these different views about teacher education is the looming shortage of teachers, especially for secondary schools, which has begun to emerge in various countries. A recent report in Australia, *Backing Australia's Ability* commissioned by federal Education Minister, Brendan Nelson, noted that up to 25% of teachers leave the profession within the first five years of teaching and by the end of the decade there will be a short fall in Australia of 30,000 teachers (Healy, 2003, p. 3). In light of these looming shortages, it is timely to discuss the quality of teacher education because a "quick fix" political solution is too easy to implement and could result in graduates of any description being placed in front of a class of children.

Different views about the quality of teacher education are reflected in the range of reforms being tried in various countries (Calderhead, 2001). England and Wales led the charge to school-based teacher education with the Education Reform Act of 1988, which legislated 25% of the teacher education budget to schools and encouraged the "cutting of ties" with local educational authorities. One consequence is that preservice teachers now spend two thirds of their time in schools and less time at university (Furlong, 2002). To establish professional standards, the Teacher Training Agency (TTA) was initiated

[2] In this book the term "program" refers to the whole teacher education experience. "Course" and "subject" are used interchangeably to refer to the content usually covered within a one semester teaching unit.

in 1993 and devised a national curriculum for teacher education. The agency produced a list of competencies for preservice students to attain as well as guidelines for managing and financing all courses. A study of this 10-year change in the UK (Furlong, Barton, Miles, Whiting, & Whitty, 2000) showed that the content of teacher education courses at university has become more prescribed and the relationship to experience in schools less connected. According to Furlong (2002), "schools' responsibilities in training programs (and the official discourse now exclusively refers to teacher "training" rather than teacher "education") have been substantially increased" (p. 23).

In Sweden, teacher education has predominantly been located in universities, although there are many different types of arrangements with schools. In New Zealand, the control of teacher education has been devolved to individual providers resulting in a large number of teacher education institutions with a wide array of course options. In Hong Kong, the government formed The Advisory Committee on Teacher Education and Qualifications to devise criterion competencies as a way of having more control over the teacher education curriculum and to assess newly appointed teachers to schools. In Spain, primary teachers complete a 3-year degree but secondary teachers undertake only a few weeks of preservice training beyond their discipline degree. In Russia, secondary teachers train for 5 years but primary teachers only receive two years of training (Calderhead, 2001).

But nowhere is the diversity of views about teacher education more apparent than in the USA. This diversity is highlighted in two opposing movements for reform (Cochran-Smith & Kries, 2001). One movement aims to *professionalize* teacher education by establishing a knowledge base and linking this to standards of teaching to get more consistency in how teachers are educated (NCATE, 2000; National Commission on Teaching, 1996). Supporters of this movement believe that preservice teachers not only need a strong grounding in discipline knowledge, but also need a grounding in aspects of pedagogy as well as an understanding of child and adult development, assessment, evaluation and teaching strategies (Wise & Leibbrand, 2000). A key driver for professionalism and standards has been the National Council for Accreditation of Teacher Education (NCATE) established in 1954 that initially focused on the quality of the curriculum. The growth of the standards movement was propelled in 1983 with the publication of *A Nation at Risk*, which led to three standards movements—in core knowledge for fields of teaching, for student achievement, and for teacher accreditation.

In contrast, an opposing USA movement aims to *deregulate* teacher education by opening the market for any institution to train teachers and leave it to schools to determine quality (Thomas B. Fordham Foundation, 1999a, 1999b, 2001). The growth of this movement is reflected in the 700 unaccredited schools of teacher education that currently exist in the USA (Wise & Leibbrand, 2000). According to Leef (2001), the curriculum of teacher education is out of touch with important aspects of schooling such as teaching reading and mathematics, and instead focuses on "trendy social critiques" centering on social justice issues, ethnicity, gender, sexual orientation and power. He believes that the trouble with teacher education is the "learner-centred progressive theory" promoted in universities by "education theorists with twisted views of schools" (Leef, 2001, p. 38). This movement for deregulation was supported in 2002 by the US Secretary of Education in the *Secretary's Annual Report on Teacher Quality*. The report stated that teachers who had undergone formal teacher education programs were academically weak and under-prepared for teaching whilst, "performance on licensure tests is higher among alternate route teachers than traditionally trained teachers in most states" (p. viii). The report concluded that, "to meet the 'highly qualified' teachers challenge, then, US states will need to streamline their certification system to focus on the few things that really matter: verbal ability, content knowledge, and, as a safety precaution, a background check of new teachers" (p. 40). Darling-Hammond and Youngs (2002) refuted many of these conclusions finding that the Secretary's report lacked empirical data to back its claims and "fail[ed] to meet the Department of Education's own standards for the use of scientifically based research to formulate policy" (p. 13).

In Australia there has also been ongoing debate about the quality of teacher education. Over the past 25 years there have been more than 20 reviews of teacher education with almost no impact. In *Quality Matters Revitalising teaching: Critical Times, critical choices*, Ramsey (2000) found that most teacher education programs in New South Wales undervalued the importance of time spent in schools. The report found that, "compared with other professions, student teachers spend minimal amounts of time in schools and other educational settings. Also, what they do there is often of doubtful value" (p. 10). The report argued that teacher education curricula should have more relevance to schools and in particular the term "practicum" be replaced with "professional experience." Ramsey recommended that time in schools should become the focus of teacher education and that university courses should be more coherent by integrating their subjects:

> It is possible to reorganise the knowledge bases of undergraduate teacher education subjects so that they are more integrated with school and classroom culture, and therefore more relevant, more meaningful, better appreciated by student teachers, with less duplication across subject areas. (Ramsey, 2000, p. 57)

The main recommendation from the report was to establish an "Institute of Teachers" to identify professional standards and a career pathway for teachers in New South Wales which would include responsibility for endorsing and deregistering programs of teacher education. Importantly, the report stated that it was not calling for a common teacher education curriculum; rather it was up to each university to design their own, however, "What matters is the quality of the end product" (Ramsay, 2000, p. 18). But how do designers identify and monitor quality in a teacher education program?

When the variety of reports and initiatives for teacher education reform in different countries are considered, it is clear that there are many viewpoints about what constitutes quality in a teacher education program. In the *Report to the American Council on Education* regarding Models of Teacher Education, Scannell (2002) concluded, "there is no one best format for teacher education programs as programs regarded to be outstanding vary in structure and conceptual formats" (p. 12). However, programs in which the elements are interrelated provide the most connected experiences for preservice teachers. This finding is consistent with research conducted by Kennedy (1991) who found that the structure of a teacher education program was not so important, but the conceptual orientation of thc program and consideration of the beliefs of the preservice teachers were the most important in terms of quality. A clear orientation is assisted by the presence of a conceptual framework that guides the design of a teacher education program. Such a conceptual framework has been highlighted as an indicator of quality by Feiman-Nemser (1990) and Howey (1996) in their relevant chapters on program design in both editions of the *Handbook of Research on Teacher Education.* A major consideration for developing such a framework is an understanding of the nature of teaching and how to best learn about it.

THE NATURE OF TEACHING AND LEARNING TO TEACH

Teacher education programs should prepare teachers for coping with the nature of the work and how to think about it. According to Carter (1990), "how one frames the learning-to-teach question depends a great deal on how one conceives of what is to be learned and how that learning takes place" (p. 307). Fenstermacher (2002) highlighted two views about the nature of teaching and how these relate to views concerning how to learn about it:

> Policy advocates who presuppose that teaching is a relatively simple enterprise are often those whose conception of "education space" is simple, and thus the teaching that navigates this space need not be highly specialized. Those who presuppose that teaching is relatively complex are typically those who perceive education space as tremendously complex and hence see a need for training and specialized competence to navigate it successfully. (p. 21)

Let us examine these two different views and consider implications for the design of teacher education programs.

Teaching as a Craft and Learning to Teach

Research by Wise, Darling-Hammond, McLaughlin, and Bernstein (1984) in 32 US cities concluded that teachers and administrators usually hold one of four conceptions of teaching—as a craft, labour, profession, or art. These four conceptions are ideal forms, but nonetheless do indicate different approaches to teaching. When conceived as a *craft*, teaching is believed to be a repertoire of skills or competencies that accrue over time. Knowledge about these techniques also means having generalised rules for when and how to apply them as, "this view of teaching assumes that general rules for applying specific techniques can be developed and that proper use of the rules combined with knowledge of the techniques will produce the desired outcomes" (Wise et al., 1984, p. 7). Similarly, when conceived as a *labour*, teaching is a set of goals, lesson plans and skills that others have designed and the role of the teacher is to implement them. Both of these conceptions represent a simplistic view of teaching that atomises classroom instruction into technical skills to be 'mastered' over time.

Readers will be familiar with the phrase, "a behaviourist view of learning," that labelled simplistic approaches to children's learning during the 20th century. Similarly, when teaching is viewed as a set of skills and knowledge to be mastered, it could be perceived as a "behaviourist view of learning to teach". Blackwell, Futrell, and Imig (2003) argue that present day schools of education have inherited a paradox that has emerged from the history of learning theories last century:

> This paradox also originated in the early 20th century and has sparked questions about how to prepare teachers and how students learn best. The focus on behaviour—what we can see—as learning, both in industry and in education, gave rise to the teaching and learning paradox. The paradox is created when we expect education to prepare technically savvy critical thinkers in a system largely devoted to mechanistic approaches to teaching and learning. (p. 356)

A consequence of assuming a behaviouristic or mechanistic view of learning to teach is that many programs focus on independent components or elements of teacher education—curriculum and instruction, practicum, foundations of education, educational psychology, assessment, classroom management, special education, technology, evaluation and discipline knowledge. Such an arrangement of courses is still underpinned by a conceptual framework—to provide student teachers with independent knowledge bases about teaching assuming that they will be accumulated and integrated by the learner. This compartmentalized course structure assumes that skills and knowledge about teaching in a classroom can be learned by the accumulation of independent components. Schön (1983, 1987) called this approach of dividing discipline knowledge into sections and delivering it to students, *technical rationality* such that, "professional activity consists of instrumental problem solving made rigorous by the application of scientific theory and technique" (p. 21). This view of knowledge assumes that learning is an "additive process" (Day, 1999) that largely ignores the experiences and knowledge of individuals as well as the social-cultural context of school settings. As such, a conception of teaching as a *craft* complements a view of learning to teach as a process of knowledge-acquisition that can be "transmitted" to preservice students. According to Feiman-Nemser and Buchmann (1989):

> The typical programs of teacher preparation treat learning to teach as an additive process that largely bypasses person and setting. None of these models illuminates the role of prior beliefs or preconceptions in teacher learning. Nor do they take into account the influence of program features, settings, and people as they interact over time. (p. 368)

Other terms used to describe this mechanistic teacher education design is a "transmission model of teacher education" Wideen et al. (1998), an "application-of-theory model" (Korthagen & Russell, 1995), and a "positivist model" (Britzman, 1991). In sum, the design of many teacher education programs is based on a mechanistic conceptual framework that presents discrete skills and knowledge to students in independent courses and is aptly named *teacher training*: "The university provides the theory, methods, and skills; the schools provide the setting in which that knowledge is practiced; and the beginning teacher provides the individual effort to apply the knowledge. In this model, prepositional knowledge has formed the basis of university input." (Wideen et al., 1998, p. 167). A different conception of teaching, however, necessitates an alternative view of learning to teach.

Teaching as a Complex Profession and Learning to Teach

In contrast to a mechanistic or behaviouristic view of teaching as a 'craft' or 'labour' that can be acquired "bit by bit", a conception of teaching as a *profession* or *art* implies that teaching is more than the development of a repertoire of techniques, but also includes personal judgments about when and how strategies should be used. To make an informed judgment means having a theoretical basis for making decisions as well as awareness of the "unpredictable, personalized nature of teaching" (Day, 1999, p. 94). Such a view acknowledges the complex setting of each classroom and accepts that there is no such thing as fail-proof teaching strategies. This means that teaching is more than the delivery of prescribed knowledge using a repertoire of strategies, but is "a dynamic relationship that changes with different students and contexts" (Hoban, 2000, p. 165). In this respect, what a teacher does in a classroom is influenced by the interaction of many elements such as the curriculum, the context, and how students respond to instruction at any one particular time.

This view of the nature of teaching necessitates 'holistic judgement' (Day, 1999) about what, when and how to teach in relation to a particular class. Developing teaching strategies in a teacher education program is still important, but reflecting upon when and how to use them, as well as thinking about reasons for changing them becomes a prime consideration. Accordingly, having a conception of teaching as an art or profession means that teachers need to develop a repertoire of strategies as well as an understanding that their application depends on making judgements about unique contexts and unpredictable classroom moments as, "the teacher must draw upon not only a body of professional knowledge and skill, but also a set of personal resources that are uniquely defined and expressed by the personality of the teacher, and his or her individual and collective interactions with students" (Wise, Darling-Hammond, McLaughlin & Bernstein, 1984, p. 8). Furthermore, aspects of classroom teaching are interrelated. In any one lesson, teachers are expected to deal with many influences simultaneously. This includes the curriculum, the number of children, the range of children's interests and prior knowledge, the resources available, how the lesson connects with previous lessons, different ways in which children learn, any special needs that children have, ways to assess the learning, a theoretical basis for structuring lessons, strategies for behaviour management and consideration of the socio-cultural background of the children. Furthermore, these influences interact creating a dynamic learning environment with many interrelated influences (Biggs, 1993). Hence, teaching is by nature, a complex profession.

Assuming that the nature of teaching is imbued with so many interrelated elements, how should student teachers best learn about it? According to Wideen et al. (1998), who reviewed 93 empirical studies on learning to teach, the design of teacher education programs should not only provide knowledge about teaching, but a dynamic and ecological approach needs to be taken to include the beliefs of preservice teachers as well as providing an infrastructure to support them in learning, "We believe that only when all players and landscapes that comprise the learning-to-teach environment are considered in concert will we gain a full appreciation of the inseparable web of relationships that constitutes the learning-to-teach ecosystem" (p. 170). In support, Kennedy (1991) argued that one-off changes in teacher education (e.g., where to place the practicum) is not the answer. Instead, the key to quality teacher education is to have a coherent conceptual orientation with interrelated elements so that, "the challenge for reformers is to find a way to help teachers in all aspects of teaching, not just the subject matter, not just the pedagogy, but both. And not just separately, but in relationship to one another" (p. 17).

One of the main arguments of this book, therefore, is that a mechanistic conceptual framework that promotes an incoherent teacher education program does not complement the nature of teaching as a complex profession. Moreover, packaging educational knowledge into independent courses is a simplistic approach to learning about teaching. This approach presents the teacher education curriculum as a jigsaw puzzle and leaves it to students to integrate the content so that they have to construct their own 'big picture' of the education landscape. Moreover, this piecemeal approach to teacher education does not embody the dynamics of a real classroom. In contrast, an acceptance of the complex nature of teaching necessitates a more integrated approach to the design of teacher education programs beyond a mechanistic "training" model. If it is assumed that teaching is a complex profession and that schools are diverse cultural and social places, then an "application of knowledge" or "training" approach is inadequate. In a review of studies about learning to teach, Wideen et al. (1998) concluded that change needs to occur in universities *and* schools:

> The focus on the knowledge base of teaching during teacher preparation, as something to be applied during the first year, has limited value for beginning teachers. . . . teacher education reform will continue to be frustrated until there is a fundamental change in the cultures and contexts of schooling that beginning teachers have to encounter. This change would create situations where greater congruity exists between teacher preparation and the schools where beginning teachers begin their teaching careers. (p. 159)

Accepting a view of the nature of teaching as a complex profession necessitates developing a conceptual framework for program design that focuses on the links amongst the elements to help students make connections and build their own knowledge about education. Importantly, such a framework should embody the dynamics of real classrooms and show preservice teachers *how to think* about the complexity of teaching.

A MULTI-LINKED APPROACH TO TEACHER EDUCATION DESIGN

When summarising the literature on teacher education design, Tom (1997) noted that the main misunderstanding about teacher education reform was the one-dimensional nature of problems and hence simplicity of the solutions proposed. He strongly argued that:

> Too many authors, however, continue to believe that the "problem" of teacher education emanates from a single cause or two, such as empty-headed and even anti-intellectual professors of education (Damerell, 1995), an inadequate emphasis on pedagogical and academic knowledge (Tyson, 1994), or the need to base professional study on a particular view of teaching (Fosnot, 1989).... we must resist attempts to reduce teacher education reform to one or two factors. For example, we must recognise that the "problem" of teacher education reform has political and institutional roots, not just intellectual and conceptual ones.... Change in teacher education programming will continue to be superficial and tenuous until the multiple sources of the "problem" of teacher education are recognized and explicitly addressed. (Tom, 1997, pp. 2–3)

His views have been endorsed by research in the USA which showed that effective teacher education programs have a coherent conceptual framework with elements that interrelate to complement the orientation of the program. Scannell (2002), reviewed six 'effective' teacher education programs and found there were many links across the program:

1. A concept of good teaching is apparent in courses and field experiences. The concept is consistent across courses and student experiences; it has a cohesive presence in the program.
2. Theory is taught in the context of practice. Theory includes growth and development, learning theory, and pedagogical content knowledge.
3. Extended field experiences are articulated and sequenced with theory. "Extended" refers to at least 30 weeks; the field experiences are designed to enhance what is studied in college classes and to provide candidates with the opportunity to apply and/or to see theory in action.
4. A well-defined, accepted standard of practice is used to guide coursework and clinical experiences and to evaluate them.
5. School/university partnerships are based on shared beliefs. The cooperating classroom teachers have the disposition and ability to extend and build on what the programs have presented to candidates.
6. Assessment and comprehensive and bonded to instruction, and results of assessment are used to ensure that candidates' learning is applied to real situations. Assessment data are collected from case studies, performance evaluation and the use of portfolios. (p. 9)

The links amongst these six characteristics of effective teacher education programs promote a coherent approach by teachers and teacher educators. Such an alignment of elements results in a more connected experience for preservice teachers which helps them to engage in sustained learning between school and university settings, and, at the same time, portrays the dynamic nature of teaching.

Developing a Multi-Linked Conceptual Framework for Teacher Education Design

Feiman-Nemser (1990) in the first edition of the "Handbook of Research on Teacher Education" used the term *orientation* to refer to a set of ideas about the goals of teaching education noting that a, "conceptual orientation includes a view of teaching and learning and a theory about learning to teach" (p. 220). Similarly, Howey (1996) in the second edition defined a conceptual framework as making, "explicit conceptions of teaching, learning, schooling, and learning to teach" (p. 143). More recently, the US-based National Council for Accreditation in Teacher Education stated that a conceptual framework:

> establishes the shared vision for a unit's efforts in preparing educators to work effectively in P-12 schools. It provides direction for programs, courses, teaching, candidate performance, scholarship, service and unit accountability. The conceptual framework is knowledge-based, articulated, shared, coherent, consistent with the unit and/or institutional mission, and continuously evaluated. (NCATE, 2002, p. 10)

The NCATE prescribes a conceptual framework with six components for teacher education. The first two refer to candidate performance and the next four refer to unit capacity:

(i) candidate knowledge, skills and dispositions about content, pedagogical and professional knowledge to help all students learn;
(ii) program assessment and evaluation to promote accountability and systematic evaluation;
(iii) field experiences and clinical practice to promote university and school partnerships;
(iv) diversity in curriculum experiences to encourage an understanding and appreciation of ethnic, racial, gender, language and religious differences;
(v) faculty qualifications, performance and development to encourage best practice in teacher education and modeling of this practice to candidates; and,
(vi) unit governance and resources to encourage appropriate workload policies, resources and information technology requirements.

To attain NCATE accreditation, faculties of education in the US have to develop a conceptual framework that addresses these six standards and show how it has been modified over time to maintain their accreditation. Importantly, a conceptual framework based on these standards should display a shared vision, coherence and a commitment to diversity, technology and professionalism.

The approach to designing a conceptual framework promoted in this book places more emphasis on the key relationships or *links* amongst the elements of a teacher education program. The two assumptions that underpin this approach are an acceptance of the complex nature of teaching and a view concerning how to best learn about it. Tom (1997) described conventional teacher education programs as "assembly-line courses offered by education professors with specialized training" (p. 4) and identified 10 issues associated with the multi-faceted problem of teacher education:

(i) unclear program goals;
(ii) fragmented courses which lack relevance and coherence;
(iii) incoherence between courses from different faculties;
(iv) discontinuities between university courses and school practice;
(v) unclear career path of teachers and their role in practicum supervision;
(vi) independent department structures in faculties of education that promote a lack of collaboration;
(vii) low status of teacher educators within a faculty of education;
(viii) too many stakeholders involved in teacher education;
(ix) lack of planning for implementing change strategies; and,
(x) vulnerability of teacher education to one-off reforms.

Tom (1997) argued for a multi-faceted approach to address these multi-faceted issues, "unless one concurrently considers normative, structural, personnel, institutional, career, governance and strategic issues, any effort to reform teacher education will be incomplete and therefore deeply at risk" (p. 8). Others also have questioned the traditional dichotomy of preservice teachers learning "theory" at university and "practice" in school settings. According to Korthagen and Kessels (1999), the debate about whether to start with theory or practice is non-sensical, "the polarization that is characteristic of this type of discussion is dangerous as it focuses on the question of whether teacher education should start with theory or practice instead of the more important question of how to integrate the two in such a way that it leads to integration within the teacher." (1999, p. 4). It was Tom's (1997) ideas about multiple issues underpinning the "problem" of teacher education as well as the work of Korthagen (2003) that informed the framework of this book.

The approach that is developed throughout this book is based on two important purposes for teacher education—for students to develop an understanding of the nature of teaching and how to best learn about it. These two aspects are of prime consideration in this book and are manifested in the four key links that underpin the conceptual framework proposed for teacher education design. In particular the sources of these four links evolved from the issues raised by Tom (1997) and Korthagen (2003):

1. conceptual links across the university curriculum to address Tom's (1997) issues (i)–(iii);
2. theory-practice links between school and university settings to address Tom's (1997) issues (iv) and (v);
3. social-cultural links amongst participants in the program to address Tom's (1997) issues (vi)–(x); and,
4. personal links that shape the identity of teacher educators (proposed by Fred Korthagen, Utrecht University, The Netherlands, in his role as discussant at a symposium entitled *Professional Development for Teacher Educators* at the 2003 Annual Meeting of the American Educational Research Association in Chicago).

The four parts of this book target these links and include chapters about existing programs to contribute ideas for addressing them. All of these programs portray a design feature that promotes coherence, so this book attempts to bring together these different features. It does not mean, however, that there is one best framework for teacher education design. Rather, there are many coherent approaches and they evolve with different emphases because of the variety of ways in which these links can be interpreted for a particular context.

CONCLUSION

The rest of this book is written in four parts to complement the four missing links identified in this chapter. Initially these links are treated separately in order to develop an in-depth understanding of them and to distil ideas from the chapters to contribute to each link. The four links are then brought together in the final chapter of this book when the complete multi-linked conceptual framework is presented. The chapters in the first three parts of the book describe exemplary teacher education programs to contribute ideas to the designated link. Although a program may offer ideas for multiple links, each author was asked to focus on one of the four. Hence, the chapters for the first three parts of the book are presented in three sections:

1. Context of the teacher education program (any national, state or political influences)
2. Structure of the teacher education program (overall structure or design)
3. Focus on one of the four links (to provide ideas for the particular link)

The two chapters in the last and fourth part of the book are different because they are not about a particular program; rather, they focus on links that shape the identity of participants in the program. These two chapters address the often unspoken issues surrounding identify formation of teachers, teacher educators and preservice students.

The four parts of this book each have an introduction to present the main ideas explained in the subsequent chapters. In Parts 2, 3 and 4, the ideas from previous chapters are represented in a diagram that is the emerging conceptual framework developed throughout the book. It should be emphasized, however, that none of the main four links of teacher education design proposed—conceptual links, theory-practice links, social-cultural links and personal links—are mutually exclusive. Many teacher education programs have these links present to different extents, but they are not made explicit in their conceptual framework or are prime considerations in the design process. However, when these four links are considered in conjunction at the planning stages of a teacher education program, I argue there is more chance that the program will be coherent and therefore more likely to improve the quality of the learning experiences of the preservice students.

REFERENCES

Biggs, J. (1993). From theory to practice: A cognitive systems approach. *Higher Education Research and Development, 12*(1), 73–85.

Blackwell, P., Futrell, M., & Imig, D. (2003). Burnt water paradoxes of schools of education. *Phi Delta Kappan, 84*(5), 356–361.

Britzman, D. P. (1991). *Practice makes practice.* New York: State University of New York Press.

Calderhead, J. (2001). International Experiences of Teaching Reform. In V. Richardson (Ed.), *Handbook of Research on Teaching* (Fourth Edition ed.) (pp. 777–800). Washington: American Educational Research Association.

Carter, C. (1990). Teacher's knowledge and learning to teach. In W. R. Houston (Ed.), *Handbook of research on learning to teach* (pp. 291–310). New York: Macmillan.

Cochran-Smith, M., & Kries, M. K. (2001). Sticks, stones and ideology: The discourse of reform in teacher education. *Educational Researcher, 30*(8), 3–15.

Darling-Hammond, L., & Youngs, P. (2002). Defining "highly qualified teachers": What does "scientifically-based research" actually tell us? *Educational Researcher, 31*(9), 13–26.

Day, C. (1999). *Developing teachers: The challenges of lifelong learning.* London: Falmer Press.

Ertmer, P. (2003). Transforming teacher education: Visions and Strategies. *Educational Technology, Research and Development, 51*(1), 124–129.

Feiman-Nemser, S. (1990). Teacher preparation: Structural and conceptual alternatives. In W. Houston (Ed.). *Handbook of research on teacher education* (pp. 212–233). New York: Macmillan.

Feiman-Nemser, S., & Buchmann, M. (1989). Describing teacher education: A framework and illustrative findings from a longitudinal study of six students. *The Elementary School Journal, 89*(3), 365–377.

Fenstermacher, G. D. (2002). Reconsidering the teacher education reform debate: A commentary on Cochran-Smith and Fries. *Educational Researcher, 31*(6), 20–22.
Furlong, J. (2002). Ideology and reform in teacher education in England: Some reflections on Cochran-Smith and Fries. *Educational Researcher, 31*(6), 23–25.
Furlong, J., Barton, L., Miles, S., Whiting, C., & Whitty, J. (2000). *Teacher education in transition: Re-forming professionalism*. Buckingham, UK: Open University Press.
Goodlad, J. I. (1993). School-university partnerships. *Educational Policy, 7*(1), 24–39.
Goodson, I. (2001). Social histories of educational change. *Journal of Educational Change, 2*(1), 45–63.
Healy, G. (2003). Unis challenged to upgrade focus on teacher training education. *Campus Review*, Vol (1) p. 3.
Hoban, G. F. (2000). Using a reflective framework to study teaching-learning relationships. *Reflective Practice, 1*(2), 165–183.
Howey, K. (1996). Designing coherent and effective teacher education programs. In J. Sikula (Ed.), *Handbook of research on teacher education* (pp. 143–170). New York: Macmillan.
Kennedy, M. (1991). Some surprising findings on how teachers learn to teach. *Educational Leadership, 49*(3), 14–17.
Korthagen, F. A. (2003). Discussant's comments on *Professional development for teacher educators*. Symposium at the Annual Meeting of the American Educational Research Association Conference, Chicago, IL.
Korthagen, F. A. (2004). In search of the essence of a good teacher: Towards a more holistic approach in teacher education. *Teaching and Teacher Education, (20)*1, 77–97.
Korthagen, F. A., & Russell, T. (1995). Teachers who teach teachers: Some final considerations. In T. Russell & F. Korthagen (Eds.), *Teachers who teach teachers* (pp. 187–192). London/Washington: Falmer Press.
Korthagen, F. A. J., & Kessels, J. P. A. (1999). Linking theory and practice: Changing the pedagogy of teacher education. *Educational Researcher, 28*(4), 4–17.
Leef, G. C. (2001). The Trouble with Teacher Training. *Ideas on Liberty, 51*(11), 38–42.
National Commission on Teaching and America's Future. (1996). *What matters most: Investing in quality teaching*. New York: Teachers College, Columbia University.
National Council for Accreditation of Teachers (2002). *Professional standards for the accreditation of schools, colleges and departments of education*. Washington, DC: National Council for Accreditation of Teacher Education.
Ramsey, G. (2000). *Quality matters. Revitalising teacher education policy: Critical choices (Executive Summary)*. Sydney: NSW Department of Education and Training.
Russell, T., & Bullock, S. (1999). Discovering our professional knowledge as teachers: Critical dialogues about learning from experience. In J. Loughran (Ed.), *Researching teaching: Methodologies and practices for understanding pedagogy* (pp. 132–151). London/Philadelphia: Falmer Press.
Scannell, D. P. (2002). *Models of teacher Education*. Report to the American Council of Education Presidents' Task Force on Teacher Education. Available: www.acenet.edu/resources/presnet/background-papers/ModelsofTeacherEducationEd.pdf.
Schön, D. A. (1983). *The reflective practitioner: How professionals think in action*. New York: Basic Books.
Schön, D. A. (1987). *Educating the reflective practioner: Toward a new design for teaching and learning*. San Francisco: Jossey-Bass.
Tom, A. R. (1997). *Redesigning teacher education*. Albany, NY: State University of New York.
Thomas B. Fordham Foundation. (2001). *Teacher certification reconsidered: Stumbling for quality*. Available: http://www.abell.org [2001, October].
Thomas B. Fordham Foundation. (1999a). *The quest for better teachers*. Washington, DC.

Thomas B. Fordham Foundation. (1999b). The teachers we need and how to get more of them: Manifesto. In M. Kanstoroom & C. FInn (Eds.), *Better Teachers, better schools* (pp. 1–18). Washington, DC.

US Department of Education. (2002). *Meeting the highly qualified teachers challenge: The Secretary's annual report on teacher quality*. Washington, DC: US Department of Education, Office of Postsecondary Education, Office of Policy, Planning and Innovation.

Wideen, M., Mayer-Smith, J., & Moon, B. (1998). A critical analysis of the research on learning to teach: Making the case for an ecological perspective on inquiry. *Review of Educational Research, 68*(2), 130–178.

Wise, A. E., & Leibbrand, J. A. (2000). Teacher Education, Quality, Standards. *Phi Delta Kappan, 81*(8), 612–618.

Wise, A. E., Darling-Hammond, L., McLaughlin, M. W., & Bernstein, H. T. (1984). *Teacher evaluation: A study of effective practice*. Santa Monica, CA: Rand Corporation.

Part I

Conceptual Links Across the University Curriculum

Introduction by Garry F. Hoban

One important question for teacher education design is what structure underpins the university curriculum? These are the "big ideas" that are embedded in the subjects or courses of the program. Traditionally, these are the knowledge bases that form the subject matter of education and are usually represented in courses such as curriculum and instruction, foundations of education, educational psychology, special education, evaluation and educational technology. Many teacher education programs still organise these areas as independent subjects or courses as this suits the teaching expertise of the instructors which is related to the department structure of faculties. However, the real world of schools is not divided in this way. Moreover, it is often difficult for teacher education students to make their own connections across these subjects when they are taught independently.

But there are other ways to present these knowledge bases to students by making the links between them more explicit. Chapter 2 by Vicki Kubler LaBoskey and Chapter 4 by Anne Phelan show how a teacher education curriculum can be linked by principles or themes that permeate all aspects of the teacher education design. The six principles used at Mills College in the USA are associated with the characteristics of teaching and learning noting that "the notion behind principled practice rests upon certain assumptions about teaching and learning—that the process is, for instance, complex, uncertain and context specific." Moreover, staff at Mills College live these principles as well and even have staff and student retreats three times each year to reinforce them. They organise the curriculum so that foundations courses are not separate, but are integrated into other courses, "we do not separate out foundations courses in the typical sense, attempting instead to infuse history, theory, and practical implication and application into all of our syllabi". Isn't this how real classrooms operate? In Chapter 4, the themes used to integrate traditional subject areas are more to do with the varied contexts of teacher education with a differentiation between the exploration of the phenomenon of learning and the phenomenon of teaching.

Another way to link the university curriculum is by having key tasks, which cross traditional subject areas, for students to investigate in schools as demonstrated by two programs in Australia. Chapter 3 by Peter Aubusson and Chapter 5 by Julie Kiggins, Brian Cambourne and Brian Ferry show how traditional subjects can be broken down by school based tasks. Interestingly, both of these forms of school-based inquiry started with problem based learning and in both cases this mode of learning evolved into other forms. The program at the University of Technology in Sydney attempted to integrate four subjects across a semester by having students identify problems in schools for them to investigate and to discuss back at university. What happened, however, is that the problems students identified were narrow and mainly focused on areas of classroom management. The program design has now evolved to use project-based learning where broader tasks are investigated by students and they are not labelled as "problems" which has a negative connotation. The program described in Chapter 5 at the University of Wollongong also started with problem based learning but did not keep with this structure because the issues in schools were also not clearly defined as "problems". Their program design evolved to set tasks that are formed to investigate the outcomes of existing subjects so that students teachers find out "how its really done" in school settings. They also present their findings in a variety of creative ways and seek the assistance of teachers to unpack why they do what they do.

Another way for preservice students to learn about traditional knowledge bases is to use different modes of teaching. In Chapter 4 by Anne Phelan, on campus subjects use lectures, case based tutorials, independent studies and professional inquiry seminars. These complement the school-based teaching modes which are practicum, field-based inquiry seminar and community-workplace experiences. In this mode, students spend two days each week at schools for three semesters and four days a week for one semester, "field inquiry seminars held on campus or at the school site, provide opportunities for students to reflect on their field experiences within a community of practice setting." In Chapter 6, traditional curriculum courses have been integrated so that a course links Maths and Health/PE and other courses such as Pedagogical Issues and Supporting Diverse Learners are linked by conducting joint activities. These include joint assignments, team-teaching activities and online discussions.

A key philosophy that underpins these different ways to link the university curriculum is that knowledge about teaching is not definitive and inert as often promoted by a traditional course based design. Ann Phelan writes about developing the capacity for discernment to promote "a teacher's capacity to see the significance of a situation, to imagine various possibilities for action and to judge ethically how one ought to act on any given occasion" and Vicki Kubler LaBoskey talks about the "complex, uncertain and context specific" nature of teaching. Similarly, Jane Mitchell, Lisa Hunter, Lisa Stevens and Diane Mayer describe multiple conceptions of knowledge about teaching such that "the contradictions, the conjoining and clashing of ideas, in the complex process of learning to teach are inevitable." The university curriculum, therefore, must promote the complexity, not simplicity of teaching. A key way for this to occur is for student teachers to have a variety of ways to integrate ideas and to compare and contrast different views on knowledge in the university curriculum which is unpacked in Part 1 of this book.

Chapter 2

Principled Practice in Teacher Education

Vicki Kubler LaBoskey
Mills College, USA

CONTEXT OF THE TEACHER EDUCATION PROGRAM

The Mills College Teachers for Tomorrow's Schools Credential Program (TTS) is the teacher education program to be discussed in this chapter. Mills is a small liberal arts college for women located in Oakland, California. Oakland is a large urban community situated in the Bay Area of Northern California that is considered to be one of the most diverse cities racially, ethnically, and socioeconomic ally in the United States. This location exerts a powerful influence on our program both in terms of its philosophy and focus and on the kind of student who attends. We give emphasis to the goals of equity and social justice and the credential candidates who come to us do so, in large part, for that reason. They are interested in learning to teach in urban schools in ways that will promote equitable and excellent outcomes for all learners; they want to become agents of change in their future classrooms, schools, districts, and beyond.

Another significant influence on TTS is the fact that the undergraduate program at Mills is for women only. Although the graduate programs, of which TTS is one, are for women and men, being situated in an institution designed for and dedicated to the education of women has a recognizable impact on the nature and tenor of the program. A related aspect of the context is its intimacy; small in numbers students and faculty form close relationships that often persist long after graduation. Each year there are approximately sixty students enrolled in the Mills credential program, fifteen in each of four subgroups: secondary mathematics and science, secondary English and social studies, elementary, and elementary with an emphasis on early childhood education.

The regulation of teacher education in the United States has been relegated in the main to the states. Although there are moves afoot in the current national administration to gain more control over this process, the policies and monitoring systems that affect us most directly at present have been designed and operated by the state of California. For the last several years teacher education in California has been a postgraduate enterprise. Indeed undergraduates have

G. Hoban (ed.), The Missing Links in Teacher Education Design, 23–36.

not been allowed to major in education. Teacher candidates were supposed to have subject specific majors and then learn how to teach those disciplines in a fifth-year teacher education program. Very recently, these regulations have been changing so that undergraduate credentialing programs of various sorts will once again become a possibility. The program at Mills is still a graduate program only and has no current plans for revision.

The state of California has historically taken a very hands-on approach to educational management; indeed it is considered by many to be one of the most highly regulated educational systems in the country. At present all aspects, stages, and institutions of teacher education in the state are being revamped under the mandate of Senate Bill 2042 passed by the California legislature in 1998. Mills, like all other istitutions of higher education (IHEs) in the state, is involved in redesign efforts in order to establish compliance with these new standards and regulations. Nonetheless, the essential design and orientation of our work has and will remain the same. In the past teacher credential programs situated in IHEs were accredited by the California Commission on Teacher Credentialing and thereby granted the right to make decisions about whether or not its graduates should be given *clear* teaching credentials. Though this responsibility is intended to shift, under SB 2042, to the K-12 school districts (an outcome that may or may not actually come to pass), IHEs will, at any rate, be responsible for determining whether or not its candidates should receive a *preliminary* teaching credential. Again, therefore, we have not changed our perspective on our mandate to both prepare our candidates well for excellent and equitable teaching and also assess their achievement of that goal. In any case we have and will continue to prepare our students to enter full responsibility teaching jobs upon completion of our program.

STRUCTURE OF THE TEACHER EDUCATION PROGRAM

As previously mentioned, the Mills College Teachers for Tomorrow's Schools Credential Program is a graduate program. Our students have all obtained undergraduate degrees, usually elsewhere; typically no more than two or three are Mills College graduates. A few enter the program right out of college, but most have worked for at least a few years before joining us. The bulk of our students are women, especially in the elementary programs, but the ratio is not much different than that in most other institutions. Though we have been improving in our ability to attract students of color to TTS, the majority is still white.

We have seven tenure-track/tenured faculty members who teach most of the courses in the program; of these, five are women and two are people of color. Depending on a variety of factors, including sabbaticals, leaves of absence, and replacement courses for administrative duties and grant management, the number of temporary visitor positions we have varies from year to year, but is seldom significant. Though most of the faculty also supervises student teachers, we only do a handful; part-time people are hired to do most of the supervision. Many of these folks are graduates of our program and several others come to this position via other work with us; for example, they may have been cooperating teachers or research grant partners.

TTS is a combination credential/master's in education program. Students in three of the four sub-groups enter the credential program first. At the end of one academic year, provided all goes well, they obtain their teaching credential and are ready to enter the work force the following year. They will have also completed one half of their requirements for the master's degree. To finish that degree they need to return to the college for one more year, which they are to do some time within five years of completing the credential program. Those courses are offered in the evenings so that students can be teaching at the same time; in fact we prefer that they be working in classrooms so that their research projects can be centered in their own practice.

The fourth group, the candidates seeking an elementary credential with an emphasis in early childhood education, enters the credential program in their second year at the college. During their first year, they take courses and engage in fieldwork focused on young children and developmental theory. At the end of their two full-time years in the department, these individuals obtain at the same time both an elementary teaching credential and a master's degree in early childhood education. In every credential program year, therefore, three quarters of our group of sixty students is in their first year and one quarter in their second. Though there are some slight variations in curriculum for the second-year folks, the program is, for all intents and purposes, essentially the same, so I will not make reference to this distinction again.

A central feature of our program structure is simultaneous fieldwork and coursework. The candidates student teach in K-12 classrooms in the mornings[1] all year long and take courses at the college in the afternoons. For the most part, they follow the schools' calendars rather than Mills' so they get to experience a full school year from the first day to the last, but in two different places. Each student has one placement in the fall, and another in the spring that varies along a number of possible dimensions such as age group, school, and subject matter. In addition, each of them has to have at least one of their placements

[1] All elementary credential candidates also need to be in their classrooms for a full day each week and take over full responsibility for at least two full weeks some time during the year. Some secondary candidates have full responsibility for the teaching of a course throughout a semester with the support of a cooperating teacher. Only rarely do any of our students have paid internship positions where they are the sole teacher of a class.

be in a classroom with English Language Learners. We are very intentional about this structure so that we can make, and help our students to make, daily connections between theory and practice. Most of our assignments are designed to include a focus on and reinterpretation of their student teaching experiences, and, on the flip side of the coin, the stories they bring to our classes provide important alternative perspectives to the research and theory we are reading and discussing.

The fieldwork is further coordinated with the coursework via the supervision structure. Each student teacher is observed every other week by their college supervisor, who reports in a weekly supervisor meeting to the group advisor, the faculty member in charge of that sub-group who is also a supervisor. In these meetings supervisors discuss student progress, engage in professional development around ways to enhance their mentoring skills, and/or plan and debrief the student teaching seminar for that week. Most of our supervisors also attend and help to facilitate the seminar, a course intended to maximize, through a variety of needs-based activities and discussions, the learning opportunity provided to the student teachers by the fieldwork. Supervisors also engage in a weekly journal exchange with their students; in these interactive professional journals student teachers are to critically reflect, with the help of their supervisors, on their experiences and developing understandings of the teaching and learning process.

The specific coursework varies somewhat for each of the four sub-programs, but all have a student teaching seminar, an age-specific development class, a course on the theory and practice of teaching English Language Learners, a technology course,[2] and a variety of subject specific and developmentally appropriate methods courses. Except perhaps for the development classes, we do not separate out "foundations" courses in the typical sense, attempting instead to infuse history, theory, and practical implication and application into all of our syllabi. One class that all sixty students share is called, *Introduction to the Profession of Teaching Diverse Learners*. In this course all of our students come together to think about teaching, learning, and schooling in ways that cross subject matter and age level boundaries. This class, being co-taught this year by three tenured faculty members, Anna Richert, Ruth Cossey, and me, is a core experience that helps to make explicit the conceptual framework for the program. In the syllabus for this year, Anna Richert included the following in the overview:

> This course is designed as an introduction to the profession of teaching. It is not a course about how to teach. Rather, it is a course on how to think about teaching. While the course is concerned with the teaching of diverse learners, it

[2] Most of the secondary mathematics and science students waive out of this class, as do some others.

> is not a comprehensive course on diversity in today's urban classroom. If we are successful, you will gain a new understanding of the challenges and complexities of teaching and a better idea of what you need to know to become the kind of teacher you decide to become. We will use the principles of the Teachers for Tomorrow's School program[3] to help build an infrastructure for examining and developing equitable practices in schools.
>
> You have undoubtedly formed strong feelings and opinions about what teaching is like, what teachers do, what teachers know, and what schools are for. In this class you will have an opportunity to examine those ideas and your assumptions about teaching and schooling in light of current ideas from research and practice, and in light of the changing demographics of California. The course is meant to broaden your perspective by providing the opportunity for you to consider anew your conception of what it takes to be a good teacher for all students.

This course is representative of our efforts to create a unified whole with regard to both programmatic ideas and personnel. Here students have an opportunity to develop relationships with everyone else enrolled in the credential program for that year and with several faculty members by engaging in an examination of the profession of teaching diverse learners via our program principles. Another venue in which these qualities reside is our thrice-yearly retreats. All sixty credential students and all regular faculty members gather together three times a year for a day in the fall and winter and an afternoon in the spring to build trust and understanding among all parties and to explore target professional issues and dilemmas utilizing our program principles. So what are these program principles to which I have been referring? They are the driving force behind our work in TTS and the goals toward which we strive; they are the glue that holds us together and the dominant characteristic of our program structure. The remainder of the chapter will be devoted to an articulation of these principles and the ways in which they serve as the conceptual links to all aspects of our program structure, content, and nature. In addition, I will summarize some of the evidence we have gathered over the years through both systematic research and anecdotal commentary for the value of our principled approach to teacher education. Our investigations suggest that program coherence around our particular principles has served to strengthen its impact both during and beyond the credential year.

PRINCIPLED PRACTICE: MAKING CONCEPTUAL LINKS AMONG ALL ASPECTS OF A TEACHER CREDENTIAL PROGRAM

The Mills College Teachers for Tomorrow's Schools credential program is guided by a vision of equity and social justice. We aim to prepare our graduates

[3] These principles, the central focus of this chapter, will be presented and discussed in the next section.

to be agents of change who will help our educational systems become more consistent with the democratic ideal by producing equitable and excellent outcomes for all learners. At present we have identified and embraced six principles that we believe embody the current wisdom of research and practice most consistent with and likely to result in these goals. They are as follows:

- TEACHING IS INHERENTLY MORAL WORK that must be *guided by an ethic of care.*
- TEACHING IS REFLECTIVE WORK that requires *active and systematic inquiry for learning throughout the teacher's career.*
- LEARNING IS DEVELOPMENTAL AND CONSTRUCTIVIST and thus teaching is best guided by those conceptions of how learners come to know.
- TEACHING IS CONNECTED IN DEEP AND IMPORTANT WAYS TO SUBJECT MATTER. A central goal of the work is to prepare students *to acquire, understand, and construct subject matter knowledge.*
- TEACHING IS COLLEGIAL in that both teachers and students learn in the contexts of relationships that matter. Colleagues and community are central.
- TEACHING IS INHERENTLY POLITICAL in that by definition, it is concerned with matters of *change* that are neither neutral nor inconsequential.

These principles serve as both guides to action and criteria for evaluation. So how does this work? What do we mean by principled practice and how do we engage in it?

What is Principled Practice and How Does It Operate as a Conceptual Link in Our Teacher Credential Program?

My colleagues and I have recently completed a book devoted to an explanation of what we mean by principled practice called *Teaching as Principled Practice* (Kroll, Cossey, Donahue, Galguera, LaBoskey, Richert, & Tucher, in press). I recommend this text to those of you interested in a more detailed discussion of this approach. In a nutshell, principled practice means a circumstance wherein a teacher, school community, or, in this instance, teacher education faculty decides to have all educational decisions be guided by a set of conscientiously selected and constructed principles. Principles are neither formulaic nor prescriptive; they are not a collection of specific strategies, nor are they dependent upon particular program structures. Rather they are a set of guidelines, of theoretical perspectives on teaching, learning, and schooling that can inform educational decision-making. They are derived from and well grounded in the theoretical and empirical literature; they "represent what is currently known about how best to insure equitable and excellent outcomes for all learners and should promote the political and ethical will to pursue these ends" (Kroll, et al., in press).

The notion behind principled practice rests upon certain assumptions about teaching and learning—that the process is, for instance, complex, uncertain, and context specific. We assume that learners have multiple intelligences (Gardner, 1983), are at different stages of development with regard to particular concepts and skills, and vary in the "funds of knowledge" (Moll, 1992) they bring to any educational encounter. There can never be, therefore, one best way, one best strategy, or one best structure. Though some are generally better than others, because they are conceptually more consistent with the relevant principles, whether they work well in a particular case will always be provisional. Thus, the aim of principled practice is to foster a deliberative educational process among the appropriate participants and to seek multiple, rather than singular, possible means for achieving the desired ends. Even the ends themselves must always be negotiable.

Principled practice means that the identified principles permeate all aspects of a teacher's, school's, or program's activity. A look at some of the different ways in which the principles of TTS operate to provide the conceptual links for our teacher credential program is illustrative. First, they serve to provide us with a vision, a set of ideals, an image of the possible toward which we try to direct our efforts. In this sense, they encourage, even require us to ask and re-ask the very important "why question"—why are we doing what we are doing? Each year the TTS credential faculty has a retreat where we revisit this question and revise, if necessary; at the very least we take the opportunity to ground ourselves again in what matters most to us, which can often become derailed by the pressures of external, and often, incompatible demands.

Second, the principles function as a set of design criteria that can help us to develop and implement approaches most likely to move us toward the envisioned ends: "These six principles have provided a set of lenses that help us to understand our practice and goals as we strive to help teachers learn to create classrooms in which social justice, equity and powerful learning can occur. They can provide us with a way to move forward, to generate reasonable, effective responses to the expected and unexpected challenges of teaching" (Kroll, et al., in press). They influence our program design, our curriculum, our pedagogy, and our general interactions. The following examples are representative:

> Program Design: We choose to have simultaneous fieldwork and coursework because it provides us with daily opportunities to engage in critical reflection, one of our program principles. It allows us to take an inquiry orientation to our practice

and to help our students do so as well. At present we have an externally funded program called the Teacher Institute for Urban Fieldwork where some of our cooperating teachers, college supervisors, and credential faculty come together to engage in action research into our efforts to mentor student teachers with regard to equity teaching. Consistent with our collegiality principle, we believe that our power to influence our candidates in desirable ways will be enhanced by messages and models in both their fieldwork and coursework experiences that are informed by our program principles.

Curriculum: The content of our curriculum is not only influenced by our principles, it is, at least in part, one and the same. That is, we engage in the explicit teaching of the principles—what they mean, why they are important, and what they imply. For instance, at our daylong fall retreat, the first substantive interaction we have with our credential students for the year, one of the activities involves the formation of six groups using the program principles. We have a short statement about each principle that has been printed out and cut apart. Each student has a piece and must find the other group members by putting together the phrases that make up one of the statements. This done, the group, led by one of the faculty members, engages in a discussion of the statement—what principle it represents and what that means, which is then shared with the whole. We thus set the stage for using the principles to frame our work for the year.

Pedagogy: Our instructional strategies are also informed by our principles. For example, in the curriculum and instruction course I teach to all of the elementary credential candidates, we engage in an activity where we examine the purpose and process of assessment through the issuance of report cards. I put the students into five groups and give to all two different report card forms. I assign to each group the role of one of the relevant constituencies: the teacher of record, the parents, the students, the administration, and outsiders who know little of the context, but will use the report card as a source of information about the student, e.g., an admissions committee. Each group is to consider the strengths and weaknesses of the two forms from the perspective of their constituency. The groups then report their reactions to the whole and we consider the academic, moral, and political implications of this practice in light of the differing and important needs of all the relevant parties. The activity is designed this way because it engages the students in an interactive (collegiality) critical analysis of an educational practice from multiple perspectives (reflection), using the criteria of educational progress (constructivism and subject matter competence) and of the moral and political implications for both the short and the long-term. The overriding question is, of course, do or could report cards promote equitable and excellent outcomes for all learners—the essential vision toward which the principles in the collective are aimed.

General Interactions: Our interpersonal interactions with one another and with our students are also guided by our principles. All of the interchanges between supervisors and the student teachers are, for instance, informed by the principles. In the observation debriefings and in the professional journal responses, the supervisors try to promote reflection. They ask more questions than they give answers, they try to offer multiple perspectives on events and a range of possible responses to those events, and they try to shift evaluative responsibility to their supervisees by asking them to begin each lesson debriefing with an examination, if relevant, of the student work produced during the lesson.

These are only some of the examples that could be provided in each of these categories; again, anything and everything we do should be a possible instantiation, if we are in fact engaged in principled practice.

The third overall way in which the principles of TTS operate to provide the conceptual links for our teacher credential program is as a set of standards by which to evaluate the consistency of our efforts and the quality of our progress. We teach according to our principles not only because we believe it will maximize the learning of our students, but also because we want to serve as role models for their practice. We want them to experience a program guided by these principles, so that, once graduated, they will embrace them as guides for their own teaching. The principles thus serve as both the means and the ends of our teacher education program. As would be consistent with this orientation, "We do not simply teach our preservice teachers a list of principles for them to memorize and be tested. Rather, we refer to these principles time and again in reflecting on our own and our [students'] experiences and practice, until [they] begin to use them to talk about their own experiences" (Kroll, et al., in press). Our fieldwork evaluation instruments use the principles as a lens through which to analyze the performance of our student teachers.[4] We judge the effectiveness of our credential program in large measure by whether or not and to what degree our students and graduates understand and enact our program principles. We do this through ongoing formative assessment, formal research, and anecdotal evidence, examples of which will be shared in the following section.

What Evidence do We Have that Principled Practice Does Operate as an Effective Conceptual Link in Our Teacher Credential Program?

For many of us a focus of our professional research agenda has been our own practice within the Mills College Teachers for Tomorrow's Schools Credential Program. Therefore, we have much to draw upon in considering whether or not principled practice is having its desired impact. Especially representative is a four-year project where several of us looked at various aspects of teacher education using a programmatic framework (Kroll, LaBoskey, & Richert, 2002; LaBoskey, Kroll, & Galguera, 2001; LaBoskey & Richert, 1999; Richert, LaBoskey, & Kroll, 2000). We were part of a larger cross-institutional effort to answer the question, "What makes a 'good' student teaching placement?" Each institution came at the question from a different direction, but, because of our principled practice approach, we always took a programmatic perspective; to us it only made sense to look at the target feature, e.g., supervision or evaluation, in relationship to the whole.

The final study summarized the work from the previous three years to come to some conclusions about how and whether our field placements were

[4] One of our research studies (LaBoskey, Kroll, & Galguera, 2001) revealed that our evaluation instrument was not as closely tied to our principles as it should be so we are currently involved in a revamping our assessment system.

serving as opportunities for our students to learn the program principles. We discovered that we were most successful when all program activities and structures were *consistent* with the program principles, when all principles and program activities were *integrated* and connected to one another, and when we were *explicit* about where and how the principles operated in program practice. In other words, when all aspects of the fieldwork component of our program were designed and implemented in accordance with the notion of principled practice, student teachers could learn to recognize, reflect upon, enact, and embrace the program principles (LaBoskey & Richert, 2002, p. 20).

In a study designed to build upon the latter research, my supervisors and I investigated what we were doing to enable student teacher learning of the program principles (LaBoskey, in press).[5] We wanted to try to keep track of our "general interactions," the more amorphous category of our means for establishing conceptual linkages through principled practice. The aim was to better understand whether and how we were affecting growth by this means. All of the student teachers involved in this study completed the program successfully. What is more, we were able to document many specific instances where they not only understood and embraced one or more of the principles, they could also enact them in practice. One of the reasons this happened is that our supervisor meeting discussions were replete with a consideration of the principles and our mentoring in relation to them.

Other studies by faculty members have focused on an examination of specific curricular or pedagogical interventions designed to promote student learning of the program principles. Anna Richert (1997), for instance, investigated the impact of an assignment she gives in the *Introduction to the Profession of Teaching Diverse Learners* course, described above, which she calls the Curriculum Project. To do the activity the 60 students are put into groups of three or four, each of which has at least one student teacher from elementary school, one from middle school, and one from high school. "The student teachers work together in these mixed groups over a four-week period to plan the teaching of a concept they have chosen within the subject area and grade levels they teach" (p. 84), which they present in a final meeting to their colleagues and to department faculty. The students then write a reflective essay on what they learned from the project. In analyzing her data, Richert found that the students gained in their understanding of the principles regarding subject matter, reflection, constuctivism/developmental learning, and most importantly, collegiality.

[5] This research was made possible (in part) by a grant from the Spencer Foundation. The statements made and the views expressed are solely the responsibility of the author.

I carried out a similar study of one of my assignments given in my course, *Curriculum and Instruction in Elementary Schools* (LaBoskey, 2002). I call the task, "Setting the Tone" and it is one of the first formal assignments the students do for any of their classes. Each must observe and interview two different teachers attempting to set the tone in their classrooms at the beginning of the year. They write narratives constructed to initiate a deliberation with a group of their colleagues about a dilemma or issue that came up for them in watching these teachers at work. In these discussions they are required to withhold judgments, to express and consider multiple perspectives, and to generate several possible solutions to the identified problems; that is, they are to begin to take a reflective stance to educational decision-making, one of our program principles. The data suggest that this exercise is very successful in that regard, not only in the immediate but also in the long term. This study included data from graduates who testified to the fact that this assignment had helped them to take a reflective approach to setting the tone in their own classrooms:

> Yes! Yes! Yes! With the reflective attitude. (I can't stop [smiley face]). I didn't like what I saw that first day but I didn't like what I saw on my first day either. There are many things that happen in my room that I don't like or that make me stop—but I appreciate my ability to reflect on my practice—good and bad—and make changes. It helps me set the tone—I feel honest when I tell the children that we are all learning together. (p. 45)

Understanding the long-term impact of our principled practice approach is very important to us; that is the ultimate intent, of course, to make a difference in the teaching they do in their own K-12 classrooms.

One of my most recent studies includes only graduates. It is part of a continuing cross-institutional study of how graduates of programs designed to prepare teachers to be agents of change are faring in this era of standardization and rampant high-stakes assessment (Freidus, H., Hamilton, M. L., LaBoskey, V. K., & Lyons, N., 2003). Eleven graduates of the TTS elementary program, all of whom had been teaching for between two and five years, responded to a questionnaire and were interviewed. The focus was on the overall impact of the program rather than on any particular principle; the questions had to do with their definitions of quality education, what was helping or hindering their ability to teach according to that definition, and what in the TTS program had or had not helped prepare them for this work. All of them felt extremely well prepared and had few suggestions for program change. Though they were often enormously frustrated with external requirements they considered to be detrimental to the needs of their students, they felt that Mills had prepared them well to manage these challenges, as the following representative comment makes apparent:

> We were given access to a range of resources and ways of thinking, like a flexibility and a diversity of thinking about the profession of teaching both from a curriculum/instruction perspective and maybe knowing the mission. I think that Mills really helped me tease out why I got into teaching and gave me that inquiry orientation. There is no way you are gonna know everything you need to know but at least you know where to start with your questions, at least you know why you are asking questions. I guess that emphasis on really being thoughtful, really being reflective: What am I doing? Why am I doing this? And what questions do I have about why I am doing it? I feel like there is no way to prepare for being a teacher, but at least Mills is willing to talk about it; how difficult it is, how little time there is. The social justice piece was huge as well—I didn't leave jaded from Mills; I left refreshed and enlightened and that that year of giving a lot of thought to that has carried me, has buoyed me when times have been difficult. I mean there are many days when I have said, "I don't have to come back after next year" and I always come back to thinking about the conversations I had at Mills, and I am continuing to have those same kind of conversations with my colleagues; that's been tremendously helpful . . . that Mills was really rigorous made me confident in myself—that that same feeling of being a learner and a teacher at the same time are always intertwined and can be a huge metaphor for your work as teachers with learners everyday, so just the orientation that we are always learners and that when we stop caring, when we stop asking questions, then we probably should get out and I see that so many times in my co-workers who just stop questioning; they just show up and they plug in and that is just never the way I want to be. That Mills was rigorous made me strong . . . it made me also clear on myself, clear on what I was doing and why I was doing it.

It is obvious from her response that this teacher has benefited from our principled practice approach and in a way that makes evident her own principled practice orientation to teaching. This inquiry stance has not only helped her to continue to try to teach in ways consistent with the goals of equity and social justice, it has helped to sustain her in that effort. Perhaps this is one reason our graduates tend to have "staying power" in the profession. We recently did an unpublished survey of our program alumni from the previous ten years and found that of those we were able to contact (576 out of 688) over 80% were still in teaching; in comparison to general trends this is a truly impressive number.

CONCLUSION

The faculty of the Mills College Teachers for Tomorrow's Schools Credential Program has chosen to have all aspects of our program design and implementation be guided by a set of six principles, principles we believe represent what current educational research and theory has to say about how best to serve the goals of equity and social justice. We do so because we believe that conceptual consistency has been a missing link in teacher education and one that stands to make a powerful contribution to program effectiveness and educational transformation. In a report written by the National Commission on Teaching and

America's Future published in 1996, Linda Darling-Hammond and her colleagues identified "what matters most" in achieving the goal of equitable and excellent outcomes for all learners: "What teachers know and can do makes the crucial difference in what children learn" (p. 5). And they characterize that knowledge in this way, a description quite similar to our notion of principled practice:

> Teaching in ways that help diverse learners master challenging content is much more complex than teaching for rote recall or low-level basic skills. Enabling students to write and speak effectively, to solve novel problems, and to design and conduct independent research requires paying attention to *learning*, not just to "covering the curriculum." It means engaging students in activities that help them *become* writers, scientists, mathematicians, and historians, in addition to learning *about* these topics. It means figuring out *how* children are learning and what they actually *understand* and can *do* in order to plan what to try next. It means understanding how children develop and knowing many different strategies for helping them learn. (p. 27)

But many, if not most, prospective teachers do not enter teacher education programs with this sophisticated knowledge base. Indeed they quite likely have spent years undergoing an "apprenticeship of observation" (Lortie, 1975) in classrooms governed by a very different philosophy of practice. Thus, previous notions will need to be deconstructed before new ideas can be developed. Howard Gardner (1991) has made clear how challenging the effort to transform a person's preconceptions can be: "Even under ideal circumstances, an education rooted in understanding takes time and effort to attain" (p. 252). We think, therefore, that our only hope for helping our students come to understand, embrace, and engage in principled practice in the interest of equity and social justice is to deliver and model a consistent, even relentless, message. In the unsolicited words of one of our current students, we seem to be doing just that: "Thus far I've been happy to find that Mills is in fact serious about the six principles they espouse around teaching. I find these principles deeply imbedded in the curriculum and in the way in which teachers and students interrelate." Principled practice is operating as the conceptual link that permeates and connects all aspects of our teacher education program.

REFERENCES

Freidus, H., Hamilton, M. L., LaBoskey, V. K., & Lyons, N. (2002, April). *Working in the margins to advance educational quality: Interrupting a discourse of standardization.* Paper presented at the Annual Meeting of the American Educational Research Association, Chicago.

Gardner, H. (1983). *Frames of mind.* New York: Basic Books.

Gardner, H. (1991). *The unschooled mind: How children think and how schools should teach them.* New York: Basic Books.

Kroll, L., Cossey, R., Donahue, D., Galguera, T., LaBoskey, V. K., Richert, A. E., & Tucher, P. (In press). *Teaching as principled practice*. Thousand Oaks, CA: Sage Publications.
Kroll, L., LaBoskey, V. K., & Richert, A. (2002, April). *What makes a "good" student teaching placement? Lessons learned from a multi-year study*. Paper presented at the Annual Meeting of the American Educational Research Association, New Orleans.
LaBoskey, V. K. (2002). Stories as a way of learning both practical and reflective orientations. In N. Lyons & V. K. LaBoskey (Eds.), *Narrative inquiry in practice: Advancing the knowledge of teaching* (pp. 31–47). New York: Teachers College Press.
LaBoskey, V. K. (In press). Speak for yourselves: Capturing the complexity of critical reflection. In K. O'Reilly-Scanlon, C. Mitchell, & S. Weber (Eds.), *Just Who Do We Think We Are: Methodologies for Self-Study in Teacher Education*. London: Routledge Falmer Press.
LaBoskey, V. K. & Richert, A. E. (1999, April). *Identifying "good" student teaching placements: A programmatic perspective.* Paper presented at the annual meeting of the American Educational Research Association, Montreal, Canada.
LaBoskey, V. K., & Richert, A. E. (2002). Identifying good student teacher placements: A programmatic perspective. *Teacher Education Quarterly, 29*(2), 7–34.
LaBoskey, V. K., Kroll, L., & Galguera, T. (2001, April). *Assessing "good" student teaching placements: A programmatic perspective.* Paper presented at the annual meeting of the American Educational Research Association, Seattle.
Lortie, D. C. (1975). *Schoolteacher: A sociological study*. Chicago: University of Chicago Press.
Moll, L. (1992). Funds of knowledge for teaching: Using a qualitative approach to connect homes and classrooms. *Theory into Practice, 31*(2), 132–141.
The National Commission on Teaching and America's Future. (1996). *What matters most: Teaching for America's future*. New York: The National Commission on Teaching and America's Future.
Richert, A. E. (1997). Teaching teachers for the challenge of change. In J. Loughran & T. Russell (Eds.), *Teaching about teaching: Purpose, passion and pedagogy in teacher education.* London: Falmer Press.
Richert, A., LaBoskey, V. K., & Kroll, L. (2000, April). *Identifying good student teacher supervision: A programmatic perspective.* Paper presented at the annual meeting of the American Educational Research Association, New Orleans, LA.

Chapter 3

Evolution from a Problem-Based to a Project-Based Secondary Teacher Education Program: Challenges, Dilemmas and Possibilities

Peter Aubusson
University of Technology, Australia

CONTEXT OF THE TEACHER EDUCATION PROGRAM

The Graduate Diploma in Education (secondary) at University of Technology Sydney (UTS) is the focus of this chapter. The program is delivered over two semesters in one year. It is an 'end-on' program, the most common type of secondary teacher education program in Australia (Committee for the Review of Teaching and Teacher Education, 2003). Students in the program have already completed an initial qualification, at least a three year bachelor's degree in their relevant teaching discipline.

A Case for Change

The first stage in developing a case for change was the consideration of what was known about the strengths and weaknesses of teacher education. That there are general problems in teacher education is not in dispute. A recent report in New South Wales, the Australian state where the University of Technology is located, identified many inadequacies in current teacher education programs (Ramsey, 2000). Internationally, systemic weaknesses (and strengths) in teacher preparation have also been identified (e.g., Darling-Hammond, 2000; Korthagen et al., 2001; Russell & McPherson, 2001; Hoban, 2002). Such general criticisms are significant and provide arguments for the future direction of teacher education including the need for greater collaboration with schools (Russell & McPherson, 2001), greater connectivity among courses and between university courses and practicum (Hoban, 2002), and wholesale change to a realistic pedagogy of teacher education (Korthagen et al., 2001). These criticisms and proposed developments do not provide information about the particular program at UTS, but do relate to similar programs.

G. Hoban (ed.), The Missing Links in Teacher Education Design, 37–55.

In a recent review of teacher education (Ramsey, 2000) evaluated teacher education programs in NSW, of which the UTS program is a part, and made recommendations for their development. He concluded, "... key aspects of initial teacher education in NSW need to be reformed.... what is needed is a new vision of teacher education, a different structure that operates according to a different logic" (Ramsey, 2000, p. 50).

While the general criticisms and the typical design of the program would suggest a need for change, further evidence was sought about this particular program. The existing program was found (Aubusson, 2003) to have significant strengths including its duration, structural features, the quality of the teaching and a good reputation. Thus one of the main obstacles to change is the apparent success of the existing program on a range of indicators, as one staff member quipped, "if it ain't broke why fix it". Yet, it seems fundamental that a teacher preparation program should be relevant and immediately so. A second obstacle to change was emerging evidence that at least some of the partnership programs, including innovations in teacher education in NSW which had been identified in the Ramsey Review were not without problems (personal communications). Consideration of the case for change led to a desire to modify rather than replace the existing program. Thus, a proposal to change the program was circulated to staff as a discussion paper. It argued that:

> ... The main challenge (it seems teacher education programs) is to increase relevance/perceived and actual usefulness of the program. A second major problem of teacher education is 'fragmentation'. Some models ... have addressed these problems successfully ... (However) Improvements may be more efficiently achieved by modifying the existing program, including:
>
> - greater collaboration among staff across courses;
> - more integration between courses and practicum;
> - enhanced partnerships between university and schools & university staff and school staff;
> - employing a unifying approach to the course across courses in at least one semester (eg. problem based learning based on practicum experience with a small number of clear broad outcomes encompassing all courses assessed by portfolio etc);
> - distributing practicum throughout semesters rather than confining it to discrete blocks;
> - promotion of more effective reflection (drawing on ideas across courses).

STRUCTURE OF THE TEACHER EDUCATION PROGRAM

The one year graduate program prepares secondary school teachers in four course areas—Mathematics, PDHPE (Personal Development, Health and

Physical education), Science and TAS (Technical and Applied Studies). There are plans to expand into other areas including English, LOTE (Languages Other Than English), and Creative Arts. The current program is four courses in each semester. Students in different discipline strands study different method courses but the other courses studied are the same. These courses include four methods/curriculum courses[1]; one professional practice course dealing with the teachers' role, responsibility and teaching practice; one psychology course; one course made up of half sociology and half philosophy; and a course catering for students with special needs. There are approximately five weeks of practicum in each semester, consisting of blocks of in-school teaching experience during which there are no university classes. The original program design, see below, is not unusual.

Orientation

During orientation students are provided with administrative information about the program, patterns of attendance and expectations.

Semester 1

Separate courses delivered: Psychology, professional practice, Science methods (2) Course delivery is interrupted by practice teaching experience.

Semester 1

Separate courses delivered.: Philosophy & Sociology, Catering for students with special needs, Science methods (2) Course delivery is interrupted by practice teaching experience.

This type of program, organised into courses according to discipline methods, (psychology, sociology etc) temporally separated from practicum would be expected to generate the problems of fragmentation identified as a general problem in teacher education (Smith & Shapson, 1999; Hoban, 2002) and to exhibit the low levels of student satisfaction reported by Korthagan (2001). Graduate teachers would be expected to suffer problems, sometimes termed 'transition shock' (Corcoran, 1981) often reported among beginning teachers (Huberman, 1989; Kane, 1991; Schuck, 2003) and the effects of the teacher education would be short term, being overpowered by the social and practical influence of schools during beginning teaching (Lortie, 1975; Zeichner &

[1] Methods/curriculum courses will be referred to a methods courses in this paper.

Tabachnick, 1981). In short, the design appears to have inherent weaknesses and requires change.

Of these efforts for change I will focus on the notion of a unifying approach and connectivity. One way to do this would be to reduce outcomes in 2nd semester, present common outcomes across courses and organise learning around a student project or problem based learning culminating in a portfolio addressing the outcomes. A student or group of students might work on a project targeting cooperative learning where they work with university staff and school teachers in their practicum schools to learn how to 'do' cooperative learning in their classes. Alternatively the student's owned problem may be "how do I teach PDHPE with my poorly motivated year 8 class" etc. The problem/projects' should be authentic but informed by practice, theory, philosophy.

USING PROBLEM-BASED LEARNING AND PROJECT-BASED LEARNING FOR CONCEPTUAL LINKS ACROSS THE UNIVERSITY CURRICULUM

In secondary teacher education at UTS, there are differences in emphasis in different courses that make it strikingly difficult for students to make connections between courses. The theoretical underpinning of some method strands was very different from those of the psychology course and the professional practice in secondary school course (a problem common to science teacher education programs, DEET, 1989). The science methods courses were based upon a constructivist view of learning and dealt with a variety of 'constructivist' teaching approaches. By contrast, students and staff reported that the success of direct instruction was emphasised in professional practice in secondary schools. In psychology an emphasis is placed on learning in terms of cognitive psychology, behaviourism, information processing and, to a lesser extent, social and humanist perspectives. The difficulty for students is characterised by one student who asked, "Where does the constructivist stuff fit into cognitive psychology, information processing and . . . ?" Furthermore, in 2002 for example, the first semester method courses were delivered independently from the other two courses with little communication among staff.

In other courses, the difficulty of links was less profound but even where there were obvious theoretical and practical connections between courses, e.g., among the methods courses and professional practice in secondary schools, these links were often not made. In particular, when teaching lesson planning in professional practice in secondary schools the lecturer did not draw on students' experience in method courses and the methods lecturers was uncertain when students were taught how to prepare lesson plans. Thus, there is a need for lecturers to know more about what is taught in other courses and when it is taught. It is unlikely that a single theoretical basis for all courses would be agreed but there is a need for lecturers to address these differences where possible.

Staff: Specialist? Generalist? and Alternative Views of the Process of Teacher Education

Universities favour the employment of scholarly researchers often with narrow fields of expertise. Lecturers in the program at UTS are scholars in their academic field with extensive teaching experience. This very strength of the teaching team is also a weakness. While it provides extensive depth of knowledge in fields such as sociology, philosophy, mathematics education etc to inform students, it tends to provide this knowledge in discrete courses associated with each lecturer. Generalist lecturers might provide an integrated knowledge base to students but less depth of understanding of particular fields. The lack of connection is in part a function of existing staff but it is also a function of the way in which academic knowledge is organised into well defined disciplines each with its own jargon, arcane practices and mystique. The problem of staffing is exacerbated by staff teaching across programs. Staff in the graduate diploma in education do not only teach in this program but also in other programs where specialist courses require specialist expertise. Even if generalists were considered desirable in the Graduate Diploma secondary they may not be well qualified to meet the requirements of other programs.

Among staff at UTS, and historically in teacher education, a continuum of views about teacher education appears to exist. These views are consistent with alternatives views of knowledge production (Gibbons, Limoges, Nowonty Schwartzman, Scott & Trow, 1994). At one extreme, learning of knowledge is followed by its application. There is a sequence where knowledge (about education) is obtained through research, information about teaching provided to practitioners and followed by application and reflection. Student teachers can first be 'taught' what research says about learning, teaching and education and asked to apply this knowledge and reflect on how to better apply the knowledge. At the other extreme of the continuum knowledge is generated by researchers with practitioners where research and application are indistinguishable. Student teachers apply their own ideas about teaching, creating a need to learn more about teaching and learning, which is engaged with as the need arises. Student teachers 'learn' how to teach through interaction, applying their ideas in an attempt to teach while interacting with others' ideas about learning, teaching and education and reflecting on practice to generate knowledge. Smith (2000, p. 1) claims that... 'with few political allies, the university based teacher education model cannot easily survive as the principal form of teacher education'. Some staff members are unconvinced and expect the current winds of change to pass as others have in the past. They, like Smith (2000), have witnessed many Government reports and reviews calling for reform in teacher education that have had little impact. Some staff with different views about how people learn in teacher education have had no difficulty in citing sources to support their position but, as often seems the case in education, 'proof' sufficient to convince an opposition often seems lacking. Whether this is a fault of education research generally (see e.g., Hargreaves, 1996) or a function of feelings, emotions and passions (see e.g., Korthagen, 2001) or a combination of the two is unclear.

It seems attractive to strike a balance between these extreme views, learning to teach and refining the application of this knowledge through practice vs. learning to teach in the attempt to teach, reflecting on this attempt and constructing understanding by engaging with ideas and others as the needs arise. Given the existing staff's rational arguments and passions about effective teacher education, balance like beauty remains in the eye of the beholder. If balance is to be realised, then these alternative views of teacher education need to be regarded as 'emphases' rather than a dichotomy of approaches. At UTS the design of the new program sets out to bring together these approaches to have the best (and perhaps the worst) of both in a single program, with an emphasis on the former in first semester and an emphasis on the latter in second semester. This division leads to Semester 1 with a situation analysis of a school establishing a context for teacher education followed by a project or problem which draws on education ideas at need. The students' situation analysis forms a context in which studies of teaching, learning, curriculum, psychology, sociology and philosophy can be realistically embedded to support teacher learning. The project (e.g., teaching my year 8 science class using cooperative learning) allows a gradual shift in emphasis to teams of student teachers, teachers and academics suggesting and trying teaching ideas, reflecting on practice and drawing on theory at need.

Developing a new program it is not so much about deciding what staff are required but deciding how existing staff may best contribute. Aligned with this is a decision, almost always made by existing staff, about the purpose the Graduate Diploma in Education and what it should be like. Its main role is teacher preparation to teach. It also should equip teachers with an understanding of education. The former is likely to be well informed by drawing on ideas from a range of disciplines often associated with teacher education;

something likely to be achieved by an integrated program. The latter may be well informed by an understanding of these disciplines; something better achieved by a discipline base program. If courses are organised into disciplines then in order for students to productively engage with learning these disciplines their learning needs to be situated in the context of their teaching. Furthermore, making connections among discipline knowledge to inform teaching has often been considered the responsibility of the student. A fundamental principle of teaching in the new program is that it is the lecturers' responsibility to make these connections and relationships more explicit. Thus, while some of the new program retains a discipline structure the aim is for each course's contribution to teacher knowledge to be related to a situation analysis of schools by students, connected with methods courses and practicum. As well, it should inform the project based phased of the program in semester 2.

Trialing a Problem-Based Approach

Design features of a modified teacher education program have been considered in passing above but the design process involves trial and evaluation. That is, trialing elements of the new program prior to making the formal program change. It seems unwise to formally alter the program and expend the extensive effort required to obtain university and NSWDET approval without investigating the merit of proposed changes. As a consequence the problem based trial, discussed below, retained a structure made up of existing courses. This was in part because significant changes to the program require university and NSWDET approvals likely to take over 12 months. The structure of the program is also restricted by university rules. These set the 'size' of the program in terms of credit points (48cpts). As each course must be 6 credit points, the number of distinguishable courses in the program is fixed by these rules.

As part of the design process, lecturers in the science methods courses, including the author, decided to try some modifications to the selected courses in the current program. Hence, in 2002 and 2003, some 'minor adjustments' to the existing program (Ramsey, 2000) were trialed with students in the science education strand of the program to address two main problems: perceived lack of relevance, links between courses and links between university and practicum. Some adjustments have been reported briefly above. Reflections on two further modifications, problem based learning and improving communication among staff, will be reported in more detail below.

One strategy trialed to address the identified shortcomings was a problem based learning approach in two method courses during semester two. During this trial the practicum and other courses remained unchanged. In this trial, the separation of the two method courses was eliminated in all but the final grade. Students were required to identify a problem in their teaching of science and to work collaboratively in teams with their lecturers' support to identify and trial ways to deal with the problem. The aim was to make the problem authentic and derived from their practice teaching so that are variety of ideas, principles and theories could be brought to bear on student teachers' problems. The problem based approach was discussed with students at the start of semester. This discussion included an outline of stages that they might go through including shock and resistance before experiencing success (Woods, 1994). Unfortunately, the timing of practicum in mid semester meant that students took some time to identify authentic problems. Furthermore, the time it took students to move from the shock to the success stage was extensive. Mid-semester the learning progress seemed so slow and haphazard that I considered abandoning the trial. Indeed, I would have done so had the portfolio assessment, which depended on the problem based approach, not been written into the course outline.

By the end of semester both method lecturers were convinced that through the problem based approach, students had learnt different things and in different ways from traditional models of delivery. They were not convinced that it was better or worse—just different. Similarly, student feedback questionnaires on the problem based delivered courses were virtually no different from feedback on the more traditionally delivered method courses in first semester. One of the concerns that one method lecturer had with the student-owned problems was that students often ignored a range of teacher education ideas many teachers, employers and academics would agree are important to teaching, such as programming. A second difficulty was that some students preferred to research issues or practices rather than problems, *per se*. While such issues or practices could be rendered as problems, such rendering seemed artificial and the problem based model was not attractive to some students.

Identification of Student Problems

During the science methods course, early on in their practice teaching experience, students were asked to share difficulties and problems they experienced in an online discussion board. It was thought that the discussion would provide authentic problems students might deal with in cooperative groups. Initially, the vast majority of the problems experienced related to classroom management. Though this changed as the course progressed, in order to have time for the extensive investigation of a problem, the problems investigated by students had to be identified early in the course. Difficulties with problem solving are illustrated with two examples below.

> On the Friday of the first week I walked into my year 9 science class and started getting ready. The class moved in and all settled into their usual places, except for one. I had never seen this kid before and didn't know who he was so I approached him and enquired, it turned out he was new to my class, fine. After I settled down the class I noticed that he had headphones on so I told him to take them off. He refused! I said two choices, take them off and put them in your bag or I'll keep them for the lesson. He then stood up and became extremely confrontational as though he wanted to fight me physically. I had to rethink my strategy as it wasn't the way to deal with a kid like this. So I said quietly but sternly you know your choices, I then turned my back on him and started the lesson. He put the headphones on his bag so I considered it a compromise. If he hadn't done it I don't know what I would have done. Did anyone have a similar bad situation or a situation that could have escalated to a bad situation? Or does anyone have any suggestions on how they would have handled it? (Student's online discussion contribution)

This problem quickly prompted ten responses from other students suggesting it was an episode of great interest to them. Unfortunately, the science methods course outcomes did not mention or deal with classroom management or such 'bad situations'. Hence, it was not an appropriate problem to pursue to address to the course requirements. Though it was discussed in another course, the opportunity to address this classroom management problem though the problem solving approach went begging. This immediately demonstrated to limitations of restricting to approach to only half of the courses studied during the semester and their specified outcomes. It also meant that the aim to have students investigate 'student owned' problems was inhibited by the specificity of course outcomes.

Although classroom management was the most frequently reported problem, classroom management difficulties were often reported as part of or as one of a number a difficulties being experienced. For example

> ... Today I spent 5 minutes trying to get some year 9 kids to think about something and write a paragraph recounting the history of a particular rock column. I'm not sure whether they are purposely trying to drive me mad, or really don't see the connection between observing and writing in science, and observation in the greater scheme of things.
>
> I have also learnt that visual aids are THE most effective way of grabbing the attention of the lower level science kids. At Peakhurst, when you get to the bottom classes like I have, you realise that a lot of the problem is based on English literacy... most have trouble reading and writing. However add a flame and some smoke randomly without telling them its going to happen, and the next thing you know its MISS, MISS DO IT AGAIN...
>
> I'll finish by saying that for the most part I am enjoying prac, the teachers (only 4) are great and help me heaps, but I find 9s5 (the lowest achieving science class) revolting most of the time and will not be sad to see them go. If anyone has any

> ideas for some interesting practical activities (not involving chemicals, out of seats, or hard throwable objects) for evolution, natural selection, please let me know...

This contribution proved more useful to me in deriving problems for investigation. I thought it would provide an authentic lead into:

- the problem of literacy and how can we address literacy needs—*they 'really don't see the connection between observing and writing in science... you realise that a lot of the problem is based on English literacy.*
- The problem of student lack of interest in an motivation to learn the science being taught at school to consider relevant science and Getting students interested—*grabbing... attention... If anyone has any ideas for some interesting practical activities*; and,
- The problem of effectively engaging schools pupils safely in genuine investigations, etc.

However, in discussions with the student who had posted this commentary, it became apparent that she had resolved the last two problems, to her satisfaction, with all her classes except 9s5, had little interest at this time in the first and was most concerned with finding ways to manage one extremely difficult class. While the outcome for the student was a good assignment meeting the course outcomes, I remained convinced that the genuine authentic problem remained unresolved, likely to manifest itself again during the first year of teaching. It had only obliquely been addressed. Indeed, it quickly became apparent that in university classes, the problem solving assignments done were typically well removed from the school situations. The real problems were arising and gradually being considered (if not solved) in discussions between student teacher, cooperating teacher and university practicum supervisor teacher while students were away from university during their block practice teaching. This rendered the methods courses' problem solving assignment somewhat artificial and untimely. Furthermore while it was not difficult for me to frame a problem based on the students reflective comments, it was difficult to address the problem when students wanted to address it and to ensure the problem they wanted to pursue was a problem consistent with the specified course outcomes—approved both by the university and major employer (NSWDET).

Limitations of Problem-Based Learning

One of the disadvantages of focussing on 'problems' was that it tended to result in students' online contributions about positive experiences being ignored, as there is a tendency for assessment to drive a course. Hence ideas and commentaries about 'interesting practicals', 'useful resources', the benefits of 'watching (and supporting) other student teachers' and 'tips' for teaching science well never became the focus of further investigation by cooperative groups. Problem based learning models seem appropriate in medicine where a patient presenting with an illness clearly poses a problem. I was not keen to have teaching or school pupils characterised primarily as problems. As a consequence, the next trial was conceptualised as a project based approach, where student will work in teams organised around self identified projects related to their teaching practice during and in preparation for practicum. It is hoped that such projects might form a context in which to consider many aspects of teacher education including effective teaching, psychology, sociology, curriculum etc. A third difficulty was that supervising teachers were generally poorly informed of the problem based approach being tried and were therefore not engaged as partners in the problem solving. A fourth difficulty with the problem based approach, which was trialed, was that it was only built around two of the four courses offered during the semester. Having half a problem based approach is a bit like having half a horse and expecting to be able to ride half way into town.

Consideration of the problem based trial led to the development of a modified model to be trialed. In this model, a student project would be used to connect ideas across courses and with schools and this project would dominate one whole semester of study rather than be limited to the mere 'assessment', as it was viewed by students, of the two science methods courses.

From Problem-Based Learning to Project-Based Learning

The trial of the project based model is now ongoing with science students. It including three courses and all lecturers in the second semester of the program. The projects require students to try and to develop approaches to teaching. They select one of the following: cooperative learning, open ended investigations, direct instruction, student performance (such as, role play and presentations) or problem solving in science. As part of this project students identify pupils in their classes with special needs and outline how they identify, address and monitor these. Throughout the semester students build a portfolio of their learning. The portfolio is submitted for assessment across all subjects. They also present selections from their portfolio to other students and staff as part of their final assessment. In this way, the project (with its product the portfolio) allows the requirements of both methods courses, as well as the outcomes of the special needs course to come together. The 'project' taken on by students can form a focus for collaboration during practice teaching for lecturer, supervising teacher and student teacher. To achieve this, teachers supervising students were provided with one day of release from teaching as part of short professional development program to meet with university staff and students to discuss the developments to the program and negotiate projects with which they would like to be involved. This process is supported by funding from the NSWDET, the main employer of graduate teachers. NSWDET staff are participating in and contributing to the professional development program.

The productive changes identified in the problem based trial have been incorporated into the project based learning model. The lack of connections among courses in the original program structure was considered a problem by both students and staff. Although, all course outlines were available to all staff, with few exceptions each staff member remains blissfully unaware of what is happening in other courses both as a whole and week by week. In semester 1, staff in three courses agreed to share more details about the content and mode of delivery of their courses prior to the start of semester and to meet regularly throughout the semester to suggest timely links and theoretical relationships to each other. The staff also shared a weekly table which listed the activities, content and main ideas being considered in sessions each week. The only course not included in this process in semester 1 was Psychology (this exclusion was accidental).

Although the communication process is currently being tried, the response from the staff and students involved has been positive. Even very small links across courses have been commented on and appreciated by students. For example, in lesson planning, a sample lesson delivered by a methods lecturer, and discussed by staff in advance, was used in the professional practice course as a 'shared experience' for students to discuss lesson planning and for which students could construct a lesson plan. Similarly, after practicum, in their first session on returning to university, students were encouraged to reflect on their practicum experiences. Students' reflections were discussed in groups, recorded and classified by students according to their importance to them and by like issues (e.g., classroom management issues, using the syllabus etc.). These were shared with all staff so that connections could be made with all courses. Students appreciated the explicit links being made across courses. As one commented, "I don't know why all these (three) courses have different names. One thing just flows into other. It's hard to distinguish why one (course) is called one thing and one is called another". One lesson here is that while the connections between courses may be apparent to academics, the connections are not always obvious to students. Simply by improving communication among staff, better conceptual and practical associations can be among ideas and practices.

As part of the project based approach being trialed, regular meetings among academics were used to share information about practices, ideas and concepts considered in sessions with students. It was anticipated that by bringing together the assessment of many courses into a single project, that greater links among the ideas across courses would be achieved. The meetings to inform supervising teachers of the plan, to negotiate their involvement and contribution to students' projects and to seek suggestions for its development also aimed to provide collaboration among all stake holders and cohesion among the ideas of students, university academics and school teachers. This project based trial was also limited requirements regarding the minimum number of courses required to form the program but in the second semester trial these courses were located within a single project and product (portfolio) assessed by specialists in different disciplines. Each project had a main theme (e.g., cooperative learning, open-ended investigations or problem solving in science) but also has relevant sub-themes, including catering for students with special needs and/or classroom management. Hence, students could investigate and report on how they introduced and developed a cooperative learning environment in a junior secondary science class and, as part of this, they would explain how they catered for the needs of a student in the class with identified learning difficulties and the strategies used to manage the class. Thus, each project consisted of a selected major theme and relevant subthemes.

In this way, issues such as classroom management, addressing needs of specific students and providing and providing engaging school science experience could remain connected. I say remain connected rather than become connected because the experience with the problem solving trial indicated that for the students dealing with authentic classes the issues are connected but we at university tend to disconnect them for the purposes of study, research or program delivery.

Initial analysis of the project based approach has shown that, at the start, students suffer similar uncertainty and discomfort to that experienced with the problem based learning in the previous trial. It seems concerns about assessment and developing a clear understanding of expectations requires time and the development of trust between lecturer/assessor and student. Many students seemed to find it difficult to accept that the lecturer/assessors want and can fairly assess very different products from different students. The period of concern and worry, although significant, was shorter than during the problem based approach. All data is yet to be analysed but this difference is probably the function of a variety of factors. With the project based approach students could identify and begin to learn about their project (a teaching approach) that was of interest to them immediately. It was also relatively easy to provide resources to support students as the range of projects was determined in advance and resources could be identified and made available at the start of the course. By contrast, in the problem based approach they were unclear of their problem to investigate until practice teaching began, at which time they were too busy to read widely to inform their problem solving. Thus the project based approach not only allowed them to learn with more confidence and address their assessment requirements but also helped them in their preparation for practice teaching.

The project approach was not without its own difficulties. Although the project 'topic' was intended to be the subject of negotiation between students and their supervising teachers the extent to which students could select their own field of interest varied widely. There was great variation in the support students received from their supervising teachers. Almost all student teacher—supervising teacher relationships seems benign and supportive. Nevertheless, some supervising teachers seemed to ignore the project while others provided extensive advice. This is typical of the range of assistance students receive during practice teaching and unremarkable that it occurred in this trial. Some students were not well informed by their supervising teachers about what they were to teach until they were about to start practice teaching. This made it difficult for these students to plan the trial of their selected teaching approach, as they had no context or content to which they could apply their strategies. It also made it difficult for lecturers to provide advice and support and to ensure that course workshops were productive for these students.

It is noteworthy that a few students selected and worked on a selected approach only to change to another project once they began practice teaching. In every case, the students changed from a more student centred approach to "direct instruction" as their project. Evidence at the time of writing suggests at least two factors influenced this:

1. the cooperating teachers lack of support for the students' selected teaching approach and 'encouragement' to adopt direct instruction; and/or,
2. a classroom environment perceived to be more conducive to direct instruction and related student teacher's concerns about classroom management.

In the delivery of courses, the provision of choice and control to the student teachers seemed an important way to engage prospective teachers in their learning. Hence, these school based influences and their interactions with students' desires and concerns require further study.

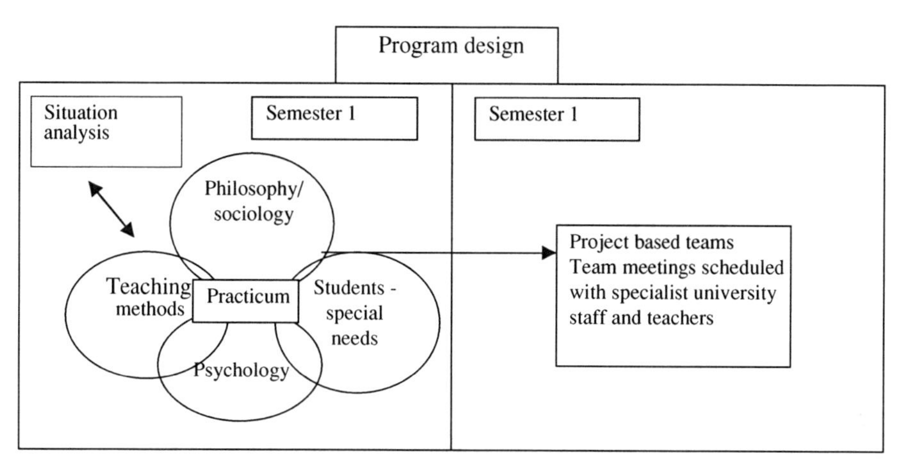

Figure 3.1. Modified program structure

QUO VADIS

Each model tried in the teacher education program informs what occurs next. The structure of the program for the next trial is shown in Figure 3.1. In first semester courses are delivered as identifiable units but connected by the situation analysis, practice teaching and communication among staff. In second semester the distinctions between courses are blurred by a common project. This structure provides a emphasis on finding out what is known about teaching and trying it in first semester but an emphasis on learning how to teach by engaging in the practice, sharing ideas and reflecting on these during second semester.

Orientation

During orientation students are provided with guidance on how to conduct a situation analysis in a school and an introduction to teacher education approach.

Situation Analysis

During week one semester 1, teams of students are placed in a small number of schools. In teaching method groups they conduct a situation analysis identifying perceptions of, issues, concerns, strengths and weaknesses, what schooling is like, how teachers teach, how students are learning, students' preferred forms of teaching, classroom management styles & strategies and propose views of why 'it' is the way it is. Its purpose is to provide shared experience to be addressed by and provide links across courses in semester 1.

Semester 1 Week 2

Students provide written summary and report on situation analysis at mini conference to staff, invited teachers and other students. Staff and invited teachers contribute to 'situation' adding issues, problems, concerns etc.

Semester 1 Week 3–Week 14

- Practicum: 3 week block + 10 days distributed throughout the semester as regular school visits.
- Courses: Teaching methods, Philosophy—sociology, Psychology, Special needs, Prof practice.
- Courses make explicit links to situation analysis and in-school experience throughout. During school experience students may collect data, trial a teaching strategy, reflection etc.
- Courses set foundation for students for more independent study in semester 2.
- Practicing teachers form part of the staff group providing sessions and advice.

Staff meet regularly to confer and make connections across courses (particularly via practice teaching experience guided activities). Partnership with selected schools and teachers developed.

Semester 2

- Teams of students work towards project and product(s) related to a few big outcomes related to all courses.
- Staff specialists are timetabled to set sessions. Teams of students book sessions with staff to gain advice and support with project—how does course related knowledge contribute to the product. Staff may choose to present occasional sessions in response to student needs etc.
- Practicing teachers form part of the staff group providing sessions and advice.
- Partnership with selected schools and teachers developed.

CONCLUSION

This chapter sets out to reflect on an attempt to improve secondary end-on teacher education as it occurred. The designs described are not 'ideal' structures for teacher education. Rather they are programs developed, within the limitations of existing rules and structures, to trial modifications to guide program design. The nature and structure of the final program will depend on outcomes form the next trial of the project based model above, as well as university limitations, NSWDET approval and the cooperation of various staff involved. An aim was to create better conceptual links throughout the program primarily by using school practice, problems arising from students' practice teaching experience, partnership with schools and better communication to unify the teacher education experience. Often developments in teacher education are reported as successful and teacher educators are exhorted to change, as if knowing what needs to be done makes the change easy and even inevitable—if only we would take steps to change. Characterisations of university academics resisting change recall the labels once applied to teachers as 'a bothersome intervening variable' (Richardson, 1989, p. 379) or 'stone-age obstructionists' (Doyle & Ponder, 1977, p. 2). Somewhere, at some time, some people thought that any current program was 'a good thing'.

Making a convincing case to change an ostensibly successful, but possibly flawed program, is difficult. Existing programs evolve and establish interlocking systems of courses, practicum, people and processes of teacher education. It is tempting to change just a little bit, but that seems to prove almost as difficult as revamping the whole program. Each little bit is connected to something else, which resists the modification or must be itself modified. Nevertheless the trial of some innovations, though difficult within an existing program, seems desirable before embarking on the wholesale change of a 'successful' program. Some innovations such as problem based learning were difficult and had outcomes neither worse nor better than previous models but have provided information leading to a 'project based approach'. Other innovations such as improving communication among staff proved easy to implement and had obvious benefits.

The gradual process of change being employed means that it will take some time for the final design to evolve. The ongoing trials and evaluation will guide its development and may provide ideas others might employ in teacher education. The extent to which the largely personal experience reported here can be generalised to teacher education or other institutions is difficult to determine. The aim here was to provide a story rich enough in detail to allow readers to make their own determination about what is familiar, what rings true and what might be relevant elsewhere.

Traditional teacher education programs have been vigorously criticised. The development of alternative ways to prepare people for the challenge of teaching is likely to raise new problems and issues that will need to be addressed. No single model is perfect or universally applicable. Each will operate in an environment rich in constraints and varied influences for good and ill. One way in which teacher preparation can improve is by teacher educators subjecting their existing models and practices to scrutiny, trying a range of models, and communicating their findings with each other. And when we do this, it is just as important to reports the failures—warts and all—as it is to celebrate the successes.

REFERENCES

Aubusson, P. (2003). Thoughts on the Graduate Diploma (secondary). Unpublished paper presented at a meeting of secondary teacher education staff at UTS.

Committee for the Review of Teaching and Teacher Education. (2003). *Review of teaching and teacher Education. Interim report: Attracting and retaining teachers of science, technology and mathematics.* Canberra: Commonwealth of Australia.

Corcoran, E. (1981). Transition shock: The beginning teacher's paradox. *Journal of teacher education, 32*(3), 19–23.

Darling-Hammond, L. (2000). How teacher education matters. *Journal of Teacher Education, 51*(3), 166–173.

Department of Employment, Education and Training. (1989). *Discipline review of teacher education in mathematics and science.* Canberra: AGPS.

Doyle, W., & Ponder, G. (1977). The practicality ethic in teacher decision making. *Interchange, 8*, 1–3.

Gibbons, M., Limoges, C., Nowonty, H., Schwartzman, S., Scott, P., & Trow, M. (1994). *The production of new knowledge: The dynamics of science and research in contemporary societies.* London: Sage.

Hargreaves, A. (1996). Transforming knowledge: Blurring the boundaries between research, policy, and practice. *Educational Evaluation and Policy Analysis, 18*(2), 105–122.

Hoban, G. F. (2002). *Teacher learning for educational change: A systems thinking approach.* Philadelphia: Open University Press.

Huberman, M. (1989). The professional life cycle of teachers. *Teachers College Record, 91*(1), 31–57.

Kane, P. (1991). *The first year of teaching.* New York: Walker & Co.

Korthagen, F. A. J. (2001). Linking practice and theory: The pedagogy of realistic teacher education. Paper presented at the Annual Meeting of the American Education Research Association, April.

Korthagen, F. A. J., with Kessels, J., Koster, B., Lagerwerf, B. & Wubbels, T. (2001). *Linking practice and theory: The pedagogy of realistic teacher education.* Muhwah, NJ: Lawrence Erlbaum Associates.

Lortie, S. (1975). *Schoolteacher: A sociological study.* Chicago: University of Chicago Press.

Ramsey, G. (2000). *Quality matters. Revitalising teaching: Critical times, critical choices.* Sydney: NSW Ministry of Education and Training.

Richardson, M. (1989). Teachers-as-learners: Images from the past and implications of a (generative) constructivist perspective for the future. In J. Novak (Ed.), *Proceedings of the Second International Seminar: Misconceptions and Educational Strategies in Science and Mathematics, Vol II.* (pp. 378–389). Ithica: Cornell University.

Russell, T., & McPherson, S. (2001). *Indicators of success in teacher education. A review and analysis of recent research.* 2001 Pan-Canadian Education Research Agenda. Symposium Teacher Education/Educator training: Current trends and future directions, Laval University, Quebec City.

Schuck, S. (2003). Getting help from the outside: Developing a support network for beginning teachers. *Educational Enquiry, 4.* (Available at http://www.literacy.unisa.edu.au/JEE/)

Smith, N., & Shapson, S. (1999). Transformative teaching: An agenda for faculties of education. *Education Canada, 39*(1), 4–6.

Smith, R. (2000). The future of teacher education: Principles and prospects [1]. *Asia-Pacific Journal of Teacher Education, 28*(1), 7–28.

Woods, D.R. (1994). *Problem-based learning: How to gain the most from PBL.* Waterdown, Ontario: Donald R. Woods.

Zeichner, K., & Tabachnik, B. R. (1981). Are the effects of university teacher education washed out by school experiences? *Journal of Teacher Education, 32*, 7–11.

Chapter 4

On Discernment: The Wisdom of Practice and the Practice of Wisdom in Teacher Education

Anne M. Phelan
University of British Columbia, Canada

> An important question for teacher education, then, is how to develop the capacity for discernment... [and] the relationship between discernment, imagination and wise practice....
>
> (Dunne & Pendlebury, 2002, p. 211)

CONTEXT OF THE TEACHER EDUCATION PROGRAM

The Master of Teaching (MT) Program at the University of Calgary, Alberta, Canada is the focus of this chapter. The program is delivered over two academic years and culminates in a Bachelor of Education Degree. Students in the program have already completed a four-year degree program in a discipline. The MT Program is inquiry-based, learner-focused and field-oriented. Grounded in the Aristotelian notion of phronesis or practical wisdom, the program makes the relationship between discernment, imagination and wise practice central to teacher education.

The MT Program emerged in the mid-1990s in the midst of a changing educational landscape in the province of Alberta. Fiscal restraints imposed on all provincial universities by the Alberta Government meant that the teacher education program at the University of Calgary could no longer be the shared responsibility of Education, Fine Arts and Kinesiology; it became the exclusive pursuit of the Faculty of Education. Additionally, a new memorandum of agreement between universities in Alberta and the provincial ministry of education (Alberta Learning) meant that all teacher education programs had to apply the new "Integrated Framework for Quality Teaching" (Province of Alberta, 1997). The framework provided a list of competencies, or Knowledge, Skills and Attributes, required for interim/initial teacher certification. Moreover, a new Dean of Education had been hired and he seemed determined to take student feedback seriously: very caring instructors but a very ineffective program. Importantly, the University of Calgary itself was undergoing a change process with a growing emphasis on inquiry-based educational experiences for all its students.

G. Hoban (ed.), The Missing Links in Teacher Education Design, 57–73.

Four faculty members were charged to review the current literature on teacher education and teacher education reform. The result was "The Blue Book" (Paul, Benson, Heyman & Kurtz, 1996) which recommended that any reform to the teacher education program be inquiry-based, learner-focused and field-oriented. There was some sense that teaching should be understood as a form of experience that is contextual, laden with values, and characterized as intentional and intuitive action. As such, a different relationship between theory and practice was called for. There was strong agreement that adult-learning principles be utilized and that self-directed and collaborative inquiry be emphasized as a way of integrating theory and practice. Finally, the authors of the Blue Book recommended that any new program should include teaching/learning experiences in community-workplace sites in addition to experiences schools. In an open vote, the Faculty of Education accepted these broad recommendations.

In 1996 the "Prototype Team" was created to develop the details of a new teacher education program based on the recommendations accepted by the Faculty. The team of seven faculty, including myself as team coordinator, two classroom teachers, two graduate students and seventy-six prospective teachers working with twenty local schools set about creating a prototype of the new program. The term 'prototype' was significant as none of the team wished for yet another pilot program which would evaporate promptly in light of daily exigencies. In action research mode, we intended to live the program as we built it collaboratively with all our partners. There were a number of key questions to be tackled: What does the practice of teaching entail? What kind of learning experiences would prepare teachers to teach well? The questions invited us to consider the reality we imply when we use terms such as "teaching" and "teacher education". What were we preparing students for? Who did we wish them to become?" What did they need to experience, know and care about? The result of two years of deliberation and practice was the Master of Teaching Program, graduating 400 students each year and currently the only teacher education program at the University of Calgary.

STRUCTURE OF THE MASTER OF TEACHING PROGRAM

The Master of Teaching (MT) Program is a two-year (four semester) teacher preparation program that provides graduates with initial professional certification in the Province of Alberta, Canada as well as a Bachelor of Education Degree.

The program is inquiry-based in that it promotes exploration and examination of teaching/learning practices presented in real life "cases" or "situations". It is learner-focused and it fosters ethical relationships between and among students, faculty and classroom teachers that facilitate and support independent and group inquiry into teaching and learning. The program is field-oriented. It provides participatory and practical learning and teaching experiences in both schools and community/workplace settings.

Learning experiences in the program are integrated conceptually around a series of interrelated themes. Foundational, policy and curriculum studies are woven into a series of thematic units entitled, "Learners and Learning", "Teachers and Teaching", "Curriculum Contexts", "Curriculum Studies", "Praxis", and "Integration". Each thematic unit emphasizes particular knowledge and professional skills. As such, each unit incorporates a number of the Knowledge, Skills and Attributes (KSAs) required by the provincial ministry of education, Alberta Learning. When one KSA's is amplified in particular thematic units, it is not contained there but continues to echo throughout other units of study in the program.

Take, for example, the KSA referring to the prospective teacher's understanding of the contextual variables that affect teaching and learning. This KSA is directly emphasized in "Teachers and Teaching" (regulatory variables

The Master of Teaching Program is characterized as:

Learner-focused *Inquiry-based* *Field-oriented*

Located in

Thematic Units of Study

Learners & Learning	*Teachers & Teaching*	*Curriculum Contexts*	*Curriculum Studies*	*Praxis*	*Integration*
(Semester 1)		(Semester 2)		(Semester 3)	(Semester 4)

Grounded in

Learning and Teaching Experiences
in

Campus	**Field**
Integrated Lecture Series	School-based Practica
Case-based Tutorials	Community-Workplace Experiences
Professional Inquiry Seminars	Field-based Inquiry Seminar
Independent Studies	Independent Studies

Regular and ongoing narrative assessment occurs in each component of the MT Program
(Faculty of Education, 2003)

Figure 4.1. The master of teaching program

such as the Alberta Teachers' Association Code of Ethics), "Curriculum Studies" (regulatory variables such as the Alberta Learning Program of Studies) and "Praxis" (social and cultural variables that exist in different school communities). The question of context is also echoed throughout "Learners and Learning" where students are asked to reconsider learning theories in light of the learners they encounter in their particular field placements. In this manner, the program is recursive; its helical curriculum allows student teachers to revisit areas of study, each time deepening and expanding their understanding.

Students are organized in both cross-route (i.e. early childhood education, elementary and secondary) and route-specific (only early childhood education, elementary or secondary) groups throughout the two years of the program, depending on the purpose of the particular thematic unit under study. For example, students are heterogeneously grouped during Thematic Unit 6: Integration when they participate in case inquiry into educational ethics.

Thematic Units

Learners and Learning: Exploration of the phenomenon of learning in psychological, sociological, philosophical and pedagogic terms. Understanding the self as learner is also emphasized. (Heterogeneous grouping)

Teachers and Teaching: Exploration of the phenomenon of teaching in terms of its purpose, history, practices, theories and its personal and ethical dimensions. Understanding self as teacher is also emphasized. (Heterogeneous grouping)

Curriculum Studies: Exploration of curriculum development and teaching practices specific to early childhood, elementary and secondary education.

Curriculum Contexts: Exploration of the political, social and cultural contexts in which curriculum is enacted. (Heterogeneous grouping)

Praxis: Exploration of teaching as a collaborative, inquiry-oriented reflective practice in the context of a 13-week practicum.

Integration: Exploration of the ethical and moral dimensions of teaching. (Heterogeneous grouping)

The thematic units are delivered in both campus and field-based experiences. The six program strands include: lecture series, case tutorials, professional seminars, independent inquiry, field experience and field inquiry seminars. Students must be successful in each strand in order to complete a thematic unit. Strands are interwoven and complement each other. The lectures provide important historical background information, identify major schools of thought, introduce current research and discuss controversial positions related to each thematic unit of study. Case tutorial engages students in the collaborative examination of specific, concrete cases and complex or ambiguous situations that characterize teaching in order to decide how a teacher ought to act in such instances (Kessels and Korthagen, 1996). Professional seminars seek to promote self-conscious learners and teachers by helping students become aware of the different and often competing values that support and frame various kinds of educational practice. The intent is to help students construct and articulate well-informed, warranted rationales for becoming particular kinds of teachers (Faculty of Education, 2003). Through their own independent inquiries students deepen their understanding in a particular area of the educational field. The independent inquiries (two per year) may be driven by the learner's own questions, developing areas of interest, and/or identified areas of need (e.g., disciplinary specialty). Field experience consists of regular periods of observation-participation and immersion in a school and community/workplace site. Each year, field experience involves a long-term (one-year) commitment to a school site. A cohort of students is assigned to a school where they spend two days each week in semesters 1, 2, and 4 and four days a week during semester 3. Field inquiry seminars, held on campus or at the school site, provide opportunities for students to reflect on their field experiences within a community of practice setting.

Assessment in the MT Program takes the form of an ongoing conversation between instructor and students about what constitutes good work in teaching and learning to teach. In order to honour the complex and collaborative quality of teaching, learning and learning to teach, assessment is based on a credit/fail system (Faculty of Education, 2003). Assessment must improve teaching and learning, promote fairness, and honour prepared accomplishment. Feedback is provided on the basis of student assignments that include field journals, case reports, independent inquiries, biographies of learning and a final exit presentation during which students declare and describe the nature of their commitment to teaching. Students are engaged in ongoing conversations with their instructors and receive regular feedback and advice on their written and oral work in the program. The final assessment for each thematic unit of study is narrative in form and describes the strengths of the student's work, the areas in need of improvement and possible directions for their future inquiry. Classroom teachers and university instructors are responsible for the narrative assessments.

The structure of the MT Program is not unlike a myriad of post-degree teacher education programs that have emerged in the 1990's. It may be the

Hour	Monday	Tuesday	Wed'day	Thursday	Friday
9:00		**Case Tutorial** 9:00 - 11:50	**Field**	**Field**	**Study Day**
9:30					
10:00	**Lecture** 10:00 - 11:50				
10:30					
11:00					
11:30					
12:00					
12:30					
1:00	**Prof. Inquiry Seminar** 1:00 - 3:50				
1:30					
2:00		**Field Inquiry Seminar** 2:00 - 3:50			
2:30					
3:00					
3:30					
4:00					

Figure 4.2. MT program, year 1, campus and field schedule (Faculty of Education, 2003)

conceptual links that underlie the program, however, that distinguish it from others.

MAKING CONCEPTUAL LINKS: DEVELOPING THE CAPACITY FOR DISCERNMENT

The MT Program embraces practical wisdom and in so doing attempts to prepare teachers that can dwell within the rough ground of experience, appreciate its complexity and deep interpretability, and respond ethically. Put simply, the program attempts to develop the capacity for discernment (Dunne & Pendlebury, 2002). *Discernment speaks to a teacher's capacity to see the significance of a situation, to imagine various possibilities for action and to judge ethically how one ought to act on any given occasion.* In the MT Program, developing the capacity for discernment takes the form of a reflective process wherein prospective teachers narrate and reflect, in written and other forms, about their direct and indirect experience in practice settings and in case studies. Those reflections on experience are characterized by three conceptual moments: (i) the play of thought between concrete particulars and abstract generalizations (Phelan, 2001); (ii) imaginative rehearsal of action (Dewey, 1985); and, (iii) the ethical claim of partiality (Nussbaum, 1986).

Curriculum as Lived

Semester 2 dawned! Two new units of study: Curriculum Studies and Curriculum Contexts. Teresa, an elementary route student, continued to observe and participate in her school placement two days each week. Her partner teacher responded to her field journal both in writing and conversation. Teresa brought forward issues and questions emerging from her experience in that Grade 3 classroom for further discussion in weekly field seminars. Her independent inquiry for the semester took the shape of a child study of Martin. She observed him closely in a variety of learning contexts and collected many artifacts to represent his learning: copies of his written assignments, audiotapes of his oral reading and conversations about stories; photographs of his social studies projects and his art work. In conversation with classmates and her professional seminar instructor (advisor on her independent inquiry), Teresa tried to make sense of Martin as a learner: What were his particular gifts? Under which conditions did he learn best?

Martin grounded Teresa's study of curriculum in case tutorial as he became the lens through which she encountered official curriculum documents, readings about the theory and practice of disciplines including Language Arts, Social Studies and Mathematics, and conversations with her case tutor and peers. In a hypothetical case on language learning, she prepared a response to parents who were concerned about their daughter's spelling errors and critical of the teacher's whole language philosophy. As she examined the artifacts of the case-samples of the child's writing, a letter from parents, statements from research and excerpts from official curriculum documents, she thought of Martin and his struggle to become literate. In the context of case discussion she and her peers identified and argued about the range of responses that the teacher ought to make to the parents.

The case discussion was further complicated when that week's lecture invited students to consider how curriculum philosophies and practices are always embedded larger political, social and historical contexts beyond their control. Teresa began to wonder how the image of her grandmother in a one-roomed, prairie schoolhouse shaped her understanding of herself as teacher and her work with Martin. She felt drawn to the plight of children like Martin who were borderline illiterate. Was her passion for their well being reflective of some sort of missionary zeal? Or was it some form of gender socialization?

In professional seminar Teresa read works by Nel Noddings (2002) and Madeline Grumet (1988) and began to wonder about the relationship between gender (literally and figuratively), teaching and the curriculum. Caring, even, seemed to be anything but straightforward. In her Biography of Learning at the end of semester 2, she wrote of her struggle during field experience to create more responsive, meaning-centered forms of pedagogy in a system that seemed bent on emphasizing measurement of predetermined outcomes . . . .

The Play of Thought

> For to be able to choose a form of behaviour appropriate for the situation, one must above all be able to perceive and discriminate the relevant details. This cannot be transmitted in some general, abstract form. (Kessels & Korthagen, 1996, p. 19)

Student teachers see field experience as the place where they really learn to teach, the "most concrete moment", as it were, in their teacher education programs (Britzman, 1990). They are anxious not only to apply what they have learned but also to accumulate a store of methods from their classroom teachers. In other words, field experience is often seen as providing access to the real (Field, 1999). In the MT Program, field experience is viewed as a site for cultivating perception, or learning to see, NOT as a site in which to acquire immediate proficiency in a so-called "real" world. As such, inquiry in the MT Program refers to the reconstruction of experience (Dewey, 1934). The reconstruction process requires prospective teachers to first learn how to make intelligent reports of what happens to them as they observe, prepare for and engage in teaching (Nussbaum, 1990). Creating an intelligent report of experience involves prioritizing the particular by writing narratives of experience and then engaging in a continual search and re-search for the significance of the experience in light of reading and in the context of conversations with one's self and others. In field inquiry seminars, instructors and students focus on their respective narratives of field experience. They burrow down in the depths of particular instances, finding images and connections that allow them to see its significance (Nussbaum, 1986). As Ricouer (in Nielsen, 1995) tells us, "All verbal significance must be constructed; but there is no construction without choice, and no choice without a norm" (p. 10). The construction of significance, and the subsequent judgment about how one ought to act on such an occasion, invites student teachers to pose value rational questions such as: What is desirable? Who gains? Who loses? (Flyvberg, 2001).

While formulated knowledge or theory contributes to prospective teachers' understanding of each concrete situation under discussion, their seeing is always in particular and cannot be determined in advance. The ethical appropriateness of the pedagogical response is inseparable from the concrete particulars of the situation. However, the concrete situation has the power to change the student's general theoretical understanding. The experience of a particular child can remind and reinforce the student teacher's understanding of child development and the importance of literacy. This is the play of thought of practical wisdom: a back and forth movement between particular experiences and general conceptual understanding: between a prospective teacher's understanding of a particular child and her knowledge of cognitive development; between identifying appropriate ways for that child to learn to read and her more general, theoretical understanding of literacy. Each reconstruction of experience in field journals or seminar discussions provides opportunities to revise their understanding of particular students or particular pedagogical moments. Inquiry, then, is potentially transformational, an endowment of meaning with significance rather than a manipulation of predetermined meaning.

Student teachers' back and forth movement between field and campus experiences echoes the play of thought by inviting them to gather images of practice and to interpret those images variously with their peers and tutors. In field inquiry seminars they may read those images in terms of particular school cultures and in light of their peers' experiences in other settings. In this manner, the specifics of context become evident as students realize that not all approaches are appropriate to a particular occasion, in a particular classroom, with a particular child. Attunement replaces application as the primary relationship between theory and practice. In the context of case inquiry, the emphasis is also on creating meaning in situ as students are confronted with the specifics of time, place and circumstance of a particular situation. Initially, students are asked to retell the case story, to examine the context in which the event unfolds, to perceive what is at stake in the situation and to begin to think about how they might act in light of that perception. However, the notion of expanded horizon is important here. Students are challenged to go beyond their initial perception of each case. They move in a spiraling fashion from their initial, individual response into a conversation with peers, classroom teachers and pupils, the research literature, and popular culture. The process of case inquiry culminates in a written analysis that utilizes the many voices of others to arrive at ethical judgment and action. By engaging student teachers in extensive deliberation about practice, the hope is that they will begin to understand that teaching can never be a simple matter of following a procedure or method as one follows a recipe in cooking; it is always a matter of perception (Risser, 1997) and experimentation.

> [T]he living relation between abstract and concrete is maintained by means of experimentation .... Inquiry always involves abstraction, since it always involves hypotheses that articulate alternative courses of action (Hickman, 1998, p. 174).

It is important, however, that student teachers have the opportunity to experiment in a safe environment; this is where imaginative rehearsal comes into play (Dewey, 1934).

The Imaginative Rehearsal of Action

> Deliberation is actually an imaginative rehearsal of various courses of conduct. (Dewey, 1934, in Garrison, 1997, p. 121)

The MT Program is premised on the notion that teaching is an intentional, situational act. The non-repeatability of situations, however, means that a teacher is always improvising... not simply going back to the textbook but by discerning the details of the particular situation. The element of risk is always present simply because teachers' intentions have to bump up against the intentions of multiple others—students, colleagues, policy-makers. While we can hope that our actions will strike a chord in others who will carry it forward to some completion, we can never be certain if our pedagogical intentions will be played out, however many times they might have done so in the past (Dunne, 1997). The unpredictability of action is only surmounted by its irreversibility; there is no going back! Flexibility, improvisation and a clear understanding of the contingencies of any particular situation, therefore, characterize practical knowledge (Dunne, 1997).

In response to cases and events drawn from their field experiences, student teachers learn to improvise by generating hypotheses that articulate alternative courses of action, knowing of course, that their inquiry is initially directed at effecting change in an imagined world. It provides student teachers with a safe place in which they can think through situations in light of conflicting goals and endemic uncertainty about how to achieve desired outcomes. Student teachers can rehearse, as it were, realizing but without having to deal with the potentially harmful consequences of their judgments and actions. Freed from the constraints of time and the pressure of having to act in the moment, student teachers can reflect at length not only in terms of "what works?" but also in terms of "why?"—the meaningfulness of their chosen actions in the short and long term (Dunne, 1997). Ironically, the absence of action in imaginative rehearsal actually underlines the relationship between pedagogical thought and action.

The space that imaginative rehearsal creates is one wrought with possibility but one that is also grounded in actuality. During their exploration of curriculum studies in semester 2 of the program, students learn to conceive of and develop learning experiences in the form of lesson and unit preparation. As part of their process, they identify and study a topic of interest to them. An example might be "structures". In addition to learning the deep structure of the phenomenon as a teacher might as part of her preparation, students are invited to recount their experience of learning—how did they first encounter the topic? What was compelling about it? What aspect of the world did the topic open up for them? What challenges in understanding did the topic present? What do they now understand about the topic? How do they now feel about it? Rehearsal in this sense is a recounting or retelling in order to cultivate insight into how a learner *might* encounter the topic at hand. Later on, students are asked to confront the possibilities they see in the same topic by imagining how three learners in their field classroom might encounter it. How might Darren, who clearly loves to draw, find an entry point into the topic? How might Deirdre, who already knows a great deal about structures, extend and enrich her understanding?

By engaging in a substantial inquiry project in semester 4, student teachers come face to face yet again with the actualities of practice while wondering about alternative possibilities:

> The intent is to have students set out to understand the dynamic relationship between current research literature (the "oughts" and the "shoulds" of the various disciplines) and the lived realities of teachers and students in their various learning contexts. For example, students might pose such questions as: "What are the issues facing teachers as they assess students?" or "What teaching approaches do students welcome when taking the Mathematics 30 course? Or "What are some of the conditions under which teachers might better implement the principle of "full inclusion"? (Faculty of Education, 2002, p. 53)

By engaging in this way, student teachers become better informed about the ethical and normative standards and traditions that exist while at the same time they begin to understand their responsibility to re-interpret those norms anew in situations that call for decisions (Smits, 1997). The (im)possibilities for moral agency and subjectivity thus emerge through the process of imaginative action.

When imaginative rehearsal gives way to action in the program, it is gradual and graduated. Student teachers observe and participate in small group settings during semester 1, moving on to prepare (with guidance), teach and assess a series of only four consecutive lesions in semester 2. In the major field experience (13 weeks) during semester 3, they progress gradually from teaching lesions planned by the classroom teacher, to lessons and units of study prepared in collaboration with the teacher, to those they prepare and enact alone. By slowing down the process of entry into so-called "solo-teaching" and by continuing to emphasize deliberation in school-based cohorts and through "living case" tutorials on campus, the relationship between the actual and the possible remains intact.

Imaginative rehearsal requires community of inquiry. There can be no deliberation without others; the intellectual stimulation and moral challenge that others present to one's ideas are at the core of practical wisdom. In the MT program, community is fostered in case tutorials, seminars, in school-based cohorts and in larger cadres tutored by a particular group of instructors. Typically, students stay together in these groupings for a minimum of one year, sometimes longer. A community not only facilitates the generation of a larger pool of possible ideas for action during deliberation, it also reminds prospective teachers of the web of relations in which they will have to act as teachers. The material existence of other student teachers, classroom teachers and teacher educators reflects the larger professional community to which they will belong. It is to this community that they will promise to engage in ethical action; it is from this community that they will ultimately have to ask forgiveness when they fall short. An emphasis on the role of others in learning to teach represents a reversal of the contemporary social emptying and the absence of a social center in many educational institutions (Wexler, Crichlow, Kern & Matusewicz, 1992). The intent is to move student teachers toward commitment and affection (vs. disaffection) as each begins to believe in, articulate and work toward something, together. At the end of the program, in the form of an Exit Presentation, students are asked to make a declaration to their peers about what they believe the profession calls forth in them. Each student develops "a metaphoric representation that focuses on the moral and ethical imperatives inherent in becoming and being an educator" (Faculty of Education, 2002, p. 59).

The Ethical Claim of Partiality

> Perceptions and beliefs are rooted in worlds of our own making that we accept as reality. (Schön, 1987, p. 222)

In the context of deliberation, student teachers encounter multiple interpretations of any given situation and they learn that not only are there no interpretations in general, but that interpretations are always situational. Every interpretation is an event in itself, involving a dialectical relationship between their fore-understandings and values and the "text" (practice) that presents itself. Prospective teachers are invited to become aware of and raise questions about "what is good or bad, what is worth doing and what not, what has meaning and importance for [them] and what is trivial and secondary" in any given situation (Taylor, 1989, p. 28). They are invited to consider those attachments that shape their decisions in light of the grounds that support them and the further conclusions to which they lead. This is the learner-focused dimension of the MT Program.

An invitation to consider one's attachments, however, requires a learning environment in which difference is fore-grounded both structurally and conceptually. To this end, students are grouped heterogeneously across disciplines and routes (elementary combined with secondary) for part of the program. As a result, students become more conscious about how their particular disciplinary background has shaped their way of knowing the world, the normative categories that they use to make sense of their experience of self, other and the world generally. When a psychology student using terms like "personality", "individual" and "development" encounters a political science student using terms such as "society", "social justice" or "body politic" in a case discussion on individual differences in learning, both can come away recognizing that different frames make for different values, desires and identities. Encountering difference across the disciplinary frames allows students to begin to see the disciplines as living frameworks for understanding rooted in different languages of practice. In addition students also begin to recognize the existence of diverse conceptualizations of reality within any one discipline. Cognitive theory and behaviourism are examples in psychology. By contextualizing so-called empirical facts within particular theories the constructed nature of those facts is more evident and questions can arise as to why certain theories dominate our thinking about reality.

The practice of heterogeneous grouping can enrich students' understanding of their own discipline as a stance or position, no better or worse than other disciplines, each with its own limitations and possibilities in given pedagogical contexts. This awareness is at once humbling and empowering in the sense that one can question and manipulate and possibly change those frameworks and their concomitant practices. The constructed nature of knowledge becomes apparent. What does it mean to know as a chemist? Why are the metaphors of "development" and "stage" so prevalent in educational psychology? A meta-narrative thus emerges that compliments the students' previous immersion in the discipline during their first degree. The distinction between fact and value appears less decisive than it once did. This in turn has implication for how student teachers begin to think about knowledge and curriculum.

However, simply grouping students heterogeneously is insufficient. We cannot assume that prospective teachers transfer the meanings gleaned from such discussions and use them to read their own experiences of practice. The difficulty with this assumption is that it neglects the role of emotions in how students and teacher educators assert, live-in and defend particular spaces. There is a certain emotional labour that is required if student teachers are to understand the import of their values. This becomes very evident when they first enter the MT Program. The thematic structure of the program, its inquiry orientation, the emphasis on collaborative work and the absence of grades disturbs their taken-for-granted understandings about knowledge, learning, evaluation and teaching. They are puzzled by the absence of courses and worry that without those cartons of abstract knowledge in educational psychology or language arts methods, for example, that they will never learn to teach. For weeks into the program, they long for the familiar course structure with its clarity of expectation and role. Their discomfort increases in the context of field experiences where they often encounter overworked teachers, diverse learners and an extensive curriculum. When they try to implement practices such as inquiry-based learning they find their desires interrupted by students, teachers and institutional policies that emphasize curriculum coverage and standardized tests.

The discomfort student teachers feel is critical, however, in developing their sense of how, as university students, they enact and embody dominant values and assumptions about teaching. Moreover, in the context of field experiences, they begin to develop a sense of the limits that are often placed on teachers when they try to counter those dominant values. While prospective teachers often express a feeling of being overwhelmed by some of these realizations, it is the emotional labour that results which enables them to question cherished beliefs and assumptions and to take responsibility and action. However, this means that teacher educators and classroom teachers have to allow student teachers to feel overwhelmed, at least temporarily.

> Experience has something of adventure.... Adventure interrupts the customary course of events, is related to the context that it interrupts. As an undergoing and return, an adventure lets life be felt as a whole, in its breadth and in its strength.... [S]omething is undergone and through it one changes. (Risser, 1997, p. 85)

In the context of Biographies of Learning, which are written at the end of each thematic unit of study, students provide an account of their "adventures". They recount critical moments of insight, identify questions for future inquiry and reexamine their reasons for wanting to become teachers. Typically, their struggle to persist in an educational system that does not honour the notion of inquiry is palpable in these writings. Part of the process of learning to teach in the MT Program becomes learning to redirect one's desires and attachments (Butler, 1997) so that they can eventually teach in the larger educational system. They begin to cultivate themselves in a different direction, beyond idealism, in some cases, and certainty, in others, towards a greater understanding of their own critical subjectivity in all its limitation (White, 2000).

An understanding of the claims values makes upon a student teacher reframes bias as a moral issue, a call to ethical action. Far from hindering action, the student teacher comes to recognize that it is those very values that enable it.

CONCLUSION

I have been going through a process of reinventing myself. These re-inventions are usually slow, occasionally painful, and often aborted. They are informed by my experiences in the field, my discussions and writings about our case study readings, and the filtering of the chorus of voices and views that I am witness to each week. While I question past assumptions-and develop new assumptions which I will in turn examine-I am recognizing that my beliefs, my values, my personal big "T" truths and this self-exploration is impacting my entire life. When I signed up for teacher education I had no idea that such a storm would ensue. (Student teacher, MT Program)

Discernment is always more than knowing. It sometimes requires courage that enables a student teacher to persist in a truthful though otherwise unprofitable or unpopular direction (Dunne & Pendlebury, 2002). It may require a sobriety that allows one to acknowledge one's limitations and yet prevents one from being easily swayed by impulse or first impressions (Dunne & Pendlebury, 2002). It requires patience in sticking with a problem, a sense of balance that keeps both details and "big picture" in focus. It requires a letting go of instrumentality and a willingness to relinquish control and certainty of outcomes. In a world that desperately wants to be sure of itself, practical wisdom offers no guarantees. However, it does allow us to recover the ontological dimension of teaching and learning to teach by reintroducing questions such as: Who am I? Where do I fit? What can we best live by and live together as social beings in our schools (Nussbaum, 1990)? Teacher educators that invite student teachers to engage in this manner "... seem to proffer only their dreams for interpretation, and then no guarantee. They are interested in mistakes, the accidents, the detours, and the unintelligibilities of identities ...." (Britzman, 1998, p. 60).

It has been exceedingly challenging to sustain the MT Program during recent years. Critics and supporters exist in the ranks of policy-makers, teacher educators, classroom teachers and student teachers themselves. To many the notion of practical wisdom appears esoteric and abstract. In fact, some have experienced an explicit statement of program philosophy as an infringement on academic freedom. To others, the historical preoccupation with technique in the form of methods courses has overshadowed the program's attempt to take up practice interpretively. Graduates' propensity to critique the educational status quo and to articulate alternative possibilities has made them unintelligible as beginning teachers.

I have come to understand that developing the capacity for discernment in student teachers is challenging, time consuming but immensely rewarding. I have also come to understand that done with inadequate understanding, it is an extremely weak form of teacher education. Practical wisdom opens up tremendous possibilities for how we think about teaching and learning to teach. In the case of the MT Program, only time will tell if the wisdom of practice will prevail in teacher education.

REFERENCES

Britzman, D. (1990). *Practice makes practice.* New York: SUNY Press.

Britzman, D. (1998). *Lost subjects, contested objects: Toward a psychoanalytic inquiry of learning.* New York: SUNY Press.

Butler, J. (1997). *The psychic life of power: Theories of subjection.* Stanford, CA: Stanford University Press.

Dewey, J. (1934). *Art as experience.* New York: Minton, Balch & Company.

Dewey, J. (1985). *Ethics. LW, Vol. 7.* (Original work published 1932).

Dunne, J. (1997). B*ack to the rough ground: Practical judgement and the lure of technique.* London: Cambridge University Press.

Dunne, J., & Pendlebury, S. (2002). Practical Reason. In P. Gwayer, R. Smith & P. Standish (Eds.) *The Blackwell guide to the philosophy of education.* (pp. 194–211). Oxford: Blackwell Publishers.

Faculty of Education, University of Calgary. (2002, Fall). *Master of Teaching Program Handbook Year II*: Author.

Faculty of Education, University of Calgary. (2003, Fall). *Master of Teaching Program Handbook Year I*: Author.

Field, J. (1999, April). Becoming field-oriented: From twin solitudes to turning towards a different landscape together. Presented at the American Educational Research Association annual meeting. New Orleans.

Flyvberg, B. (2001). *Making social science matter.* London: Cambridge University Press.

Garrison, J. (1997). *Dewey and eros: Wisdom and desire in the art of teaching.* New York: Teachers College Press.

Grumet, M. (1988). *Bitter Milk: Women and Teaching.* Amherst, MA: University of Massachusetts Press.

Hickman, L. (1998). *Reading Dewey: Interpretations for a postmodern generation.* Bloomington, IN: Indiana University Press.

Kessels, J., & Korthagen, F. (1996). The relationship between theory and practice: Back to the classics. *Educational Researcher, 25*(3), 17–22.

Neilsen, H. B. (1995). Seductive texts with serious intentions. *Educational Researcher, 24* (1), 4–12.

Noddings, N. (2002). *Starting at Home: Caring and Social Policy.* Berkeley, CA: University of California Press.

Nussbaum, M. (1986). *The fragility of goodness: Luck and ethics in greek tragedy and philosophy.* Cambridge, UK: Cambridge University Press.

Nussbaum, M. (1990). *Love's knowledge: Essays on philosophy and literature.* New York: Oxford University Press.

Paul, J., Benson, G., Kurtz, S., & Heyman, R. (1996). *The blue book.* Faculty of Education. Calgary: University of Calgary Publication.

Phelan, A. (2001). The death of a child and the birth of practical wisdom. *Studies In Philosophy and Education*, Vol. 20, 41–55.

Province of Alberta. (1997). *Teaching Quality Standard Applicable to the Provision of Basic Education in Alberta, Government of Alberta Ministerial Directive 4.2.1.* Edmonton, AB: Author.

Risser, J. (1997). *Hermeneutics and the voice of the other: Re-reading Gadamer's philosophical hermeneutics.* New York: SUNY Press.

Schön, D. A. (1987). *Educating the Reflective Practitioner.* San Francisco: Jossey-Bass.
Smits, H. (1997). Living within the space of practice: Action research inspired by hermeneutics. In T. R.Carson & D. Sumara (Eds.), *Action research as a living practice* (pp. 281–297). New York: Peter Lang.
Taylor, C. (1989). *Sources of the self: The making of the modern identity.* Cambridge, UK: Cambridge University Press.
Wexler, P., Crichlow, W., Kern, J., & Matusewicz, R. (1992). *Becoming somebody.* London, UK: The Falmer Press.
White, S. (2000). Sustaining affirmation: The strengths of weak ontology in political theory. Princeton and Oxford: Princeton University Press.

Chapter 5

Re-Organising and Integrating the Knowledge Bases of Initial Teacher Education: The Knowledge Building Community Program

Julie Kiggins, Brian Cambourne & Brian Ferry
University of Wollongong, Australia

CONTEXT OF THE TEACHER EDUCATION PROGRAM

Reviews of beginning teachers over the past 80 years continually identify a number of key skills that are not well developed by traditional preparation programs. These include: student discipline, motivating students, dealing with individual differences, insufficient and/or inadequate resources, organisation of classwork, assessing student work, and relationships with parents (Koetsier & Wubbels, 1995; Commonwealth of Australia, 2002). Interviews conducted with final year preservice teachers report that they leave university with feelings of being under-prepared for life in classrooms and confused by what confronts them when they arrive at schools (Armour & Booth, 1999). Further, the schools that employ beginning teachers claim that a majority of recent graduates are unaware of how classroom cultures operate and find it difficult to transfer what they've studied at university into effective classroom practice (MACQT, 1998; Vinson, 2002). The Ramsey (2000) review of teacher education in NSW supported these findings and also asserted that preservice teachers do not understand how classroom practice produces effective student learning.

Hoban (1999) asserts that many teacher education courses present a fragmented view of learning and this hinders preservice teacher development into flexible, progressive teachers. Studies of learning in schools and universities support this view and regularly assert that knowledge is presented in a fragmented and decontextualised way (Entwhistle, Entwhistle & Tait, 1993). As a result essential knowledge is not retrieved when it is required in real-life situations because there is no link to the situation in which it applies during the teacher education program (Bransford et al., 1990).

The Ramsey (2000) review of teacher education in NSW supported these findings and recommended that preservice teachers receive quality classroom-based experience supervised by an accredited teacher mentor. However,

G. Hoban (ed.), The Missing Links in Teacher Education Design, 75–94.

providing more extensive classroom-based experience is no guarantee of quality (Darling-Hammond, 1999) and Ramsey (2000) admitted that school-based practical experience often consists of a series of isolated, decontextualised lessons prepared and implemented according to the requirements of the supervising teacher; or at worst it can be an unsupported and disillusioning experience.

The time had come to re-think school-based practice teaching programs. In late 1997, a small group of our Faculty of Education staff initiated an informal, but searching series of discussions that centered on developing an alternate mode of delivery for the Bachelor of Teaching (Primary) Program. The outcomes of these discussions can be summarised thus:

1. Given that the rapidity at which socio-political change was impacting on all levels of the education system, as teacher educators, we faced a 'double whammy'. Not only was it becoming obvious that schools, more than ever, would need increasing numbers of teachers who were both knowledgeable 'thinkers' and highly flexible' doers', but it would be our responsibility to lay the foundations for their life-long professional growth and development.
2. Like most pre-service teacher education providers we had both anecdotal and empirical evidence which indicated that many of our graduates arrived at schools after graduation very much unaware of how school and classroom cultures operated, were unable to see the relationships between what they had studied in the courses they'd completed, and how it should be translated into effective classroom practice. (Grant, 1994; Armour & Booth, 1999).
3. We were also aware that the system which employed most of our (and other providers') graduates (the NSW Department of Education [DET]), had a long-standing concern that teacher education graduates in general did not know how to solve the kinds of problems which would confront them on appointment to schools, and that as the main employing authority, they were looking for ways to reduce the cost, both in terms of time and personal stress, of the 'induction period' that many newly graduated teachers seemed to need.
4. After several long, drawn-out 'restructurings', our program evolved to what could be described as an eclectic mix of key features of what Reid and O'Donoghue (2001) refer to as the 'traditional dominant models'. Our model was underpinned by basic, 'non-negotiable skills and knowledge', to which was added layers of a 'teacher-as-skilled artisan' ethos, and this was then wrapped in a mantle of 'standards of professional competency'.

5. Despite this our graduates didn't seem to change in ways that were commensurate with the constantly changing needs of the profession and/or the systems that employed them.
6. We therefore needed to explore, design, trial, and evaluate alternate models of pre-service teacher education

Given this rationale, the faculty supported a proposal to design a research project that would investigate, as a pilot, an alternative approach to initial teacher education through:

- implementation and evaluation of an inquiry and problem-solving approach such as that used in medicine and the health sciences; and,
- greater integration of the practical field-based component of the teacher education program with the theoretical.

As a consequence of a wide ranging review of relevant literature we concluded that we needed to begin a process of challenging, and subsequently changing, the traditional paradigm of pre-service teacher education to which we'd been wedded for as long as we cared to remember. We decided that given the complexity of effecting such change, given our particular University/Faculty socio-political context, our best chance for starting and maintaining such a shift would be to design a project which would produce at least the following changes:

- a shift in the mode of program delivery from the traditional 'campus-based-lecture-tutorial' mode to a '*problem based-learning-within-a-school-site*' mode;
- a shift of from the traditional *clinical supervision* model of practice teaching to a *problem-based-action-research-mentoring* model that brought the relationship between the specialised knowledge in Education courses and the nature and culture of schools and how they 'do business', closer together; and,
- a shift in the traditional roles and responsibilities the major stake holding groups in teacher development, namely, the professional employing authorities, (e.g. NSW DET, local non-government school systems), the university, local schools, and the Teacher's Unions (NSWTF), so that a new form of 'School-based Learning' might be developed.

We argued that if we set these three processes in motion, an important by-product would be the opportunity to identify and explore the logistical, cultural, and political barriers to effecting changes in:

- the teaching/learning culture of undergraduate teacher education (in our context); and,

- the traditional mindset and culture associated with practice-teaching/the practicum (in our context).

By late 1997, the faculty agreed to support the proposal *'in principle'* provided that any structural and/or procedural changes that were set in place were:

- resource-neutral;
- maintained academic standards, and met professional standards of competency; and,
- maintained equity of workload and assessment procedures, with respect to students/staff locked into the mainstream program.

This 'in principle' support was followed by a further two years of formal and informal meetings with the major stake-holding groups, including senior management within the NSW DET Directorates, local superintendents, principals, whole-school staffs, individual teachers, faculty committees and diverse university power brokers, as well as the teacher unions. In these two years different formal committees, working parties, reference groups met, negotiated and discussed, for an estimated total of 1200 to 1500 hours. By the beginning of the 1999 academic year a pilot program had been designed. We were ready to begin.

STRUCTURE OF THE KNOWLEDGE BUILDING COMMUNITY PROGRAM

It was soon realized that the prospect of implementing a new program with a full cohort of more than 240 incoming first year students, while at the same time maintaining the pipe-line of second, third, and fourth year students who were already enrolled in the existing program, was logistically impossible. We therefore decided to impose two caveats.

***Caveat #1*:** We would begin with a small sub-group comprising approximately 10% of the new intake, to a maximum of 24 students; and,
***Caveat #2*:** The KBC model would operate only in those sessions when practice teaching was scheduled, (Session 1 in first and second year, Session 2 in third year). This meant that the 10% of students who were admitted to participate in the KBC version of the program would be engaged in this form of pre-service professional training for approximately half their total program. For the other half they would join their mainstream peers and engage in the traditional 'lecture + tutorial + formal examination' form of program delivery. Figure 5.1 below is a schematic representation of this caveat showing the year-by-year progression for the cohort of 24 students who became part of the KBC project, vis-à-vis the other 90% of their mainstream peers.

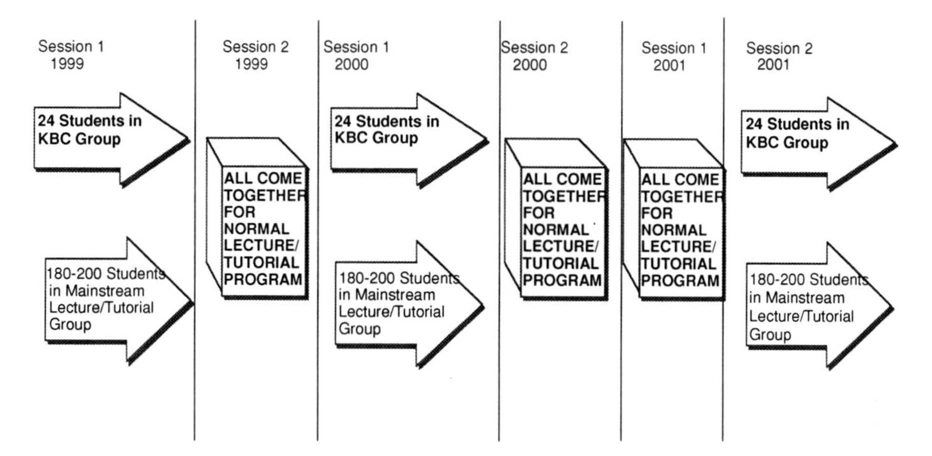

Figure 5.1. Session-by-session progression

With these caveats in place we anchored our alternative model of teacher education to a robust constructivist theoretical model based on a concept by Berieter and Scardamalia (1993) who proposed the concept of a Knowledge Building Community. They described a Knowledge Building Community as a group of individuals dedicated to sharing and advancing the knowledge of the collective. Members of this community invest its resources in the collective pursuit of understanding.

The notion of students and teachers working together in collaboration has been in educational conversation since Dewey but in the last decade has been taking a more definite shape in various programs (Scardamalia & Bereiter, accessed January 2000). These various experimental programs have taken place predominantly in school settings. Scardamalia and Bereiter (1993) present the Knowledge Building Community as a means of reforming the culture of the classroom. The adoption of this approach sees the class become a research team aimed at advancing its own "collective, intellectual growth through sustained, collaborative investigations". Based on the principles espoused by Scardamalia and Bereiter (1989, 1991, 1993, 1996) the student teachers involved in the KBC project at the UOW work in a learning environment that supports the continuous social construction of knowledge (Vygotsky, 1978).

The Knowledge Building Community in operation at the UOW is a teacher education model specifically designed to deal with the issue of contextualising the delivery of instruction. One of its important tenets is that instruction should be linked as closely as possible to the contexts and settings to which it applies in the real world. Furthermore KBC's are based on the creation of learning environments that:

(i) Support the continuous social construction of knowledge,
THROUGH,
(ii) The constant construction, de-construction, and reconstruction and sharing of meanings,
SO THAT,
(iii) The community's knowledge needs are advanced and maintained.

The UOW's KBC applied these principles through the creation of a setting that provided opportunities to engage in three modes of learning:

- Community learning (CL).
- School-based learning (SBL).
- Problem-based learning (PBL).

Community Learning

Community learning (CL) is a major shift from the traditional teacher education model of lectures and tutorials and serves to strengthen the working link between the University and the participating local primary schools. It requires the development of a community of learners, which is made up of preservice teachers, the school-based teachers and University lecturers who act as facilitators on campus. This community is designed to establish a sense of trust among all of its members who are dedicated to working together to educate and develop competent and sensitive professionals.

School-Based Learning

School-based learning (SBL) is the second learning principle of the KBC project. Schools are more than a conglomeration of buildings and people rather they are a set of individual cultures which have evolved in response to the wider cultural values (Bullough, 1987). To function, and indeed survive a beginning teacher must understand this culture. This component of the KBC structure aims to develop a sophisticated understanding of school-based culture. It is important for preservice teachers to understand how schools do business and how classroom cultures operate and support the learning of all students. It is also necessary as a part of this understanding of classroom culture to know and appreciate how to create and sustain this culture. This part of the KBC project is particularly aimed at reducing the 'reality shock' by increasing preservice teachers' understanding of a teacher's multiplicity of roles in both the school and the classroom.

Problem-Based Learning

Although problem-based learning has been extensively used in medical and other health professions over the last 30 years it has not widely crossed over into teacher education. The literature to support problem-based learning in preservice teacher education provides relatively few examples. Higher education has become characterised by structured subject based learning. Subject based learning has at its centre the lecture. The lecture rates poorly as a means to motivate students because the core issue of the lecture is the lecturers intent to cover set material (Margetson, 1994). However, effective student learning does not necessarily result from the lecturer's presentation of material. It appears that no matter how well the lecturer performs during the course of the lecture, students still sit passively and are seldom involved (Margetson, 1994). Subject-based learning means that subjects are viewed in isolation from each other and it is the subject that is driving learning. This style of learning assumes that the learner is unknowledgeable (Woods, 1994) and the instructor is the source of knowledge.

Current Problem-based Learning (PBL) theory asserts that PBL encourages and motivates students to 'learn to learn' (Duch, 1995). The critical difference in PBL is that it is characterised by instruction, which involves the students working in small groups to solve 'real world' problems. In this process the students develop skills of negotiation, communication and collaboration (Aldred, Aldred, Walsh & Dick, 1997). Problem-based learning is believed to promote life-long learning, making knowledge relevant by placing it in context (Aldred et al., 1997). Above all problem-based learning challenges students to take charge of their education (White, 1996). The common characteristics of PBL are:

- abolishing the traditional lecture–tutorial format;
- changing the lecturer's role from transmitter of facts to facilitator of learning; and,
- the facilitator will ask open-ended questions, monitor progress, probe and encourage critical reflection, and make suggestions thus helping students to create a positive learning atmosphere.

Duch, (1995), says that faculties that incorporate problem-based learning into their courses empower their students to take a responsible role in their learning and as a result must be ready to yield some of their authority in the classroom to the students. The transition to a PBL mode of delivery should not be considered as an easy option or a quick fix. Just as the tutor needs to adopt changes to practice the students involved in the transition to PBL also go through certain changes and these need to be understood for a smoother transition to PBL for all concerned. Students involved in PBL need to become self-directed learners and it must be realised that the benefits to this mode of learning are neither immediate nor automatic; the learning curve required with such an undertaking is very steep.

> The students, whose teachers have been telling them everything they needed to know from the first grade on, don't necessarily appreciate having this support suddenly withdrawn. Some students view the approach as a threat, some students may gripe loudly and bitterly about other team members not pulling their weight or about having to waste time explaining everything to slower team mates. (Felder & Brent, 1996, pp. 1–2)

Initial glitches involved with implementing PBL are both common and natural (Felder, 1995) and if an understanding about them is present they can be overcome without too much pain, panic or discouragement. These learning principles are represented diagrammatically in Figure 5.2:

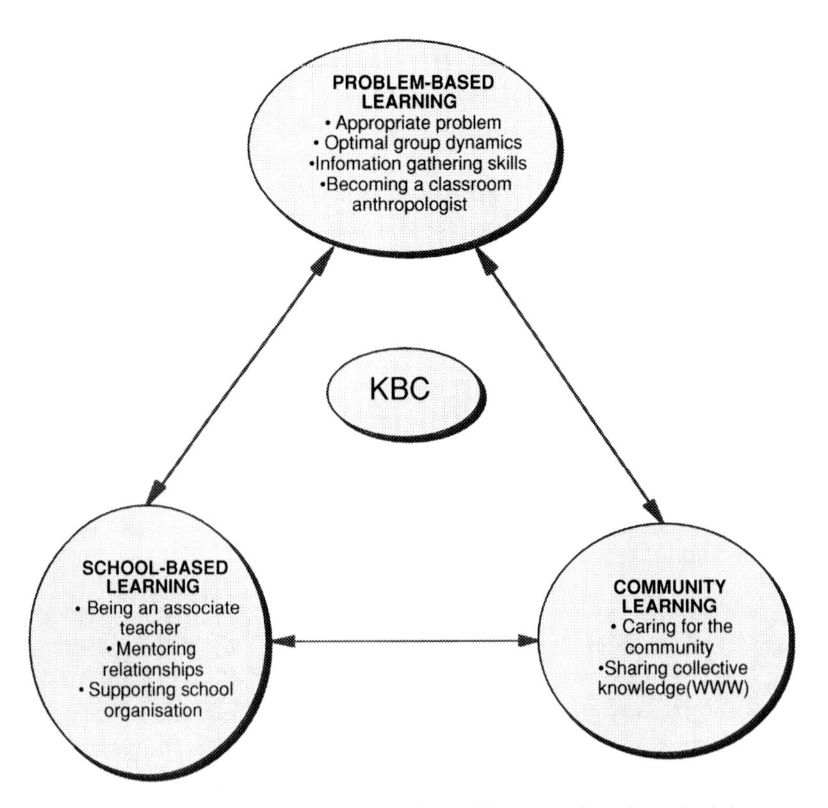

Figure 5.2. Diagrammatic representation of the KBC's learning principles

THE KBC PROGRAM: FORGING RELATIONSHIPS, INCREASING LEARNER IDENTITY AND RESPONSIBILITY

As the students work through the above learning principles of the KBC a tripartite relationship is built. This relationship highlights the importance of social interaction between the main participants. When students are given the opportunity and support of the KBC facilitators, school-based teachers and each other they can develop ownership of and responsibility for their own learning. This tripartite relationship is known as the community triad. With the support of this triad students are able to link theory to practice as well as developing an increased understanding of the culture of schools and the way that they operate.

The partnership between university facilitators and school-based teachers meets one of Ramsey's (2000) recommendations—that the re-energising of teacher education needs to be supported by reconnecting universities and schools. It also demonstrates to the students that they are part of an established team and this team can only become the community triad with their inclusion.

Just as the students had reflected on the relationships that they had established through their involvement in the KBC program so to did the school-based teachers.

> Having KBC students in the school has led to discussions about teaching philosophies and organisational matters better professional conversations not whingeing and whining... (Steve)

> The students were making comments and asking questions that as a teacher I have longed to hear because what it did was reassure me that as graduates they were going to be effective teachers. (Jane)

Comments such as those above from the school-based teachers involved in the KBC-Mentoring Program support the existence of the community triad. However, the university facilitators also take on this role and their role cannot be underestimated.

The role of KBC facilitator differs from the traditional role of the lecturer. They take on multiple roles including counsellors, confidantes, co-learners, mediators, and "buffers" between the Community and the University bureaucracy and the school system.

University facilitators are responsible for the coordination of the program, the school liaison and the recruitment of students. In terms of the coordination it is the facilitators' duties to ensure that students meet the outcomes of the subjects in which they are enrolled. This aspect requires meetings with mainstream subject coordinators and lecturers, as well as regular KBC facilitator meetings that discuss and debrief the students' progress.

EVOLUTION OF WOLLONGONG'S KBC PROGRAM

The UOW program has been evolving for almost 5 years now. Although we've had to abandon some of the original organisational and procedural ideals we started with in 1999, the underlying constructivist rationale and philosophy has remained firmly in place.

The current, 2003 KBC model is best described as a:

> negotiated-evaluation-of-a-non-negotiable-curriculum-based-on-a-constructivist-model of-learning-and-knowledge-building.

This over-nominalised phrase captures the essence of UOW's KBC program since 2001. While the program is still delivered along the original guidelines of the KBC ideals (i.e., CL, SBL, and PBL), a significant addition has been the addition of what we call, *'the four pillars of professional wisdom'* which now frame and guide the KBC learning process.

These four 'pillars' of UOW's KBC are:

- taking responsibility for mine and others' learning;
- learning through professional collaboration;
- identifying and resolving professional problems; and,
- becoming a reflective practitioner.

The four pillars allow students to practice empowerment and responsibility and ultimately enable the integration of the curriculum. Therefore it is important to fully investigate what activities the students need to undertake in each of the four pillars of the KBC.

Taking responsibility for own learning

Within pillar number one it is expected that the students will:

- Demonstrate that they understand the importance of becoming autonomous, self- directed, independent learners.
- Demonstrate that they know how to make effective, productive, learning decisions.
- Identify a set of learning "strategies" and/or "tactics" that responsible, self-directed, independent learners can use and/or draw on.
- Apply some of these strategies and/tactics to their own learning.

Learning through professional collaboration

Pillar number two expects the students to:

- Demonstrate understanding of the value and power of collaborative learning.
- Demonstrate ability to work productively and professionally as a member of a team.

- Demonstrate the ability to deal with inter-group conflict in productive ways.
- Understand how "group dynamics" work and be able to apply principles and "know-how" to maintain group cohesion.
- Demonstrate that they can collaborate in the generation of professional knowledge which all who are members of the KBC community can share and use.
- Understand the difference between "competitive" and "collaborative" learning and know when either is appropriate.
- Actively support each other's and the whole community's learning.
- Be honest, "up-front" and professional with each other, especially with respect to opinions and behaviour of others in the community. (Even if you don't like members of your group you need to show you know how to deal with this in ways that will not destroy or destabilise the learning or problem solving that the group/community is involved in).

Identifying and resolving professional problems

Pillar number three encompasses the principles of PBL and therefore expects that the students will:

- Demonstrate the ability to identify and articulate professional problems, which need to be addressed and resolved.
- Demonstrate the ability to analyse the key elements in a range of professional problems.
- Make explicit and apply a set of problem- solving strategies and tactics with can be used to address and resolve such problems.
- Demonstrate the ability to identify resources that might be needed to address and resolve a problem, and subsequently find and use such resources.
- Demonstrate the knowledge and ability to use time effectively in the problem-solving process.

Becoming a reflective practitioner

The fourth and final pillar of KBC learning engages the students in reflective practice; therefore the students will be carrying out the following activities:

- Demonstrate the ability to engage in the process(es) inherent in reflective learning.
- Students will be expected to make regular, honest, and systematic judgments of the degree to which they believe they have demonstrated the four broad specific outcomes of KBC in the various settings (School, KBC home-room, and via Self-Directed Learning).

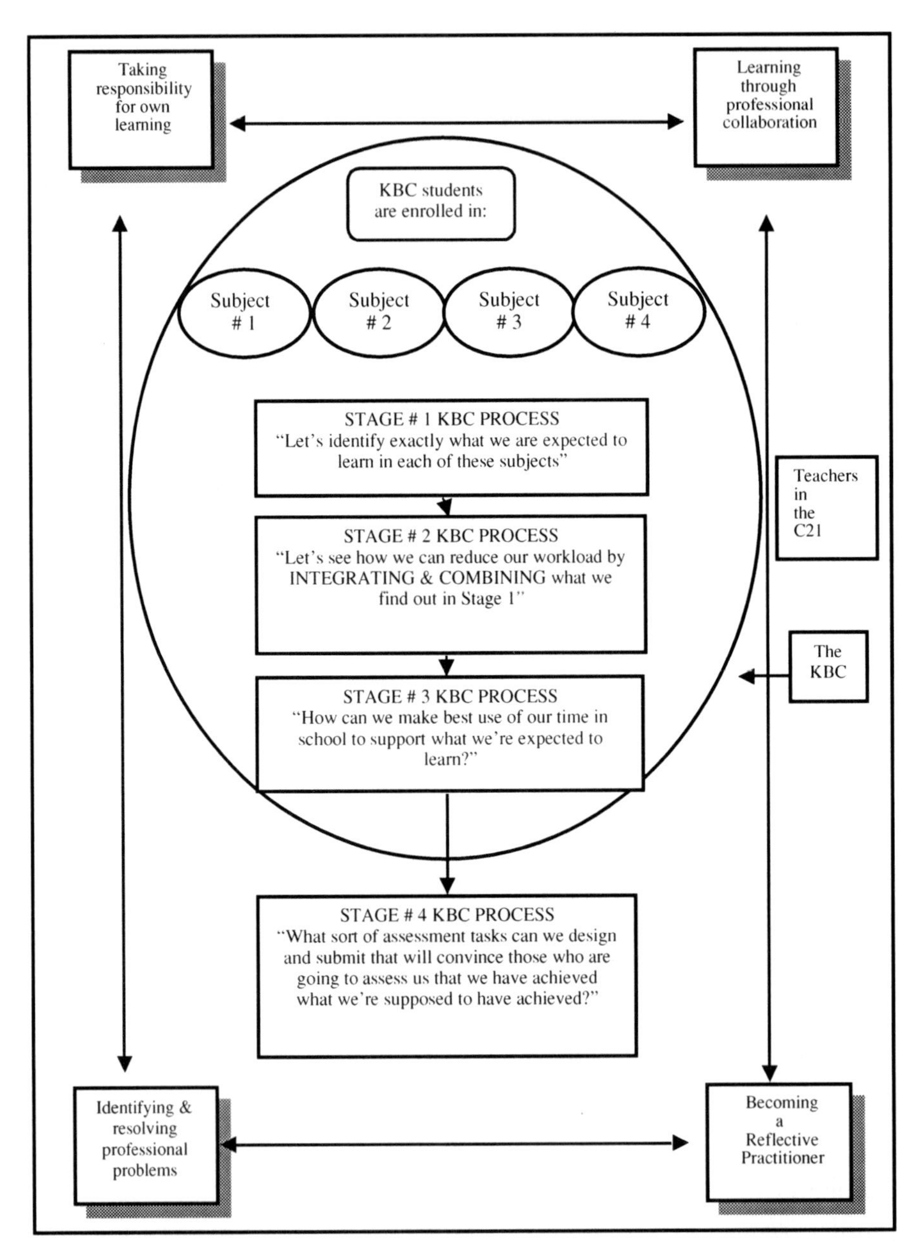

Figure 5.3. The four pillars of professional learning & the KBC processes and structures of integration.

The four pillars of the KBC are a set of complex interactions that are interrelated. When these interactions are working they will serve to drive any assessment task that is to be investigated. When the expectation that all members of the KBC have to acquire skills in using, and demonstrating conceptual understanding of these four 'pillars' is made explicit, it sets in train a range of complex interactions within the KBC.

Figure 5.3 describes the relationships between the 4 pillars of professional learning, processes and structures inherent in the KBC process, and how these are distributed across the session to allow for the creation of an integrated curriculum.

INTEGRATING THE KNOWLEDGE BASES ACROSS THE UNIVERSITY CURRICULUM

The KBC models of 1999 and 2000 had large overarching problem-based learning style assessment tasks that had been written in an attempt to integrate the knowledge bases of the four compulsory subjects which was consistent with Ramsay's recommendation:

> ... it is possible to reorganise the knowledge bases of undergraduate teacher education subjects so that they are more integrated with school and classroom culture, and therefore more relevant, more meaningful, better appreciated by student teachers, with less duplication across subject areas. (Ramsay, 2000, p. 57)

These problems proved cumbersome and in the end served only to hinder the learning of the students. In the Figure 5.3 it is shown that the Four Pillars of Professional Learning are also supported by a series of four questions which have been designed to guide the students in their quest to master the outcomes of the compulsory subjects in which they were enrolled. These four questions were intended to guide students as they worked towards designing their own assessment tasks. The four guiding questions as shown in Figure 5.3 are:

- Stage 1 "Let's identify exactly what we are expected to learn in each of these subjects".
- Stage 2 "Let's see how we can reduce our workload by integrating and combining what we find out in Stage 1".
- Stage 3 "How can we make best use of our time in school to support what we're expected to learn?".
- Stage 4 "What sort of assessment tasks can we design and submit that will convince those who are going to assess us that we have achieved what we're supposed to have achieved?".

It is timely to investigate what processes the students carry out at each stage/guiding question in order to achieve subject integration:

Stage 1: "Let's identify exactly what we are expected to learn in each of these subjects"

At stage one the KBC students are expected to deconstruct the subject outlines for each of their enrolled subjects. This process will highlight each subject's outcomes. The students will then be able to compare each subject for commonalities. In 2002 this process revealed that the compulsory subjects of Language and Literacy, Curriculum and Pedagogy I and Education 1 required that students "read and demonstrate understanding of specified theory and knowledge; describe examples of how the specified theory and knowledge is applied in practice; demonstrate progress in developing the skills and values needed to become a reflective practitioner". The deconstruction process then revealed that the major themes of these subjects were classroom management and discipline, developing a teaching Program (Curriculum), creating, implementing and evaluating daily lesson plans; assessment and evaluation of student learning theories of child growth and development including physical, social, emotional, psychological, learning, and cognitive growth. Once this stage is complete the students are now ready to identify how these theories and themes relate to teaching, learning and classrooms.

Stage 2: Let's see how we can reduce our workload by integrating and combining what we find out in Stage 1"

In regards to the students' findings at stage one the KBC 1 groups discuss, question and brainstorm different school-based research that will illuminate the practice behind the theory. The facilitators then take the students to the next level where they ask them to consider the type of actions and resources that could be involved in addressing their fledgling ideas. Questions are posed to the students such as: "What kinds of actions/ activities / tasks etc would you need to engage in to address your assessment plan?" The students are asked to think and plan how they can organise themselves to maximise their learning and minimise their stress, they are asked to consider what kinds of collaborative processes and structures they could create and set up and use to ensure that they make full use of the KBC opportunities and resources.

As well as considering how they may undertake their in school investigations the students must consider what options they have for presenting the results of their school-based research.

Stage 3 "How can we make best use of our time in school to support what we're expected to learn?"
The following is a summary of how the one school group planned to link the main concepts and themes of their subjects to their school-based experiences.
In school and self-directed learning as a group we need to take the opportunity to:

- Read and summarise the text books.
- Plan and allocate tasks for each group member.
- Appoint a student subject coordinator to keep track of the data we are collecting.
- Make sure we see and experience all the different stages at school.
- Ask our mentor teachers lots of questions.
- Keep minutes of group meetings.
- Record our definitions and our brainstorm lists.
- Share them with the rest of the KBC group.

Stage 4: "What sort of assessment tasks can we design and submit that will convince those who are going to assess us that we have achieved what we're supposed to have achieved?"
The following is an example of one group's planned responses for the compulsory subjects:

Curriculum & Pedagogy
After the students had analysed the subject outlines, compulsory texts and consulted with the KBC facilitators they proposed that the core components for this subject were:

- Classroom management and discipline.
- Developing a Program (Curriculum).
- Daily Lesson Planning and Evaluation.
- Assessment & Evaluation of Student Learning.

Based on this analysis they proposed to address these following three questions:

1. What do teachers at our school believe about each of these components?
2. What practical examples of these beliefs did we witness, or hear about while at the school?
3. Describe some of our own experiences with each of these components in our roles as a Teacher Associates.
4. What links can we make between what we find out in 1,2,3, and the prescribed textbook.

Education 1

The students proposed to carry out a mini-research project which addressed these two questions:

1. What is the link between the theories of growth & development described in the prescribed text and real primary school children?
2. What do the different theories of learning/ cognitive development described in the prescribed text book (Piaget, Vygotsky, Gardner) actually look like in the classroom?

Language and Literacy

The KBC students proposed that the core components of Language and Literacy were:

- The content of the official NSW K-6 English Syllabus.
- The content of the prescribed text book.
- Identifying how theory is put into practice especially in the early years.
- The links we can make between what we find out in 1, 2, & 3 above and our own SBL experiences, through the processes of individual & group reflection".

Figure 5.4 shows how this group integrated their assessment tasks. It is a summary of the processes that they followed as they developed their final set of assessment tasks based on the above proposals.

The final product was based upon the organizational metaphor of a "Reading Program-cum-Library Box" reflecting a very effective home-school reading program, which is a special feature of the school that they were at. The artifacts and documentation included in the final product were a set of documents which recorded the reading, writing, collaboration, research, and connections between theory and practice which the group made while at the school during their school-based learning time. This assignment consisted of 7 bound books. Three were an integrated Education 1 and Language and Literacy compilation and consisted of a total of 127 pages. Four were labeled Curriculum and Pedagogy and consisted of 102 landscape pages of matrices of observations and links to other core subjects. The students also included a volume devoted to appendices and artifacts.

Also included in the 'library' was a key document which outlined the processes and responsibilities of each of the members of the group. Within this document there were details that highlighted how the group:

1. Negotiated an equitable group contract.
2. Created and refined structures, roles, and responsibilities to ensure workload was completed in ways that resulted in a knowledge-collective that each group member "owns" and internalises.

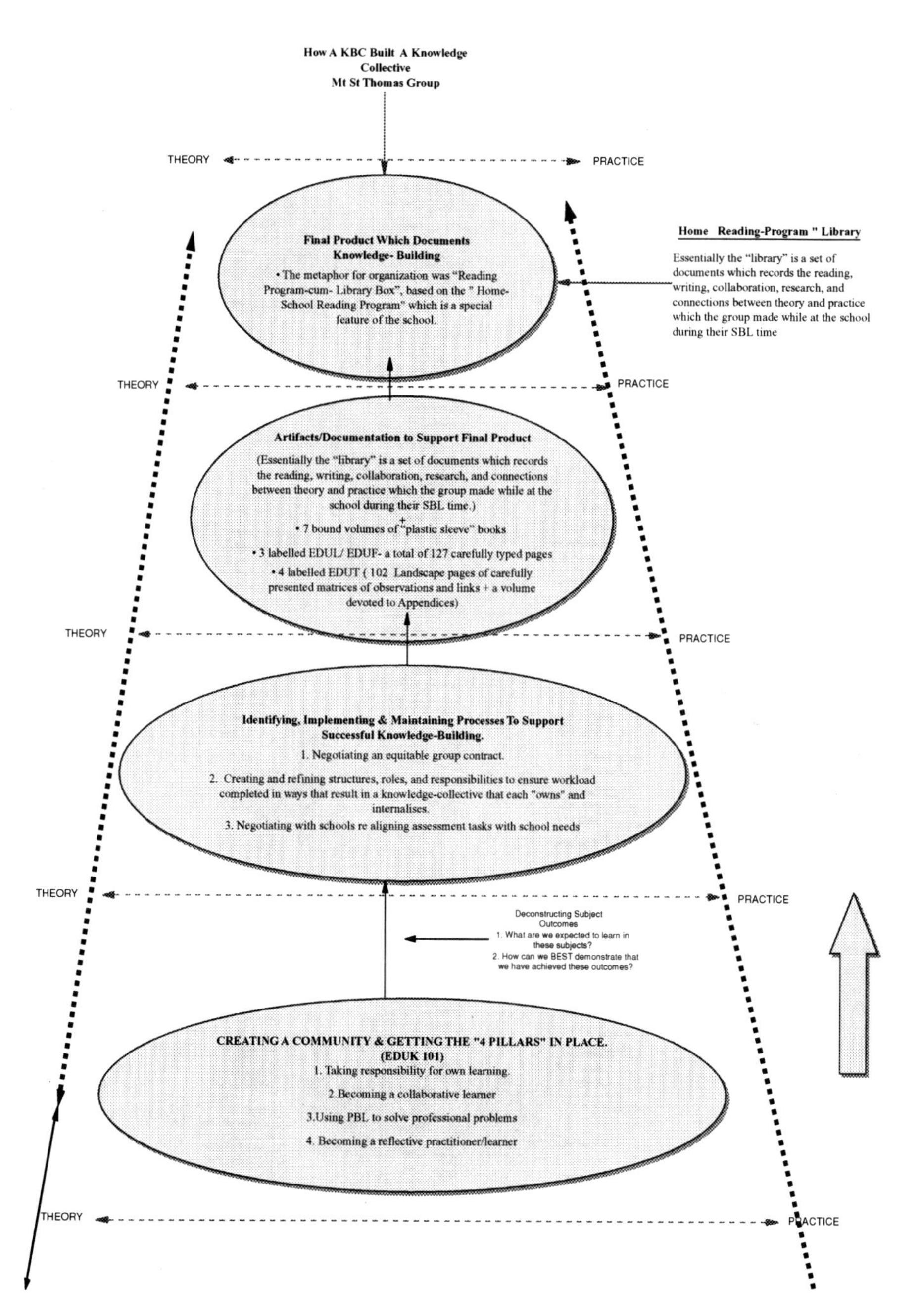

Figure 5.4. The knowledge integration process.

3. Negotiated with the school regarding how they aligned assessment tasks with school needs.

MAINTAINING QUALITY CONTROL

The purpose of the guiding questions serves to focus student attention so that they develop learning tasks that meet the compulsory requirements for individual subjects. The form of any facilitator guidance takes, is dependent upon the maturity and experience of the students. Often the facilitators' responses are often in the form of feedback on the students' plans or via probing questions designed to highlight weaknesses in their plans. Often the wording of these questions was critical to the success of the next stage of the process and time and thought must be devoted to the wording of these questions.

In addition students and facilitating lecturers consulted with subject co-ordinators to receive critical feedback on proposed tasks. This ensured that the tasks meet the expectations of all stakeholders. Further, each KBC group was given the opportunity to convince a critical audience of experienced staff of the quality of their work at a final presentation day held at the end of the session.

CONCLUDING COMMENTS

We believe that the KBC process acts as a stimulus for the achievement of one of the long-term goals of most teacher education courses i.e. a strong commitment to life-long professional learning. The four pillars together with the four-stage approach to curriculum integration provide a set of structures, processes, and a form of discourse for KBC students, university facilitators and participating school-based teachers. This discourse assists all participants in on-going construction and refinement of understandings about their role(s) in the profession and of the transformative nature of their profession. To achieve this they need to be involved in ongoing discourse that will both challenge and affirm strongly held knowledge and beliefs. Such a process requires participants to be exposed to opposing views and alternatives to 'accepted' practices. Thus participants are exposed to a wide range of information and views about what teachers know, do expect and value and this has the potential to significantly influence the nature, extent and rate of future learning of their pupils. In addition the process stimulates all stakeholders to explore innovative approaches to learning and assessment in a university context that is increasingly regulated by stringent quality controls.

During their careers in education graduates of teacher education courses will be continually challenged to revisit many of the issues initially raised during their undergraduate course. We believe that the principles of professional learning that were articulated and experienced through the four pillars model of the KBC will serve as a scaffold allowing graduates to re-apply the principles and processes used in the undergraduate degree to the professional context of the full-time classroom teacher. Further, if the KBC process is achieving its stated goals, we should be able to observe that graduates are applying such processes in their professional lives.

Finally, it is important to restate that there are many education faculties throughout the world who are experimenting with alternative approaches to teacher education and our story represents one contribution to this growing body of knowledge about alternative approaches to initial teacher education. Indeed our own faculty has adapted the processes described in this chapter to trial an integrated assessment approach with the entire first-year primary education intake in 2004.

REFERENCES

Aldred, S. E., Aldred, M. J., Walsh, L. J., & Dick, B. (1997). *The direct and indirect costs of implementing problem-based learning into traditional professional courses within universities.* Department of Employment, Education Training and Youth Affairs: Australia.

Armour, L., & Booth, E. (1999). Analysis of a questionnaire to primary educators at schools accepting students for the six week extended practicum. Report by Faculty of Education: University of Wollongong.

Bereiter, C. & Scardamalia, M. (1993). Surpassing ourselves: An inquiry into the nature and implications of expertise. Chicago, IL: Open Court.

Bransford, J. D., Sherwood, R. D., Hasselbring, T.S., Kinzer, C.K., & Williams S.M. (1990). Anchored Instruction: Why we need it and how technology can help. In D. Nix & R. Spiro (Eds.) Cognition, Education Multimedia: Exploring ideas in high technology, (pp. 115–141). Hillsdale: Lawrence Erlbaum.

Bullough, R. V. (1987). Accommodation and tension: Teachers, teacher role, and the culture of teaching. In: J. Smyth. *Educating teachers: Changing the nature of pedagogical knowledge.* (pp. 83–94). London: The Falmer Press.

Commonwealth of Australia (2002). *An Ethic of Care—Effective Programmes for Beginning Teachers.* Canberra: Department of Education, Science and Training.

Darling-Hammond, L. (1999). Teacher Education: Rethinking Practice and Policy. *Unicorn 25*(1), 31–48.

Duch, J. B. (1995). What is Problem-Based Learning? from The Newsletter for the for the *Centre for Teaching Effectiveness*, University of Delaware. Available URL: http://www.udel.edu/pbl/cte/jan95-what.html. Accessed: 29/03/98.

Entwhistle, N., Entwhistle A., & Tait H.(1993). Academic Understanding and the Contexts to Enhance It: A perspective from research on student learning. In T.M. Duffy, J. Lowyck & D.H. Jonassen (Eds). *Design Environments for Constructive Learning*, (pp. 331–357). Heidelberg: Springer-Verlag.

Felder, R. M., & Brent, R. (1996). *Navigating the bumpy road to student-centred instruction*. Available URL: http://www2.ncsu.edu/unity/lockers/users/f/felder/public/Papers/Resist.html. Accessed: 28/07/00.

Grant, L. M. (1994). *An evaluation of the effectiveness of preservice language education in one university* Unpublished Honours Thesis, Faculty of Education, University of Wollongong. University of Wollongong: Australia.

Hoban, G. H. (1999). Using a reflective framework for experiential learning in teacher education classes. *Journal of Experiential Education, 22*(2). 104–111.

Koetsier, C. P., & Wubbels, J. T. (1995). Bridging the gap between initial teacher training and teacher induction. *Journal of Education for Teaching. 21*(3), 333–345.

MACQT (1998). Teacher preparation for student management: Responses and directions. *Report by Ministerial Advisory Council on the Quality of Teaching, October, 1998*. Sydney: NSW Department of Education and Training.

Margetson, D. (1994). *Current educational reform and the significance of problem-based learning*. Griffith University: Carfax Publishing Company.

Ramsey, G. (2000). *Quality matters. Revitalising teaching: critical times, critical choices*. NSW Department of Education and Training: Sydney.

Reid, A., & O'Donoghue, M. (2001, September). *Rethinking Teacher Education Policy*. Paper presented at Australian Teacher Education Association Conference. Melbourne.

Scardamalia. M., & Bereiter, C. (1991). Higher levels of agency for children in knowledge building: A challenge for the design of new knowledge media. *The Journal of the Learning Sciences, 1* (1), 37–68.

Scardamalia. M., & Bereiter, C. (1996). Student communities for the advancement of knowledge. *Communications of the ACM, 39*(4), 36–37.

Scardamalia, M., & Bereiter, C. (1999) *Schools as knowledge building organisations*. Available URL: http://csile.oise.utoronto.ca/abstracts/ciar-understanding.html Accessed: 08/01/00.

Vinson, T. (2002). *Report of the Independent Inquiry into Public Education in New South Wales*. NSW Government: Sydney.

Vygotsky, L. (1978). *Mind in Society: The development of higher psychological processes*. Cambridge: Harvard University Press.

White, H. (1996). *Dan tries problem-based learning: A case study*. Available URL: http://www.udel.edu/pbl/dancase3.html. Accessed: 29/03/99.

Woods, D. (1994). *How to gain the most from problem-based learning*. McMaster University: McMaster.

Chapter 6

Teacher Education for the Middle Years of Schooling: Making Connections between Fields of Knowledge, Educational Policy Reforms and Pedagogical Practice

Jane Mitchell[1], Lisa Hunter[2], Lisa Patel Stevens[2] & Diane Mayer[2]
Monash University[1]
University of Queensland[2], *Australia*

> I propose a dialogic restructuring of teacher education that begins with the recognition that multiple realities, voices, and discourses conjoin and clash in the process of coming to know.
>
> (Britzman, 2003, p. 49)

Britzman's notion of dialogic restructuring and the 'clashing' and 'conjoining' of ideas provides a framework for examining the development of a reform initiative in teacher education in Australia—a program concerned specifically with preparing teachers for the middle years of schooling. The middle years of schooling have been the focus of education reform efforts in Australia over the last decade, with a growing interest at grassroots and systemic levels in policy and practice related to the education of young adolescents. In the Australian context, middle schooling developments have not been accompanied in any systematic or on-going way by specialised teacher preparation programs. This chapter discusses one programmatic response to middle schooling initiatives by a teacher education institution—the development of a new Middle Years of Schooling Teacher Education (MYSTE) program at The University of Queensland (UQ). Considering the emergent state of middle schooling in Australia, alongside the rapidly changing social, economic and technological context underpinning the current and future educational needs of young people, this new teacher education program represented a conceptual and practical opportunity and challenge for the UQ team, including the authors of this chapter. Working collaboratively, the team sought to design a pre-service teacher education program that was both responsive to school reform initiatives and generative of new theories and practices associated with teacher education.

G. Hoban (ed.), The Missing Links in Teacher Education Design, 95–112.

A common theme in both the literature on middle schooling and teacher education is the notion of connection and integration across subject areas, courses, and fields of practice (Beane, 1997; Tom, 1997). This chapter explores some of the background to these concepts and how they play out in the context of the MYSTE program. Two brief case studies that highlight connections across disciplinary fields and between campus-based courses will be presented. Through the descriptions we focus on ways in which particular pedagogical tools mediate connections between the people and ideas integral to the program. In each case we consider how these connections align with policy reforms in the school sector in Queensland, and what they might mean as part of challenging taken for granted knowledge, and taken for granted ways of coming to know, in teacher education programs. As with any reform initiative, this teacher education program has experienced a mixture of successes and failures. Thus, the chapter does not claim to be a blueprint for change; rather it seeks to identify the instructive elements emerging from this effort at curricular and pedagogical reform in teacher education.

THE CONTEXT FOR 'MIDDLE YEARS' INITIATIVES—SCHOOLS AND TEACHER EDUCATION

The design of a teacher education program focussed on the 'middle years' rests on two premises. First, that schools need to develop specific practices that meet the needs of students in the 'middle years'[1], particularly given the rapidly changing world in which students of this phase of schooling are shaping their identities and ideas of the future. The second premise is that initial teacher education programs need to prepare teachers to work specifically with this group of students. The social and educational background to these two premises is described below.

The School Context

While the notions of middle school and middle schooling have been common, particularly in parts of North America for some years, it is only over the last decade or so that middle schooling has attracted attention in the Australian educational context. The literature pertaining to the need for specific curricular practices in the middle years converges around some key and related themes. First, young people in this phase of schooling have particular social, emotional,

[1] Although a somewhat ill-defined term, we use the concept 'middle years' to refer to students in Grade 5 to Grade 9 (aged 10–15 years). While no hard and fast rules exist in terms of defining the age group and year level for middle years, most typically it is used to talk about the upper years of primary school and the lower years of high school. Middle Schooling is often used to refer to sets of school practices perceived as relevant to students in these grade levels.

physical and intellectual needs that have not been adequately catered for in the traditional primary/high school structures (Hargreaves, Earl, & Ryan, 1996). Second, many students in the middle years find school alienating and become disengaged from learning. Consequently a 'year 8 dip' is noted in terms of student outcomes (Hill & Russell, 1999) and quality of pedagogy (Lingard, Ladwig, Luke, Mills, Hayes, & Gore, 2001). Third, the current and future needs and young people are changing rapidly in light of new communications technologies, changing patterns of work and family, 'knowledge-based' economies, and global movements of people (Luke, Luke, & Mayer, 2000). A criticism levelled at schools is that current, and what may be termed traditional approaches to school curricula, are unresponsive to the ways in which many young people are negotiating new forms of popular culture, communicating using digital technologies, and creating their identity in a context of rapidly shifting social, cultural and economic relations both within families and the wider community (e.g., Green, Reid, & Bigum, 1998; Hagood, Stevens, & Reinking, 2002).

In the state of Queensland there has been a flurry of educational activity over the last five years in terms of developing school policy and practice that more adequately meets the current and future needs of students in the 'middle years'. This activity has been in response to both the findings of a major piece of research in Queensland state schools, the Queensland School Reform Longitudinal Study (QSRLS) (Lingard et al., 2001), as well as other national and international literature concerned with schooling in the middle years, see for example, *From Alienation to Engagement* (Australian Curriculum Studies Association, 1995); *The National Middle Schooling Project* (1996–1998); *Extending reform in the middle years of schooling: Challenges and responses* (Cumming, 1998). While there are numerous curricular and pedagogical emphases in this literature, two broad and related themes relevant to this chapter include the need for curriculum that is connected to the particular academic, cultural and social needs of young people in a rapidly changing social and economic context, and secondly an integrated or transdisciplinary curriculum in which connections are made across curriculum fields in ways that address real world problems, and/or in ways that are responsive to new forms of knowledge that extend and challenge traditional curriculum boundaries.

Key among the initiatives in Queensland schools has been the trialing a 'New Basics' curriculum in 50 of its government schools.[2] While the New Basics curriculum has been designed for Grades 1–9, its relationship to the demands for curricular reform in the middle years is obvious. The New Basics initiative is a radical refashioning of the curriculum that seeks to address

[2] Further detail regarding the New Basics curricular project developed by Education Queensland can be found at www.education.qld.gov.au (or refer to Education Queensland, 2000).

broad-brush social and technological change; reduce and revamp the number of 'subjects' in the curriculum through transdisciplinary study and a focus on content that is intellectually engaging and connected to students' lives; and align curriculum content with pedagogy and assessment. Other examples of what could be termed 'middle schooling' practices developed in Queensland schools include: the creation of Year 1–Year 12 campuses which have within them junior, middle and senior structures; transition programs between primary schools and high schools; a focus on integration across subject areas in high schools (e.g., transdisciplinary projects, rich tasks); and the use of the Productive Pedagogies as a planning tool.[3] While there are numerous initiatives in schools in Queensland, it is important to keep in mind that the level of reform is still in its initial stages, and the social and academic outcomes associated with these reforms have yet to be comprehensively evaluated.

Most recently the Queensland State Government released new policy related to what it has termed the Middle Phase of Schooling (Grades 4–9). The State School Action Plan (Education Queensland, 2003) that is part of this policy, identifies key challenges and actions in the following areas: focus and accountability (at a school level); curriculum, teaching and assessment; achievement (literacy, numeracy and extra-curricular opportunities); transition from primary to high school; teachers (professional development, pre-service provision, recognition of MY as a specific area of expertise). In the context of this paper, a key action pertains to the last point, the professional learning of teachers, particularly in the pre-service phase.

The Teacher Education Context

Recent Queensland policy notwithstanding, a noticeable silence in the discussion of middle schooling in Australia has been the link between the development of new curricular practices and teacher education. While some attention has been paid to the professional development needs of teachers working to create teaching and learning approaches relevant to young people, there has been little by way of response, until recently, of the role that could be taken by faculties of education to develop postgraduate or undergraduate degree programs that credential teachers to work in middle years settings.

[3] Productive Pedagogies was the term used in the Queensland School Reform Longitudinal Study to describe and subsequently rate classroom practice. The four dimensions of productive pedagogy in this study were: levels of intellectual engagement; connectedness of the curriculum to factors outside of school; degree of safety and supportiveness in the classroom; and extent to which social and cultural difference is taken into account in curriculum and pedagogy. Following the study Education Queensland instituted a program of professional development for teachers in which they are introduced to the Productive Pedagogies Framework.

The lack of alignment between schooling practices and teacher education practices, and any reform of those practices, is not new. In his analysis of teacher education and its future in the Australian context, Smith noted that: "not one of the fundamental training sector and school transformations presently underway in Australia advantages teacher education institutions or teacher educators" (2000, p. 10). He argues further that in the current climate of restructuring taking place in both schools and universities in Australia, the divisions between these two institutions are widening. In the middle schooling context we would argue that practices have developed in ways independent of teacher education programs and any reform of teacher education. That this is problematic is obvious and reflects, not only the marginal status of teacher education with respect to school reform, but also the endemic ideological and pragmatic divisions related to conceptions of curriculum and teacher education, and held by those in school sectors and universities.

The problem mentioned above is one example of the more generic problem of program fragmentation (across courses and between campus and schools, between content and pedagogy, knowledge and interest) that has been well-documented in the teacher education literature (Britzman, 2003; Gore, 1995; Lowenberg Ball, 2000; Tom, 1997). In conceptualising models of teacher education that seek to make alignments across sectors, courses, and local and global contexts, Luke et al. (2000) make the case that there is a need to go beyond the usual reforms that seek to simply rearrange the relationship between foundations, curriculum and practice-based parts of teacher education programs. As an example of such reform, Smith argues that there is a need in teacher education to generate new types of knowledge that are not reliant on the traditional methods of knowledge production, and traditional methods of learning that knowledge. Central to his ideas are broad-based platforms and networks for teacher education in which schools, universities, professional associations, parent groups and unions take a role in the process of teacher education. Smith bluntly argues that:

> University-based teacher education is no longer essential to the self-reproduction of the school system in anything more than the accreditation of awards role... What exactly is taught or produced as knowledge has mattered less and less in teacher education over the last few decades because increasingly, it does not matter. (2000, p. 13)

Such arguments provide a critical stimulus to rethinking program design in teacher education in ways that are related to the broad social context of schooling and knowledge production, and that align more specifically with current school reforms such as those taking place in the middle years of schooling in Australia.

THE MIDDLE YEARS OF SCHOOLING TEACHER EDUCATION PROGRAM

It is within the context described above that we discuss the establishment of the MYSTE program at The University of Queensland. The task as we see it is to make explicit the content focus for professional development around which bridging between school reform and teacher education reform can take place. The process of designing, staffing and establishing procedures for the recognition and approval of this degree program began four years ago. The first cohort of students entered the program in 2002.

The Middle Years of Schooling Teacher Education program is located on the new Ipswich campus of The University of Queensland.[4] The 'newness' of the campus has enabled a form of program design that has been, to some degree, free of long-standing institutional structures and routines that often constrain the reconceptualisation of teacher education programs. The purpose underpinning the development of the Ipswich campus has also been an important contextual variable in program design. The campus was created in order to make university education more accessible to those in the Ipswich region. Ipswich, with a population of 135,000, is a city 45 kilometres west of Brisbane, the capital of Queensland. The city's economic base was in coal mining and servicing the rural communities to its west. However, its economic prosperity has wavered over the last two decades, which in turn has put pressure on the social fabric of the community. The development of the campus is part of an attempt to shift and regenerate the social and economic base of the Ipswich region by providing infrastructure for a 'knowledge economy', and for community-based research and education. Designing programs that are relevant to the needs of individuals and institutions in the local community is a key part of the vision associated with this campus.

Conceptual Framework for the Program

The curricular and pedagogical framework central to both the teacher education program at UQ and the middle years initiatives being developed particularly in Queensland schools, can be broadly conceived in relation to the following:

(i) changing conceptions of knowledge and what it is important for teachers and students to know in a global society (Britzman, 2000; Luke et al., 2000);

[4] The campus opened in 1999.

(ii) changing ways in which knowledge is communicated, represented and translated in pedagogical and other settings, particularly through new technologies (Burbules & Callister, 2000; Willinsky, 1999); and,

(iii) models of pedagogy that emphasise dialogue and debate, intellectual engagement, connections across fields of practice, and problem solving (Wells, 1999).

The above three points and the ways in which they have been built into the design of the teacher education program presuppose particular assumptions about knowledge, inquiry and processes of learning. Central to these assumptions are social theories of learning and knowledge construction that explicate the inter-relationships and inter-dependence between 'knowers', 'knowing' and 'known'. Wells (1999), for example, argues that 'knowing is not done in isolation' and that it is the connections and inter-relationship between people, artefacts, resources, and mediational tools that are crucial to the process of understanding. Britzman (2003, p. 50) likewise contends that that knowing is not separate from values and experiences, or from pedagogy. Importantly, Britzman (p. 54) also argues that the social negotiation associated with processes of coming to know are not always seamless and complementary, and that the connections between ideas, and the translation of ideas from one context to another, can be contradictory, competing, and contested. In the context of this paper we focus in particular on aspects of pedagogy that provide the mediational tools for connecting ideas and people across courses and curriculum areas.

The inter-relationship between knowers, knowing and known also presupposes the importance of context for knowledge construction. Given the current context of rapidly changing and expanding bodies of knowledge, the program curriculum is underpinned by a futures orientation, one that seeks to challenge traditional curriculum boundaries in both teacher education and school contexts by taking account of the needs and interests of young adolescents in a highly technologised global society.

Program Design

The teacher education program is part of a dual degree set of offerings that enable students to complete two years of study in a general degree area—social science, behavioural studies or contemporary studies—and two years of study in a professional degree such as education. Particular requirements in the selection of courses in the initial degree provide students with an understanding of the social and psychological experiences of adolescents, as well as the disciplinary knowledge relevant for teaching specific subject areas in schools.

Integral to the Bachelor of Education degree is a strong programmatic commitment to study that is inter-disciplinary and connected to student teachers' experiences. Thus, for example, an inter-disciplinary approach to course design and the teaching of curriculum methods has been adopted in ways that coincide with the trial of the New Basics curricular reform in Queensland schools, and integrated curriculum studies advocated in the middle schooling literature. Courses that combine specific curriculum areas and that seek to develop an interdisciplinary and futures-oriented approach to the curriculum have been termed 'Frames'.[5] The assessment in the program is in part underpinned by collaborative research tasks that bring together issues that are of a cross-course nature.[6] In addition, there is a coursework focus on curricular and pedagogical problems that emerge from topics considered in the initial degree, from educational research relevant to middle years, from developments in local schools, and from students' own experiences as students and student teachers. A further important contextual feature is the size of the program. There is a core group of seven faculty and the anticipated maximum enrolment in any one year is 80 students. In the cases described below there was a cohort of 50 students. The program, by comparison with many others, is not large and this enables regular face-to-face and electronic communication between faculty, and between faculty and students.

In the sections that follow we examine the design and implementation of two of the MYSTE programmatic connections, and the mediating tools employed to make those connections. The first example discusses the third 'Frame' course. This course considers and seeks to connect the curriculum fields of mathematics and health/physical education, and more broadly numeracy and embodiment. Examples of assignments, teaching approaches and student work are considered in this case study. The second example describes the connections between two courses, one focussed on pedagogy in the middle years and the other focussed on diversity and social justice in schools. In this case we describe one pedagogical tool designed to enable students to consider the ethical dimensions underpinning their teaching practice, and particularly to consider how specific pedagogical and curricular choices are framed by broad discourses of identity and subjectivity. In both cases we have sought to systematically investigate aspects of our own teaching practice. This process has involved video-recording lessons, observing and providing feedback on each others' teaching, collecting and analysing samples of student work,

[5] The Frame combinations include: English education and Technology education; Science education and the Arts education; Mathematics education and Health/Physical Education. Studies of Society and its Environment is a stand along Frame.

[6] The research tasks model the 'Rich Task' assessment projects that are part of the New Basics trial.

interviewing students, and documenting our reflections. In the examples presented we do not want to make the case that these connections are in any way the solution to problems of fragmentation in teacher education, or that they coherently link with school reform. Rather we present examples of ways in which the MYS program has experimented with making connections in order to consider some of the possibilities these connections offer, as well as some of the problems.

MAKING CONCEPTUAL LINKS ACROSS THE UNIVERSITY CURRICULUM

Case Study 1: Connecting Maths and Health/PE (Written by Lisa Hunter)

Frame 3 was a semester long course in the third semester of the two year program. The frame brought together two Key Learning Areas (KLAs), namely Health and Physical Education (HPE) and Mathematics. While the curricular practices associated with these KLAs are not typically seen in an integrated way, this Frame sought to find points of connection between some of the broad concepts embedded in these disciplinary fields. The Frame had a particular focus on numeracy, embodiment and movement in relation to the curricular and pedagogical experiences of young people in the middle years of schooling.

To connect the course with pre-service teachers' experiences I conducted a survey prior to the course to determine students' values, beliefs, knowledges and experiences related to numeracy, health, physical activity and personal development. Many of the students reported negative experiences and a lack of knowledge with regards to the depth and scope of both of these learning areas. Reports of this kind are common amongst those entering primary teaching and in some ways were not surprising within this cohort because most had completed specialist degrees, or the initial part of their dual degree, in disciplines not connected to mathematics or HPE. The responses provided by the students in the initial survey provided an important starting point for the design of the course. An approach was developed that enabled students to explore the pedagogical tools and discipline content associated with both the Queensland mathematics and HPE syllabus documents. At the same time the course sought to interrupt the traditional and 'balkanised' school curriculum organisers by questioning traditional knowledge within these subject areas, and making connections across the two disciplinary fields with reference to, for example, methods of thinking associated with relatively new fields such as biomechanics.

The following descriptions of some of the assessment and class tasks illustrate aspects of the pedagogical practices put in place to achieve the above intent. The first assessment task required students to conduct an autoethnography in which they put themselves in the position of being new learners in relation to a physical activity for six weeks. Students undertook a range of activities such as yoga, medieval fighting, cycling and squash. Students documented their responses to that learning, noted the physical, emotional and intellectual aspects of that learning, and compared it to their own learning about physical activity in their school experience. Some of the key learnings documented by students through this experience included: that some of their prior assumptions about movement and physical activity were incorrect; that particular physical activities have their own culture that needs to be learned in order to participate; and that for the first time they had had a positive experience in a sport or recreational club.

The second assignment involved in-class peer teaching in which students sought to both teach through movement and to integrate this movement with the knowledge represented in a range of curriculum areas. The medium for movement was Tai Chi. I have some expertise in Tai chi and would teach a small group of students one movement, they would then practice and teach the larger group of students. This provided students with an opportunity to think about their own learning through movement and then to process how they might teach this movement to others. In the peer teaching activity the students would also consider how they could integrate ideas from a range of curriculum areas into an integrated unit on Tai Chi. Most students made the connections more broadly to aspects of ancient Chinese culture by considering language, mathematics and artistic symbols, the history of Tai chi and its links to Taoism. Other students connected Tai Chi to science and technology by considering the physics of the body in relation to balance and gravity. Certainly some of the integrations made by students were to some degree forced or overly generalised, yet the debriefing after the peer teaching activities provided a forum in which to consider some of these issues and how they might play out in the design of integrated units in school contexts. Aspects of student learning through this activity included: an understanding of ways in which learning areas could be integrated, and the creative as well as forced ways that integration can sometimes occur; ways in which something that looked easy to do was difficult to teach; and ways in which parts of teaching could be made explicit through teaching movement.

Other in-class activities likewise involved seeking connections across maths and HPE. One task involved an examination of issues pertaining to human bodies and the use of mathematical data to describe and inscribe bodies. Thus students considered issues pertaining to the following: obesity, body image, the measurement of size and shape, and the interpretation of demographic statistics; athletics and the measurement of speed and distance; the biomechanics of the human body and the interpretation of measurement and statistical data pertaining to biomechanics.

On the one hand making these connections across disciplines and curriculum areas proved to be relatively straightforward as the students had minimal and sometimes misinformed information regarding the syllabus documents and the conceptions of knowledge embedded in those documents. On the other hand because many of the students had negative experiences of their own in mathematics and HPE classes, or had not pursued these subject areas in higher degree studies, the degree to which they were able to build on strong disciplinary knowledge, have confidence in their knowledge base, and make complex connections, was limited.

The pragmatics of practicum placements also created some dilemmas in the structuring of this Frame. Students were placed in a variety of school settings for the practicum, from traditional primary and secondary school settings to purpose-built middle schools using a New Basics curriculum. On the one hand, in those instances in which students were placed in more traditional settings, especially high schools, they were able to recognise how tightly knowledge was claimed and reproduced through school structures and teachers' attitudes. On the other hand, the nature of the placements constrained the freedom of many students to develop integrated units, particularly units that related to mathematics or HPE. These two areas are not often considered sites for integration in schools and moreover, are not necessarily the areas in which student teachers have disciplinary knowledge or confidence. Some students were, however, able to more broadly extrapolate some of the concepts pertaining to movement and numeracy into their teaching units in the social sciences or language arts areas. For example one student created an integrated social science unit that examined ways of portraying the body in historical and contemporary times. These broad extrapolations hold considerable possibility as a way of extending approaches to integration and learning, without necessarily having the specialist knowledge in a disciplinary field.

Case Study 2: Blurring Boundaries between Courses (Written by Jane Mitchell and Lisa Patel Stevens)

This case examines the blurring of boundaries between two courses: Pedagogical Issues in the Middle Years of Schooling and Supporting Diverse Learners. Within and across each course we have sought to blur boundaries between two aspects of teacher education programs that are often tightly drawn: the day to day aspects of teaching, and broad social, cultural and political theories of identity, diversity and social justice in educational settings. In this case we do want to argue that both courses are underpinned by theories of pedagogy and diversity that presuppose the importance of connections between theory and practice, campus and school, experience and research. However, we argue that by conducting joint activities across both courses, we can work to make more explicit ways in which pedagogical and curricular decision-making, and associated interactions, both shape and reflect particular discourses of identity and difference. In so doing the key purpose of these joint activities is to assist students to identify some of the values and ethics underpinning any pedagogical interaction, and to consider how these ethical issues might inform their decision-making as teachers.

Connections are made throughout the two courses through joint assignments, team-teaching activities, and online discussions. In this particular case we want to examine one specific teaching and learning activity that is employed in the two courses. It is a values clarification exercise in which students consider the specific intersection between day-to-day pedagogical relations, curricular decision-making, and discourses of gender and sexuality. Questions pertaining to gender and sexuality in school contexts are of considerable interest and importance in this teacher education context for two reasons. First, there is an emerging body of educational literature documenting the alignment between shifting patterns of relationships, behaviours, learning outcomes, and responses to school amongst young adolescents, and the social constructs of gender and sexuality .(Lesko, 2001; Mills, 2001; Renold, 2003). Second, there is similar body of literature documenting ways in which gender and sexuality play out in teachers' identities and relationships with students in classrooms (Britzman, 2003; Thorne, 1993).

Prior to the values clarification exercise students had considered some of the sociological literature pertaining to young people, gender, sexuality and schooling in relation to both concepts of identity and subjectivity, and issues of social justice and equity. Moreover, the activity occurs well into the joint timeline of our courses, to ensure that an established sense of community which provides the foundation for dialogic exchange.

In this activity, our goals for the students are to participate in an example of recognitive pedagogy (Gale & Densmore, 2000) and to consider ways in which difference and diversity can be affirmed through day-to-day classroom practices. The activity sought to complicate the often taken for granted, or rarely discussed, gendered and heteronormative assumptions underpinning curricular and pedagogical practices in schools. At the same time, our key concern is to enable students to identify, discuss and justify their own beliefs and values in relation to a particular set of educational and ethical questions.

The activity takes place in a room cleared of furniture. The room is divided into halves using a piece of tape along the floor. Students are presented with four scenarios in which an ethical dilemma is posed in relation to pedagogy, gender and sexuality. The ethical issues posed in each dilemma contain at least two 'rights'. In each of the four scenarios students are positioned as a middle years teacher and are asked to make choices about their actions in relation to the following: how explicitly they acknowledge and support two young people who are 'going out' together; teachers' disclosure of their sexual identities to students; curriculum choices that explicitly and deliberately confront questions pertaining to gender and sexuality; communication with parents and community about curriculum choices concerned with sexualities.

The detail of each scenario is read to the students. At the end of each scenario a question is posed in which students consider the degree to which they agree or disagree with a particular pedagogical action. Students are asked to consider the strength and standpoint of their opinion by physically positioning themselves in the room, using the tape as a neutral marker of agreement or disagreement. The tape and the self-determined location of the students act as an embodied Likert scale as students spread along the scale of strongly agree to strongly disagree. Following each question and students' self-positioning, we facilitate whole group discussion, encouraging dialogue that articulates the reasons for taking particular stances on issues.

For example, one scenario builds the case around whether a teacher reveals his/her non-heterosexual identity to a school student. If the university student teachers strongly agree with disclosure, they move to the far left of the tape, and to the far right if they oppose disclosing. Students are asked to situate themselves silently, to sit down on the floor, and then we open up the discussion, asking students to share why they chose their position. In facilitating the discussion, we strived to clarify students' positions, make connections and comparisons among various perspectives, and to probe further about issues relevant to diversity, schooling, and pedagogy.

In each scenario there was inevitably a wide range of positions taken up by the students along the agree/disagree continuum: some students to the extremes and a spread of students in between. In the scenario mentioned above, for example, the following array of opinions and questions were aired: that teachers should not reveal their sexual identity because it brings a personal dimension to teacher/student relationships; that teachers should reveal their identity because it is important to have role models and it is nothing to be ashamed of; that teachers should not reveal their sexuality because it may be seen as influencing a student with ramifications for both the student and teacher; that by wearing a wedding ring many teachers are revealing their sexuality, so it is a double standard if teachers are unable to reveal their homosexuality. In discussing their location along the continuum with peers, students were able to explain their decisions, take account of the opinions of others, and then draw on a range of ideas to inform and justify their own point of view.

Through the discussions following each scenario students identified their beliefs and values, not only about sexuality and gender, but also about teaching, about young people, and the curriculum. They also noted how their positions shifted and/or strengthened through the contributions of others to the discussion. We aimed to hold back our own opinions during the reading and discussion of the four scenarios, so that students' viewpoints are privileged, and to emphasise that there is no one answer to these dilemmas. As facilitators our concern is not to simply ensure that all opinions are given equal weight, instead we favour the more difficult but necessary stance of asking students to consider various positions in re-evaluating and reconsidering their own values, and to ask students to make clear the tools they were drawing on to justify their points of view (Gale & Densmore, 2000; Nieto, 2000). Once all four scenarios and various issues have been discussed, a larger debriefing was facilitated, and we considered how points raised in the discussion can be connected back to broad theories of curriculum and gender/sexuality.

In this case the mediational or pedagogical tool—the values clarification exercise—was central to enabling students to make a three-fold set of connections between discourses of identity/subjectivity; day-to-day pedagogical and curricular decision making; and their own beliefs, values and assumptions. In making these connections students were able to identify, clarify and justify their own position and the actions they would take in relation to a set of ethical dilemmas. The breadth and variation of opinion expressed in each discussions served to illustrate Britzman's .(2003) concern that multiple voices 'conjoin and clash through the process of coming to know'. The activity in this respect enabled students to consider the ways in which pedagogical interactions are underpinned by sets of personal, cultural and political values and discourses.

CONCLUSION: THEORISING CONNECTIONS

A key purpose of the pedagogy in the two examples documented above is to provide the conditions that will support student teachers' engagement with not only the complex practice of teaching, but also the emerging practices of middle schooling. In each case the pedagogical tools provided the means through which ideas about curriculum, students, teachers and pedagogy could be connected and mediated. While one layer of connections existed between courses or curriculum areas, there was a second layer of connections between the people involved (their values, actions, beliefs, experiences), the mediational processes (the pedagogical tools and activities), and the

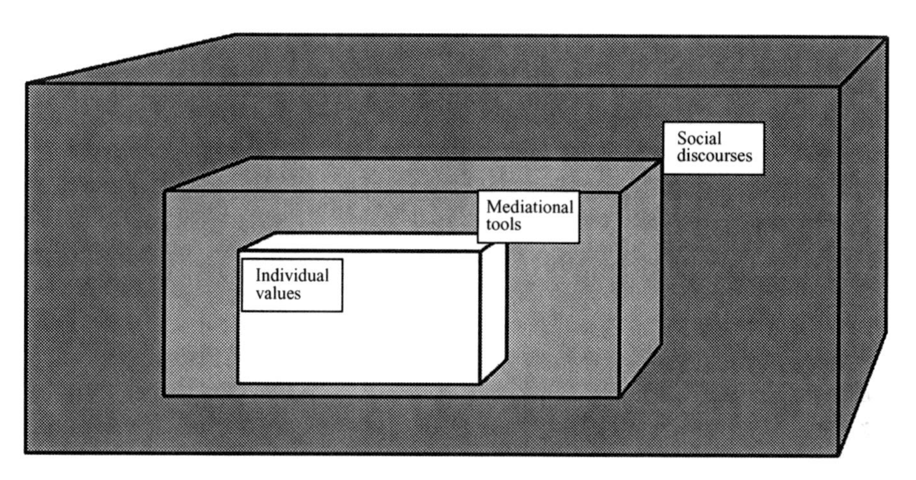

Figure 6.1. Theory of pedagogy diagram.

content/disciplinary/curriculum fields. These connections are represented in Figure 6.1.

These connections are responsive to the call made by Wideen, Mayer-Smith and Moon (1998), who argue that students in teacher education programs need to be able to examine their own experiences in light of a wider set of experiences, theories and practices. They also serve to make explicit the multiple, uncertain, and sometimes contradictory, subject positions one can take up as a teacher and a student (Britzman, 2003). In this respect the connections have not sought to develop a unitary conception of teaching in the middle years, rather they have sought to expand and complicate thinking in ways that both make explicit and challenge the values underpinning curricular and pedagogical practices. Moreover and more specifically, the connections sought to orientate students to new curricular and pedagogical possibilities relevant to young people.

While our intention, and the intention in much of the literature on middle schooling, has been to create learning contexts that require students to integrate understandings in ways that address real problems, we are also aware of some of the pitfalls associated with this model. The connections, as the case studies demonstrate, created some of their own contradictory and competing discourses, and it is being able to understand and work with these contradictions that is crucial to the program. The contradictory and competing discourses also manifested themselves most strongly through the relationship between the campus-based and school-based parts of the program.

As mentioned earlier the practices constitutive of middle schooling are new, emerging, or yet to be constructed, and as a consequence are subject to debate in schools. During the practicum students are placed in a range of settings, traditional primary and high schools, as well as purpose built middle schools, and have been asked to teach within the confines of traditional subject divisions as well as cross-curricular units. Not surprisingly, questions have been asked about the degree to which the MYSTE program prepares students with adequate content knowledge to teach across a range of curriculum areas in the middle years, and/or in ways that enable them to design and teach integrated units that connect fields of knowledge in rigorous and worthwhile ways. While questions about the adequacy of teachers' curriculum content knowledge are relevant to all teacher education programs, they seem to have a sharper focus in this program because of its newness, because of the newness of the policy directions and practices pertaining to middle schooling in Queensland schools, because there are multiple and competing views regarding the nature and value of middle schooling practices, and because they challenge some of the taken for granted assumptions about the organisation of secondary schools. The focus is also sharpened by the very fact that student teachers are required to show a degree of proficiency in establishing a set of teaching and learning practices in classrooms. This means that student teachers are caught in the 'push-pull' not just between theory and practice, but also between what is and what might/should/will be in the future. A key question for those working in schools and teacher education programs, and more particularly given the focus of this paper, for teacher educators in both contexts, is to work out what might be termed the 'complication threshold' or the degree of complication that can be managed without rendering practices unworkable.

Farr Darling argues that: "In an important sense, learning to teach is learning to examine existing practices and promising alternatives" (2001, p. 8). This requires making connections between traditional or current practice and future practice, and provides a useful clue for conceptualising the sorts of alignments necessary between teacher education and schools in times of reform. The dilemma for student teachers is that not only do they have to examine classroom practice, but they also have to effectively participate in it across a range of settings in both school and university contexts. The degree to which pedagogical and curricular practices are rendered problematic or something that is simply conformed to varies across each setting. Thus learning to engage in those practices as a beginning teacher takes on multiple forms and can require participating in practices that contradict ones own values and/or in which there are contested values represented in different aspects of the school and teacher education curriculum. On one level it would seem to make sense to iron out these competing values so that connections between ideas in a teacher education program are seamless. However, on another level it is perhaps more useful to suggest that the contradictions, the conjoining and clashing of ideas, in the complex process of learning to teach are inevitable. Thus the purpose of the dialogue, the pedagogy that makes possible connections between people and ideas and between past and future, is to make explicit the multiple discourses and the processes of interpretation and negotiation required to engage in learning to teach.

REFERENCES

Australian Curriculum Studies Association. (1995). *From alienation to engagement: Opportunities for reform in the middle years*. Canberra: Australian Curriculum Studies Association.

Beane, J. A. (1997). *Curriculum Integration: Designing the Core of Democratic Education*. New York and London: Teachers College Press.

Britzman, D. (2000). Teacher education in the confusion of our times. *Journal of Teacher Education, 51*(3), 200–205.

Britzman, D. (2003). *Practice Makes Practice: A Critical Study of Learning to Teach* (Revised ed.). Albany USA: State University of New York Press.

Burbules, N. C., & Callister, T. A. (2000). *Watch IT: the Risks and Promises of Information Technologies for Education*. Boulder, Colorado: Westview Press.

Cumming, J. (1998). *Extending reform in the middle years of schooling: Challenges and responses*. Canberra: Australian Curriculum Studies Association.

Education Queensland. (2000). *New Basics Project*. Brisbane: New Basics Branch Queensland State Education.

Education Queensland. (2003). *See the Future. The Middle Phase of Learning State School Action Plan*. Brisbane: Queensland Government.

Farr Darling, L. (2001). When Conceptions Collide: constructing a community of inquiry for teacher education in British Columbia. *Journal of Education for Teaching, 27*(1), 7–21.

Gale, T., & Densmore, K. (2000). *Just Schooling: explorations in the cultural politics of teaching*. Buckingham, England and Philadelphia: Open University Press.

Gore, J. (1995). *Emerging Issues in Teacher Education*. Perth, Australia: NPDP Project.

Green, B., Reid, J., & Bigum, C. (1998). Teaching the Nintendo generation? Children, computer culture and popular technologies. In S. Howard (Ed.), *Wired-up: Young people and the electronic media* (pp. 19–41). London: UCL Press.

Hagood, M. C., Stevens, L. P., & Reinking, D. (2002). What do THEY have to teach US? Talkin' cross generations! In D. Alverman (Ed.), *Adolescents and literacies in a digital world* (pp. 68–83). New York: Peter Lang.

Hargreaves, A., Earl, L., & Ryan, J. (1996). *Schooling for change: Reinventing education for early adolescents*. London: Falmer Press.

Hill, P., & Russell, J. (1999). Systemic, whole-school reform of the middle years of schooling. In R. Bosker, B. Creemers & S. Stringfield (Eds.), *Enhancing educational excellence, equity and efficiency: Evidence from evaluation systems and schools in change*. Dordrecht: Kluwer Academic Publishers.

Lesko, N. (2001). *Act Your Age!: A Cultural Construction Of Adolescence*. New York: Routledge.

Lingard, B., Ladwig, J., Luke, A., Mills, M., Hayes, D., & Gore, J. (2001). *Queensland School Reform Longitudinal Study: final report*. Brisbane: Education Queensland.

Lowenberg Ball, D. (2000). Bridging Practices: Intertwining Content and Pedagogy in Teaching and Learning to Teach. *Journal of Teacher Education, 51*(3), 241–247.

Luke, A., Luke, C., & Mayer, D. (2000). Redesigning Teacher Education. *Teaching Education, 11*(1), 1–3.

Mills, M. (2001). *Challenging Violence in Schools: An issue of masculinities*. Buckingham, UK: Open University Press.
Nieto, S. (2000). *Affirming diversity: the sociopolitical context of multicultural education*. New York: Longman.
Renold, E. (2003). 'If You Don't Kiss Me, You're Dumped': boys, boyfriends and heterosexualised masculinities in the primary school. *Educational Review, 55*(2), 179–194.
Smith, R. (2000). The future of teacher education: Principles and practices. *Asia-Pacific Journal of Teacher Education, 28*(1), 7–22.
Thorne, B. (1993). *Crossing the Gender Divide*. Buckingham, England: Open University Press.
Tom, A. (1997). *Redesigning Teacher Education*. New York: State University of New York Press.
Wells, G. (1999). *Dialogic Inquiry: Toward a Sociocultural Practice and Theory of Education*. New York: Cambridge University Press.
Wideen, M., Mayer-Smith, J., & Moon, B. (1998). A critical analysis of the research on learning to teach: Making a case for an ecological perspective on inquiry. *Review of Educational Research, 68*(2), 130–178.
Willinsky, J. (1999). *Technologies of Knowing*. Boston: Beacon Press.

Part II

Theory-Practice Links between School and University Settings

Introduction by Garry F. Hoban

Part 1 of this book focused on ideas to provide links across the university curriculum. These ideas, identified and discussed in the previous six chapters are summarised in Figure A.

Part II of the book focuses on ideas to create links between theory and practice. Importantly, a common agreement amongst many student teachers, no matter what country they are in, is that they learn more about teaching in schools rather than in university classes. Green, Hamilton, Hampton and Ridgeway in Chapter 9 confirmed this belief with research from the University of Kansas in the USA. They found that students believed that their practicum was the most valuable part of their teacher education. In particular, students who stayed in teaching were often those that had extensive practicum experiences accompanied by quality supervision by their cooperating teachers. Beginning teachers with extensive practicum experiences during their education degree were the ones most likely to cope with the challenging first few years of teaching.

But why is learning in school settings most valued by student teachers? In Chapter 8, Tom Russell from Queen's University visits the fundamental assumptions that underpin the conventional "theory first, practicum later" approach versus the "practicum first, theory later" approach. He argues that having students experience schools first gives them a need and context for learning about educational theory. According to Russell, school experiences provide a context for learning as "we hear calls for constructivist approaches to learning, we hear about the potential of communities of learners, but we have no experience of creating, maintaining, and defending such approaches." Importantly, Tom Russell highlights ways in which teacher educators can draw on student experiences in schools such as modelling good practice, using reflection indirectly and using school experiences as content in teacher education classes.

A question that arises from considering alternative approaches to the placement of practicum is what is the relationship between schools and universities?

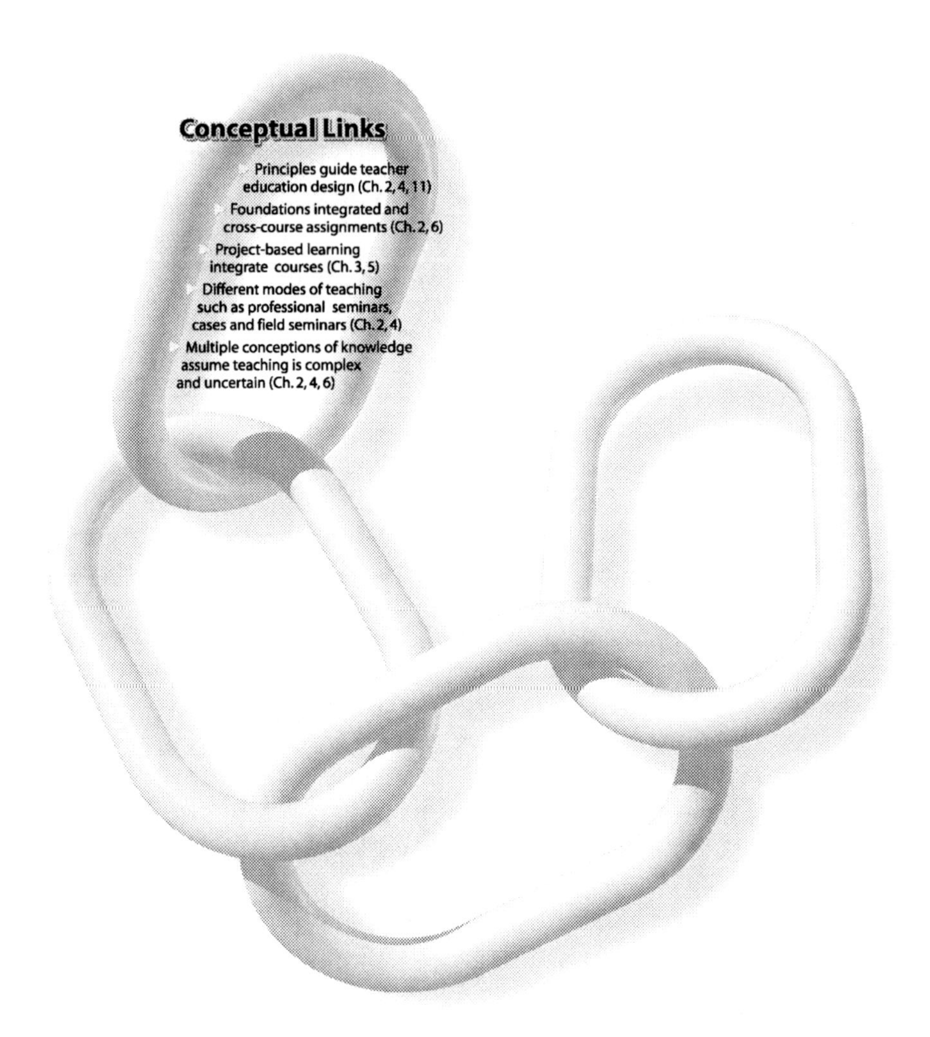

Figure A. Key ideas for conceptual links across the university curriculum

A conventional view of schools is that they are places to apply theory that is presented in university classes. A different type of relationship views both schools *and* universities as settings for generating theory. This means making connections between theoretical ideas generated in university classes and comparing these to practice in school settings. Conversely, it could involve theorizing from experience in school settings and discussing and comparing these to ideas from educational literature in university classes. Accordingly, there should be a reciprocal relationship between school and university settings.

Developing such a relationship implies that school and university experiences should be concurrent, not consecutive. Such a dialectic relationship is a feature of several programs in this book as exemplified in Chapters 2, 4, 5, 7 and 12. In Chapter 7, Anne Freese describes an innovative program developed at the University of Hawaii that is an "inquiry, reflective and collaborative approach to teacher preparation". Not only do the preservice teachers progress through the two-year degree in a cohort of 20–30 students, but a centrepiece of the program is that "schools should be centers of inquiry and places where knowledge is generated and produced, as opposed to merely transmitted." This view of the role of schools requires substantive time in the action setting and so students spend 12 hours per week in the field in the first two semesters of the program. To assist students to make connections between theory and practice, professional and field based seminars are conducted with common assignments and students are encouraged to research topics of interest in small groups and to present their findings in seminars. Various modes of learning are encouraged such as portrait research, action research, inquiry/problem based learning with reflection encouraged throughout. Hence, an important consideration as you read Part 2 of this book, is not only thinking about the quantity and placement of practicum, but the quality of the experiences as well.

Chapter 7

Innovation and Change in Teacher Education: An Inquiring, Reflective, Collaborative Approach

Anne Reilley Freese
University of Hawaii, USA

BACKGROUND AND CONTEXT OF THE TEACHER EDUCATION PROGRAM

Recent reforms in teaching and schooling have led teacher educators and educational researchers to rethink their conceptualizations of how learning about teaching takes place. The "theory first, practice later" approach that often characterizes preservice programs has been under criticism (Darling-Hammond, 1996; Darling-Hammond & Sykes, 1999; Goodlad, 1994; National Commission on Teaching & America's Future, 1996). The University of Hawaii began the journey of reinventing teacher preparation twelve years ago when it implemented the Master of Education in Teaching (MET) program. This two-year graduate program was developed as an innovative way to prepare teachers that challenges the traditional transmission approach to teacher education. The program has inquiry into practice as the core focus, a collaborative learning community as its cultural norm, and the development of effective teachers who are reflective practitioners as the goal. The integration of theory and practice is accomplished through the close school/university partnership. In the MET program students learn about teaching as they are immersed in real schools, interacting with real teachers teaching and with real students learning.

PHILOSOPHY UNDERLYING THE MET PROGRAM

The MET program can be described succinctly as an *inquiring, reflective, collaborative approach* to teacher preparation. The program operates very differently from the traditional model of student teaching which involves an apprenticeship structure, where preservice teachers learn the dominant curriculum in the schools (Zeichner & Tabachnick, 1981) and do not have time to engage in action research and reflective inquiry. Unlike many preservice programs in which the participants are placed in schools with only one or two other preservice teachers, the MET preservice teachers progress through

G. Hoban (ed.), The Missing Links in Teacher Education Design, 117–133.

the program in cohort groups of approximately 25 to-30 students, providing a cohesive element throughout the program. The program provides certification in the areas of elementary and secondary education. Students who select elementary certification are placed in an elementary partner school. Those who desire secondary certification are placed in a secondary partner school. In the partnership school context, conditions are established to promote collaboration, self-reflection, action research, and extensive field-based experiences. In this section, I will describe each of the components and discuss how they contribute to an innovative approach to teacher preparation.

Inquiring

Current research in learning and teaching emphasizes that students need to understand concepts and modes of inquiry as opposed to memorizing facts and formulas. Learning theorists believe that students do not develop this kind of understanding by merely absorbing the facts and information delivered by their teachers and books (Gardner, 1995). Schools should be centers of inquiry and places where knowledge is generated and produced, as opposed to merely transmitted. An inquiry-based approach, designed to promote reflection and critical thinking skills, actively involves the students in their learning and makes them responsible for their learning.

Reflective

Research that has guided the development of the MET program includes Dewey's theory that new understandings are expected to result from the process of reflective inquiry (Dewey, 1929). Teacher development and learning require problem identification and problem solving through continuous reflection and professional inquiry into one's practices. Students integrate theory and practice by researching and reflecting upon schools and classroom teaching. Schön (1983) argued that practitioners must generate their own professional knowledge in the context of practice. They cannot take the "expert" knowledge developed in universities and simply apply it, as technicians, since such knowledge is largely unusable in real-world contexts.

Collaborative

The MET Program views the classrooms and schools as "research sites and sources of knowledge that are most effectively accessed when teachers collaborate, interrogate and enrich their theories of practice." (Cochran-Smith & Lytle, 1993, p. 63) In the program, preservice and inservice teachers and university faculty together co-construct, co-reflect and co-inquire into their teaching and learning. As Cochran-Smith (1991) argues, this is the best possible situation for students who are learning to become teachers because it encourages them to participate in the co-construction of knowledge with experienced teachers and fosters "continuous inquiry into practice" for both preservice and inservice teachers (Cochran-Smith & Lytle, 1993). Collaboration includes all stakeholders working together and engaging in collaborative decision-making, planning, teaching and continuous inquiry into their practice.

STRUCTURE OF THE TEACHER EDUCATION PROGRAM

The MET two-year graduate program is structured in the following way. The preservice teachers take six credits of university coursework (professional studies seminar) during the first two semesters of the program. Simultaneously they are involved in field-based experiences at the partnership school, spending twelve hours per week in the field both semesters. During the first semester, they observe and participate with students and teachers in classrooms and attend field-based seminars. They develop and teach two three-week units during the second semester. In the third semester, the conduct their student teaching. In the fourth semester the preservice teachers are referred to as "interns" and are placed in public school classrooms where they replace and assume the full time teaching responsibilities of teachers who have retired, quit, or gone on sick or sabbatical leaves. The preservice teachers receive guidance and support throughout this semester from university faculty and mentor teachers who frequently visit them.

The seminars and field experiences are closely linked and are organized around the following four components: the professional studies seminar, field experiences, the professional specialization and research. The professional studies seminars, field experiences and school-based seminars are collaboratively planned and delivered by a team of university faculty members. The coursework is designed to connect what the student is experiencing in the field with what is being discussed in the university seminars. The curriculum is flexible so that questions/problems that arise in the field become the focus of the students' inquiry and research. The university faculty team and the mentor teachers connect the field-based experiences with the university coursework.

Professional Studies Seminar

The professional studies seminar consists of twelve credits the first year of the program and is designed to help students develop theoretical knowledge and skills for analyzing teaching issues and problems. In the professional studies seminars, students select topics of interest, research their topics in small groups, and present their findings. The professional studies seminar emphasizes an inquiry-based approach and meets two times per week to research and inquire into four broad areas of educational inquiry. During the first semester the students are allowed to select areas of interest within the following broad areas of inquiry: The Learner and Learning, The Teacher and Teaching, School Organization and Developing a Philosophy of Education. Each inquiry lasts approximately three weeks. Through the inquiries, the preservice teachers learn to identify issues and problems, and explore solutions. The areas of inquiry for the second semester include: Curriculum Development, Assessment, Technology in the Classroom and Action Research Projects. The objectives of the inquiry-oriented approach are to provide learning experiences that help develop critical thinking, effective communication and collaborative skills, as well as a theoretical knowledge base. To assist students in making the connections between theory and practice, projects and assignments from the professional studies seminar link the university coursework with the field experiences. All of the assignments are discussed and planned in the professional studies seminar and the research projects are conducted in the schools. The seminars include educational theory which, in large part, arises from the questions and the students' desire to make sense of what is being observed in the schools. The professional studies coursework is collaboratively planned and taught by the MET faculty team.

Field Experiences

During the first year of the program the preservice teachers are required to spend a minimum of twelve hours per week in the partnership schools developing a knowledge base of pedagogical practices and principles, connecting theory with the practice, and developing an understanding of the culture of the school. The preservice teachers conduct guided observations, participate in teaching activities, and conduct research projects in the schools to develop an understanding of the school culture and the community. While the first semester focuses on the school as a whole, the second semester focuses primarily on the classroom. In the second semester students develop lessons and unit plans and teach in the classrooms of two mentor teachers. In the third semester students do their student teaching under the guidance of a mentor teacher. The teachers are encouraged to adopt a collaborative, mentoring relationship with their students as opposed to a supervisory one. The emphasis is on the co-construction of knowledge and practice. In the final semester, students are placed in a full time teaching internship. The internship is similar to a beginning teacher's first year, except that the interns receive support and guidance throughout the semester by the university faculty and intern mentor teachers. The field experiences are designed to become progressively more challenging and focused each semester. The MET faculty team coordinate the field experiences and teach the field based seminars.

Field-Based Seminars

The field experiences are supported by discussions and assignments in weekly seminars which explore issues that arise in the field. The three-hour long seminars are conducted on site at the partner schools. The students and professor meet together for the first two hours and the mentor teachers participate in the third hour. The seminars foster the creation of a learning community in which "teachers support and sustain each other's growth" (Ziechner & Liston, 1996). The weekly seminars for the preservice teachers provide an opportunity to connect theory with practice by discussing and reflecting on classroom experiences and dilemmas, as well as co-planning lessons and conducting collaborative projects, such as action research, with the mentor teachers. The seminars encourage dialogue between the preservice teachers and the mentor teachers and also provide opportunities for the participants to develop a shared understanding and shared language of the program philosophy and goals. During the summer between the first and second year, the preservice teachers and their mentor teachers co-plan the curriculum they will be teaching in the third semester.

Professional Specialization

The professional specialization component includes 12 semester hours of coursework in the students' area of specialization: elementary education or a secondary content area. These courses are not cohorted and are taught by faculty outside the MET core faculty.

Research

The research component includes the following requirements: school portrait, action research and the program culminates in a Master's research paper. The preservice students are required to do more than write theory to practice papers, they are engaged in translating theory to practice and engaging in their own action research in conjunction with a mentor and university professor.

Professional Development

In addition to the goal of creating and offering a high quality teacher preparation experience, the MET Program was designed to provide on-site professional development for inservice teachers. Teacher professional development takes on a variety of forms including involving teachers in the MET seminars, providing graduate courses for teachers on-site, creating time for teachers to meet and plan, and providing opportunities for mentor teachers to serve as adjunct faculty.

Governance

The MET Program has a governing structure, the Executive Council, which meets monthly and is designed to foster communication, collaborative decision making and formative evaluation. The Executive Council consists of university faculty, school principals, mentor teachers, and student representatives. This *unique* participatory governing structure provides opportunities for constant collaboration among stakeholders and for program evaluation and refinement.

INTEGRATING THEORY AND PRACTICE WITH LINKS BETWEEN THE UNIVERSITY AND SCHOOLS

This section will include a discussion and analysis of how the program structure and components provide integration between the university program and the field experiences. This section will also discuss how the program establishes a learning community which provides a foundation for an inquiring, reflective, and collaborative approach among the preservice teachers and the mentor teachers in the partnership schools.

The philosophy of connecting theory with practice pervades the whole program, on the university campus and in the field (Darling-Hammond, 1994; Goodlad, 1990, 1994; Zeichner, 1990, 1999). Instead of offering a series of discrete courses followed by student teaching, the university courses and field experiences are interconnected and occur simultaneously throughout the program. The faculty team meet regularly and collaboratively plan and teach the professional studies and site based seminars. This results in links and connections being established "between the ideas in these courses and teaching practice" compared with programs in which "foundational courses are offered by faculty unconnected to the professional semesters" (Tom, 1997, p. 143). The faculty team remains with the cohort of students for the entire two years and divide their responsibilities between teaching the university coursework (professional studies seminars) and spending approximately two days per week in the professional development school conducting the on-site seminars and working with the preservice and mentor teachers.

LEARNING TO TEACH IN THE CONTEXT OF TEACHING AND LEARNING

Immersion

From the first day of instruction in the partnership schools, the cohort of preservice teachers are immersed in classrooms. The university professional studies seminars do not meet during these two weeks, so that the students can fully experience what schools, teachers, and students do during the opening weeks of school. Spending the first two weeks in the field gives the preservice teachers an opportunity to see how teachers greet their students, implement routines, and establish goals and expectations. The preservice teachers keep a reflective journal in which they write down their observations and reflections on what occurred in the classrooms: student-teacher interactions, classroom activities and routines, management issues, student learning, etc. From these focused observations, the preservice teachers construct questions about teachers and students, learning and teaching, based on their observations in the classrooms. These questions arising from the field become the topics of discussion and inquiry in the professional studies and field based seminars. The reflective journals become an ongoing record of the preservice teachers' thoughts, reactions, shifts in thinking, and growth. These journals are often shared with the mentor teachers and provide an interactive dialogue between mentors, preservice teachers and university faculty. In a number of instances, preservice teachers have used their journals as invaluable data sources for their narrative inquiry and self-study research of their growth and development over the two years of the program. They have written master's papers in the fourth semester which charted their journey of becoming a teacher, including their framing and reframing of their thinking. In the following quote, the preservice teacher attests to the value of reflection and self-study.

> Just the other day I spoke with a classmate who shared her frustration due to her detachment from her master's paper topic. . . . . Looking back, I would feel exactly the same way had I done anything other than narrative self-study. I feel that I have wrestled with some of the greatest dilemmas one can face when choosing any career. Now, I feel as though I not only know how I have gotten to where I am today, but also where it is I hope to be going. At this point I feel excited to keep moving forward. (MET student, 2002)

THEORY TO PRACTICE LINKS

Specific assignments (portrait research, first semester; action research projects, second and third semesters; master's paper, fourth semester) are introduced in the university courses and researched in the field. Students integrate theory and practice by researching and reflecting upon school and classroom teaching.

Portrait Research

During the first semester, the MET students use qualitative research strategies to discover and uncover the complexities of schools and schooling. The school portrait assignment, which is discussed in the professional studies seminar, combines qualitative research methods and an inquiry approach to learning and teaching. The "School Portrait" is modeled on the work of Sarah Lawrence-Lightfoot's portraiture methodology as described in her book, "The Good High School" (Lawrence-Lightfoot, 1983). The portrait assignment provides the preservice teachers with an opportunity to apply research methods to questions and issues they encounter in their partnership school. The portrait topics arise from the preservice teachers' observations and involvement at the school site. Students learn about the roles and responsibilities of school personnel by shadowing and interacting with administrators, counselors, custodians, and coaches via interviews, surveys, observations, and document analysis. Following are examples of topics preservice teachers have explored in the portrait research:

- The Future of Schooling—Multimedia Uses and Application in the High School.
- A Portrait of Assessment Methods used in the Partnership Schools.
- Creating Futures: Helping Students Prepare for College and/or Work.
- Ability grouping: An Ethnographic Study of Heterogeneous and Homogeneous Classrooms.
- Instructional Strategies in the High School.
- At Risk students: A Portrait of the School.
- The Role of Student Athletics and Academics.
- The School's Perspective on the Hawaii Content Standards.

The sample of titles indicates the range of issues students select to explore. Some studies focus on the learners, while others focus on the school as a whole. The research process provides the students with a deeper insight into the complexities of schooling. The preservice teachers orally present their portraits to the faculty of the partnership schools at the end of the first semester.

The written portraits are also given to the schools. The school faculty have commented that the portrait research makes a valuable contribution to the school because the preservice students provide a fresh perspective on school issues and see things through "new eyes". Changes in the schools have resulted as a result of the portrait research. The school portrait assignment is an example of how students combine "reflective practices, an inquiry approach to learning and teaching, qualitative research methods and collaborative peer relationships to explore what it means to work in schools" (Marble, 1997, p. 55).

Action Research

Action research projects are introduced and discussed in the professional studies seminars in the second semester. Students select issues or topics which arise out of their classroom teaching experiences. Action research projects are done collaboratively with other preservice teachers as well as with mentor teachers. The introduction of action research into preservice teacher education programs is an important step in promoting teachers as researchers and helping them adopt and practice an inquiry approach to teaching (Ross, 1987, 1995; Russell, 1997; Zeichner, 1983, 1996).

Both the action research and portrait research provide opportunities for the preservice teachers to become effective problem posers and problem solvers through their "hands on" experiences conducting research. Action research is a powerful means of assisting preservice teachers to reflect on their practice, increase their self knowledge, and improve their teaching and their students' learning, and integrate theory with practice. The action research projects often provide practice for the master's paper required for graduation.

The quality of the action research has been at a high level. A number of preservice teachers have presented their research at peer reviewed educational conferences. Three presented at the American Educational Research Association Conference and others presented at the Hawaii Educational Research Association Conferences.

Inquiry/Problem Based Learning

Faculty and mentor teachers assist the preservice teachers in making sense of the dynamics of the classroom (disruptive behavior, reluctant learners, classroom climate, classroom organization), by emphasizing the inquiry/problem based approach in seminars. Based on personal experiences in the classroom, preservice teachers write critical incidents which become the problems that are discussed in seminar collaboratively with the mentor teachers. The critical incidents are examples of how the questions can drive the curriculum and connect the experiences in the classrooms with theory and pedagogical practices. In a detailed manner, the preservice teachers write their critical incidents by describing the context, the dialogue that takes place, and the issues and concerns raised by the situation. The students construct meaning and often reframe the problem through dialogue with their peers, mentors, and professors during the seminars. Examples of critical incidents include specific classroom management situations, student learning, parent-teacher relationships, assessment, etc. The following preservice teacher's words illustrate how the inquiry based approach and active engagement in one's learning are effective ways to make sense of the teaching experience.

> It's interesting how an experience can raise more questions than it answers. All the classroom observations in the world, all the readings about teaching, will not have as much significance for you as the actual doing. It is perhaps the strength of the MET program that observations and actual teaching are wedded. One affects the other in an endless cycle—observations gives rise to theory and expectations, teaching sharpens future observations. Journal writing enables us to chart the course of the journey. (MET student, 1996)

Reflection in Practice

In this program, reflection is not merely a solitary activity, but also occurs as a social process within the context of the learning community. Collaborative planning and reflecting are considered to be important aspects of the preservice teachers' development. The inquiry and reflective activities are grounded in a constructivist approach in which preservice teachers construct their understandings, and collaborate with their peers, university faculty, and mentor teachers. The mentor teachers and the university faculty, assist the preservice teachers in considering multiple perspectives as they co-reflect and co-construct teaching incidents together. The practical and theoretical elements of teaching and learning are examined and explored through this co-inquiry, co-reflection and co-construction of knowledge. An example of this occurs in the first semester when the mentor model of reflection and lesson planning.

During the first semester when the preservice teachers visit the mentor teachers' classrooms to observe their classes, the mentor teachers analyze several of their own lessons. The mentor teachers make their thinking explicit for the preservice teachers. Before teaching the lesson, the mentor teachers discuss with the preservice teachers what they are thinking about when planning the lesson and what they anticipate may occur during the lesson. The mentor teachers encourage the preservice teachers to write any questions or reactions that arose while observing the lesson.

Since preservice teachers generally observe the end products of the mentor teachers' thinking, they may not be aware of the reasons why a classroom is organized the way it is, why a particular teaching strategy is used, or how the learners' responses influence future lessons and approaches. Preservice teachers are encouraged to ask questions and inquire into the mentor teachers' thought processes about the lesson. Debriefing the lesson together allows the preservice teachers to see that even the highly skilled mentor teachers may not anticipate everything that may arise during the course of the lesson, and that teachers are continuously making adjustments in their lesson in response to the students and the context. After the lesson the mentor teachers address the preservice teachers' questions and share any surprises or "on the spot" decisions they may have made (Freese, 1999).

The university faculty and mentor teachers assist the preservice teachers make meaning out of their field-based experiences by helping the preservice teachers co-construct and co-reflect on their teaching with experienced teachers. To help the preservice teachers in constructing their practice as inquiry (Cochran-Smith & Lytle, 1993), the mentor teachers and university professors probe the preservice teachers' thinking and help them make sense of their experiences. Through guided reflection, the preservice teachers develop strategies which they use throughout the program.

In the second semester when the preservice teachers begin teaching lessons, they become actively engaged in analyzing their own teaching. In collaboration with the mentor teachers and university faculty, the preservice teachers engage in collaborative conversations similar to the conversations the preservice teachers and mentors had the first semester. However, during the second semester the focus is on the preservice teacher's thinking. In the pre-lesson conference, the mentor teacher assumes the role of "question asker" rather than expert or provider of information. The discussion takes the form of an inquiry into the lesson. The preservice teachers are encouraged to make tentative hypotheses about what they think may occur in the lesson. The mentor teachers ask questions and probe to help the preservice teachers visualize the classroom context, the students, and the expected learning outcomes.

The following excerpts from several collaborative planning sessions provide a snapshot of how a mentor teacher uses probing questions to guide two preservice teachers' planning and reflection on their teaching and decision making. Instead of telling the students what to do, the mentor walks the preservice teachers through their lesson plan and encourages them to visualize what will happen.

> Would you go through this with me? Visualize what a class will look like. The bell has rung; the students are walking in. How will they know what the journal writing is for the day? What will they see?

The mentor continues to probe the preservice teacher's thinking and encourages the preservice teacher to articulate how the group activity will work.

> What will the role groups look like? You have sixteen children in this classroom. How many will you have in each group? How will the groups be determined?

Students inform mentor that while the students are writing in their journals that they will handle attendance, notes, trades, other possible interruptions. They indicate an awareness of the structural issues in a lesson.

> All right, so your students have picked up their journals, they are now writing. What's on the board, are they standing up to put their journals away?
>
> One of the things you might consider is mentally, just the two of you, going through the activity yourself. It gives you a sense of the pacing. There's one thing I'd like to interject and that is the directions, directions giving.... The objective of today's lesson is... or however you give the direction giving. Is it something you will do orally? Is it something you will write on the board?

(Note: The interactive dialogue went on like this throughout the unit and lesson planning session. The dialogue, which consists of probing questions, guides and encourages the preservice teachers and to move beyond the technical aspects of teaching by visualizing what the students will be doing, what the classroom will look like and what they want the students to learn content-wise. This example illustrates that planning a lesson involves more than just developing a technical lesson plan. The process of collaborative planning goes beyond reviewing a preservice teacher's lesson plan. It provides a way for the preservice teacher to think aloud and clarify his/her thinking with the guided assistance of the mentor. Context issues such as the nature of the students, their age and ability levels, classroom setup were raised through the questioning).

The preservice teachers are encouraged to make personal connections and meaning from their experiences. Following is one of the preservice teachers' reflections after the dialogue with the mentor teacher.

> I'm more sensitized as to what to look for. The key things I need to concentrate on are the following:
>
> - pacing is important;
> - keeping students meaningfully engaged from beginning to end;
> - do not sacrifice student comprehension in order to keep on track;
> - maintaining awareness of what is happening around the room.
>
> linking assessment with my objectives. (MET student, 1996).

How much easier it might be to provide a checklist of possible solutions to the preservice teacher? But the end result may not be as meaningful nor will the preservice teachers feel the same ownership of the solution.

Collaborative Planning and Reflection

Schön (1990) stressed that teachers acquire professional knowledge primarily from continuous action and reflection on everyday problems. Reflection is ongoing throughout the program through journals, video analyses of lessons, seminar discussions, and dialogue with mentor teachers. Preservice teachers gain practice analyzing their teaching by reflecting on videotapes of their teaching collaboratively with peers, mentor teachers, and university professors. Since teaching is an activity in which the unique set of circumstances can influence what a teacher does, there are times when a teacher cannot anticipate what may arise. The following quote demonstrates how teaching involves the process of reflecting on the unanticipated events that arise in our teaching and the students' learning.

An example (of reflection) was when we were taking a quiz and a couple students asked "Oh, can we use notes?" And then I spent a couple of minutes, what do you call it, reflection on the spot. I never let them use notes. Then I thought, "Will the notes really help them?" or "at what point will it be fair for everybody?" I (reflected) for several minutes, and after holding off their questions, I said, "Okay you can use your notes." In my mind when I let them use them, I determined that it was fair because I knew that as far as what goes on their quiz and what was on their notes, it would help them only if they understood their notes, or if their notes were good enough. I thought. "Oh well now I have another teachable moment where I can go back and say, "Were your notes helpful and if they were, what was good about them? And if they weren't, what do you think you could have done in your notes that could have helped you with your test? That's how reflection helps me. If I didn't think about, reflect on it, I wouldn't come up with that kind of idea. (MET student, 1998.)

The preservice teacher quoted above thought about the consequences and implications of his decision, particularly in terms of student learning. By thinking about their "on the spot" decisions during the lesson, they develop into flexible, thoughtful problem solvers and decision makers who can make adjustments to the lesson.

As discussed in the section above, the inquiring, reflective, collaborative approach in the MET Program emphasizes the theory practice links in a number of ways. However, it should be noted that one of the most critical links is the establishment of a learning community that closely involves all participants in a shared understanding and commitment to bridging theory, pedagogy, and practice. By working closely with the mentor teachers and providing professional development opportunities, the field experiences become "an opportunity for personal and professional growth rather than as application of predetermined teaching strategies" (Beck, Freese, & Kosnik, 2004). The classrooms becomes sites of inquiry, reflection, and collaboration instead of places where traditional practice is reinforced and where the preservice teachers are expected to be clones of the mentor teacher.

An example of this is the way the preservice teachers, mentor teachers, and university faculty develop and create curriculum together. The following quote describes how this collaborative planning contributes to the professional growth and development of all the participants. "From the student teachers' perspective the ongoing spiral of planning, implementation and monitoring of curriculum change became their context for learning to teach. For the teachers, the teaming experiences became the context for curriculum inquiry and professional renewal. For university faculty, the project was a chance to promote group reflection." (Phelan et al., 1996, p. 338)

The preservice teachers have commented in their evaluations of the program about how the professional studies seminars, linked with the field based seminars and field experiences provided them with opportunities for personal and professional growth rather than merely applying pre-set teaching strategies. They valued the opportunities to construct meaning from their shared experiences and shared reflection. The benefits of the learning community and peer sharing and collaboration are shown in the following quote.

> Reflection works for me. It helps me look at different ways of learning, teaching, and being a teacher. Instead of being given to us, we had to discover for ourselves and we heard our peers talking instead of our professors talking. It makes it more meaningful if you see your friend or peer up there telling me what she found out. (Freese, 1999, p. 904)

SUMMARY AND CONCLUSIONS

This chapter has focused on an important dimension of teacher education design: the theory to practice links between the school and university. Based on my experiences teaching in the MET program for the past eight years, I have attempted to show how this teacher education program makes the theory to practice links between the university coursework and the field experiences. To achieve this integration, I believe the following five components are essential: (i) a shared philosophy of teaching and learning among the participants; (ii) a team of faculty who collaboratively plan, teach, and coordinate the coursework and field experiences; (iii) a school/university partnership in which inquiry, reflection and collaboration are modeled and practiced by the faculty, preservice teachers and mentor teachers; (iv) early and ongoing field experiences which are linked with the university coursework through inquiry, problem based assignments, portrait and action research; and finally, (v) extensive "hands on" teaching experiences which include the continuous inquiry and reflection on one's practice in the company of experienced teachers.

Challenges and Opportunities

The program described in this chapter has involved a major effort to change the way teachers are prepared. The program has received high praise from its graduates, principals who hire the graduates, and the teachers who work with the graduates. Although the program has met with a high level of success, implementing and sustaining an innovative program of this nature requires that everyone involved in the program, professors, teachers, and principals, have had to reconceptualize their roles, and reexamine long-held beliefs and assumptions about how teaching and learning occur. Because the program requires personal and professional change, tensions and challenges have arisen. One source of tension for faculty is the fact that the program involves a major commitment of time, resources, and effort (Freese et al., 1998).

In the College of Education many faculty are reluctant to assume the new roles and commit to the extensive fieldwork, collaborative planning, and teaching. Faculty are aware that there are no rewards from the university for the extensive amount of time devoted to working in partnership schools. Tensions also occur from the commitment tugging at faculty from two institutions, the university and school. The challenge is particularly difficult for untenured faculty because the demands of publishing and conducting research compete with the expectations of the preservice and mentor teachers at the partner schools. These tensions and challenges are not unique to this program. However, they are important issues that cannot be ignored and raise questions such as the following. Are there ways to implement programs of this nature that do not require additional demands on the faculty who teach in these programs? If faculty are required to spend more time in the field, can incentives and/or rewards be offered? Are there ways that the programs can be modified to retain the essential elements and reduce some of the tensions and challenges? While I have no answers to these questions, they do require further inquiry.

Reform in teacher education is challenging. I believe these challenges need to be addressed and examined if universities are going to continue to implement ways to enhance teacher education programs by linking theory and practice. A systematic analysis of programs that successfully integrate theory and practice between the university and schools would be a beneficial way to find out how different universities have dealt with the challenges resulting from implementing innovative approaches to teacher education. Identifying and addressing these challenges will ensure that the innovative approaches to preparing teachers will not just be another passing educational fad.

REFERENCES

Beck, C., Freese, A. R., & Kosnik, C., (2004). The preservice practicum: Learning through self-study in a professional setting. In J. Loughran, M. L. Hamilton, V. K. LaBoskey, & T. Russell (Eds.). *The international handbook of self-study of teaching and teacher education practices.* Dordrecht: Kluwer Academic Publishers.

Cochran-Smith, M. (1991). Learning to teach against the grain. *Harvard Educational Review, 61*(3), 279–310.

Cochran-Smith, M., & Lytle, S. (Eds.) (1993). *Inside/outside: Teacher research and knowledge.* New York: Teachers College Press.

Darling-Hammond, L. (Ed.). (1994). *Professional development schools: Schools for developing a profession.* New York: Teachers College Press.

Darling-Hammond, L., & Sykes, G. (Eds.). (1999). *Teaching as the learning profession: Handbook of policy and practice.* San Francisco: Jossey-Bass.

Dewey, J. (1929). *Experience and education.* New York: Macmillan.

Freese, A. R. (1999). The role of reflection in preservice teachers' development in the context of a professional development school. *Teaching and Teacher Education, 15*(8), 895–910.

Freese, A., McEwan, H., Bayer, A., Awaya, A., & Marble, S. (1998). Reinventing teacher preparation: The master of education in teaching program. *National Forum of Teacher Education Journal, 8*(1), 7–13.

Gardner, H. (1995). Leading Minds. New York: Basic Books.

Goodlad, J. (1990). *Teachers for our nation's schools.* San Francisco: Jossey-Bass.

Goodlad, J. (1994). *Educational renewal: Better teachers, better schools.* San Francisco: Jossey-Bass.

Lawrence-Lightfoot, S. (1983). *The good high school: Portraits of character and culture.* New York: Basic Books, Inc.

Marble, S. (1997). Narrative visions of schooling. *Teaching and Teacher Education, 13*(1), 55–64.

National Commission on Teaching & America's Future (NCTAF). (1996). *What matters most: Teaching for America's future.* New York: Author.

Phelan, A., Hunter, H., & Pateman, N. (1996). Collaboration in student teaching: Learning to teach in the context of changing curriculum practice. *Teaching and Teacher Education, 12*(4), 335–353.

Ross, D. (1987). Action research for preservice teachers: A description of why and how. *Peabody Journal of Education, 64*, 131–150.

Ross, D. (1995). Professional development schools: Prospects for institutionalization. *Teaching and Teacher Education, 11*(2), 195–201.

Russell, T. (1997). Teaching teachers: How I teach IS the message. In J. Loughran & T. Russell (Eds.), *Teaching about teaching: Purpose, passion, and pedagogy in teacher education* (pp. 32–47). London: Falmer Press.

Schön, D. (1983). *The reflective practitioner.* New York: Basic Books.

Schön, D. (1987). *Educating the reflective practitioner.* San Francisco: Jossey-Bass.

Strong, A., Freese, A., & Ing, M. (2000, April). *The value of action research in preservice teacher education: Two preservice teachers frame and reframe their teaching.* Paper presented at the American Educational Research Association Conference. New Orleans.

Tom, A. (1997). *Redesigning teacher education.* Albany, NY: State University of New York Press.
Zeichner, K. (1983). Alternative paradigms of teacher education. *Journal of Teacher Education, 34*, 3–9.
Zeichner, K. (1990). Changing directions in the practicum: Looking ahead to the 1990s. *Journal of Education for Teaching, 16*(2), 105–132.
Zeichner, K. (1996). Designing educative practicum experiences for prospective teachers. In K. Zeichner, S. Melnick, & M. L. Gomez (Eds.), *Currents of reform in preservice teacher education* (pp. 215–234). New York: Teachers College Press.
Zeichner, K. (1999). The new scholarship in teacher education. *Educational Researcher, 28*(9), 4–15.
Zeichner, K. M. & Liston, D.P. (1987). Teaching student teachers to reflect. *Harvard Educational Review, 57* (1), 23–48.
Zeichner, K. & Tabachnick, B. (1981). Are the effects of university teacher education "washed out" by school experience? *Journal of Teacher Education, 32*(3), 7–11.

Chapter 8

Using the Practicum in Preservice Teacher Education Programs: Strengths and Weaknesses of Alternative Assumptions about the Experiences of Learning to Teach

Tom Russell
Queen's University, Canada

> Because of its casualness and narrow scope, . . . , the usual practice teaching arrangement does not offset the unreflective nature of prior socialization; the student teacher is not forced to compare, analyze, and select from diverse possibilities. The risk is, of course, that practice teaching may simply expose the student to one more teacher's style of work. The value of practice teaching is attested to by many who have participated in it, but there is little indication that it is a powerful force away from traditionalism and individualism. It may be earthy and realistic when compared with education courses; but it is also short and parochial.
>
> (Lortie, 1975, p. 71)

One basic feature of many preservice teacher education programs is the *gradual* introduction of the future teacher to experiences in schools and classrooms. In programs in which education elements span two or more years, it is common to begin practicum experiences with visits to schools and to classrooms for purposes of observation, tutoring and assistance to teachers. Gradually, it is assumed, the teacher candidate becomes increasingly ready to assume full-class teaching experiences; short practicum assignments usually lead to placements of greater length near the end of the preservice program. Recently, we have seen changes that increase the amount of time spent in practicum settings, but this type of change has not been accompanied by more fundamental analysis of the role of *experience* in learning to teach. Lortie's (1975) conclusions about the practicum drawn more than 25 years ago still ring true. Critiques of teacher education in terms of tensions between theory and practice have not disappeared, nor have they been resolved. Structural links between theory and practice are often missing from the practicum experiences in most preservice teacher education programs.

This chapter focuses on identifying strengths and weaknesses of two major alternatives—the familiar and traditional *gradual* introduction to teaching responsibility versus a *rapid* introduction approach that would place teacher

G. Hoban (ed.), The Missing Links in Teacher Education Design, 135–152.

candidates into an extended teaching practicum with minimal formal introduction and preparation. The goal is to explore strengths and weaknesses of the two sets of assumptions. Although I have strong personal interest in the potential of immersion approaches, my purpose in this chapter is to call attention to what appears to be an *extreme reluctance* on the part of teacher educators (collectively, in their programs, more than individually, in their classrooms) to explore the assumptions underlying a traditional approach. (I take 'traditional' to imply repeating past practices for their comfort and familiarity, even though they may have lost their original rationale). Teacher educators tend not to ask if there might be alternative approaches to preservice teacher education that could make greater academic and practical use of *experience* in the introduction to the teaching profession. By calling attention to implicit premises, it may be possible to understand better why the highly sought goals of teacher education reform seem so rarely realized. The central issue might be summarized by asking, 'How are assumptions about the place of the practicum in teacher education programs related to new teachers learning to learn from their own teaching experiences, including the perspectives of their students?'

CONTEXT FOR CHANGE IN A TEACHER EDUCATION PROGRAM

There seems to be no end to calls to improve our schools, and the same can be said of calls to improve teacher education. In this section I draw on perspectives from Sarason, Bruner, and Kessels and Korthagen to indicate the extent to which traditional approaches to the preservice practicum have failed to examine underlying premises of how practicum experience can contribute to learning to teach.

Whether in schools or universities, change processes appear to be similar; fundamental change is rare (Sarason, 1971). When Sarason (1996) revisited and extended his earlier (1971) analysis of school change, he concluded that changes in conditions for learning must occur in parallel for students and for teachers. He also singled out the teacher-student relationship of 'asker-answerer' as the most fundamental feature requiring change. I argue here that the pattern of 'teacher asks and student answers' is at the core of the 'theory first, practice later' approach that characterizes not just how teachers teach but also how teachers learn to teach. In *The Case for Change: Rethinking the Preparation of Educators*, (Sarason, 1993) summarizes his position with the following points:

- The primary aim of education is to nurture the sense of discovery and growth in students and teacher. (p. 138)

- The arena of classrooms and schools contains mammoth obstacles to actions consistent with the primary aim. (p. 138)
- Those who seek to become educators have a major asset: they have spent years as 'learners' in classrooms. (p. 139)

Sarason discusses the need to prepare future teachers to deal with the obstacles to fostering discovery and growth, and his third point indicates the need to deal with future educators' prior classroom experiences as students. Dealing with past and present experiences of school has rarely been a fundamental feature of learning to teach.

The importance of dealing with future educators' previous experiences of school is supported in a related perspective from Bruner (1996), who has used the term *folk pedagogy* to refer to our deep-seated sense of pedagogy formed from our perceptions of teaching:

> In theorizing about the practice of education in the classroom . . . , you had better take into account the folk theories that those engaged in teaching and learning already have. For any innovations that you . . . may wish to introduce will have to compete with, replace, or otherwise modify the folk theories that already guide both teachers and pupils. (Bruner, 1996, p. 44)

Most would-be teachers appear to approach a preservice teacher education program with the assumption that they themselves are 'empty vessels' with respect to the art and craft of teaching. This tragic assumption is a natural consequence of 15,000 hours of school and classroom experiences that have given no explicit consideration to how students are taught. What Bruner sees as 'folk theories' about pedagogy are probably just as powerful as students' prior conceptions of scientific phenomena, conceptions that prove to be highly persistent outside the science classroom despite the best efforts of science teachers.

> Folk pedagogies . . . reflect a variety of assumptions about children: they may be seen as willful and needing correction; as innocent and to be protected from a vulgar society; as needing skills to be developed only through practice; as empty vessels to be filled with knowledge that only adults can provide; as egocentric and in need of socialization. Folk beliefs of this kind, whether expressed by lay people or by 'experts,' badly want some 'deconstructing' if their implications are to be appreciated. For whether these views are 'right' or not, their impact on teaching activities can be enormous. (Bruner, 1996, p. 49)

Those learning to teach may be assumed to enter the preservice practicum with significant folk theories about pedagogy, yet the elements and sequence of events in that practicum are, traditionally, quite unprepared to deal with these folk theories.

Perhaps the most obvious challenge to change in any aspect of teacher education is our individual and collective unfamiliarity with anything that we might change to. Despite the countless differences between teachers, the commonalities of telling and testing leave us with limited imaginations and little sense of possible alternatives. 'Genuine innovation begets incompetence' (MacDonald, 1975, p. 11) is one way of pointing to the problem. We hear calls for constructivist approaches to learning, we hear about the potential of communities of learners, but *we have no experience* of creating, maintaining, and defending such approaches. 'Experience' plays a role somewhere; most people agree that learning from experience is powerful and longer-lasting than learning from being told.

A significant contribution to this challenge has been provided by Kessels and Korthagen, writing in the context of teacher education reform. They build their argument on a fundamental contrast between *episteme* and *phronesis*. Episteme, closely associated with our familiar *epistemology*, is the bedrock on which knowledge rests; it is the foundation of the university itself, and the institution of the textbook is its most visible embodiment. Phronesis, closely linked to perception, is generally foreign to the school and university context. Kessels and Korthagen have argued that phronesis holds considerable promise for addressing the perennial theory-practice problem that is so readily glossed over from the perspective of episteme.

> Someone may acknowledge the importance of practicing periods in teacher education programs and still completely miss the point of phronesis. In fact, many teacher educators who stress the value of practical experience nevertheless work on the basis of an epistemic conception of knowledge; they struggle with the gap between theory and practice, they worry and puzzle about transfer problems, and they brood on how best to connect to the students' existing knowledge.... *The point of phronesis is that the knowledge a student needs is perceptual rather than conceptual.* Therefore it is necessarily internal to the student, *it is in the student's experience* instead of outside it in some external, conceptual form. It is thoroughly subjective.... *And so there is nothing or little to transmit, only a great deal to explore.* And the task of the teacher educator is to *help the student teacher explore and refine his or her perceptions.* This asks for well-organized arrangements in which student teachers get the opportunity to reflect systematically on the details of their practical experiences, under the guidance of the teacher educator—both in group seminars and in individual supervision. (Kessels & Korthagen, 1996, p. 21; emphasis added)

> The danger of an emphasis on procedural knowledge in teacher education is that student teachers learn a lot of methods and strategies for many types of situations *but do not learn how to discover, in the specific situations occurring in everyday teaching, which methods and strategies to use.* (Korthagen & Kessels, 1998, p. 7, emphasis added)

Important insights into the use of a *phronesis* perspective in preservice teacher education are provided in Kortagen et al. (2001), although complete understanding of such an unfamiliar perspective is unlikely without extensive personal experience of attempting to use that perspective in one's own settings of practice. In the following sections I describe the innovative structure attempted at Queen's and explore the issue of assumptions about learning to teach within the preservice practicum. I then contrast gradual introduction and rapid immersion in experience to highlight the unexamined nature of these assumptions.

STRUCTURE OF THE TEACHER EDUCATION PROGRAM AT QUEEN'S UNIVERSITY

As recounted elsewhere (Russell, 1999, 2000), Queen's University's Faculty of Education transformed its preservice program structure in 1997–98, after two years of planning, consultation, and a pilot project involving 60 volunteers. In the initial two years (1997–1999), all teacher candidates began their practicum experiences on the opening day of the school year, after a week-long introduction and orientation at the university. The placement ran from September through December, a period of 16 weeks interrupted by a two-week return to the university near the midpoint of the placement. In briefest terms, it worked, and it worked very well; with a few inevitable exceptions, teacher candidates seemed very pleased. Many associate teachers were also pleased, but many others were not. Teachers' discomfort with being observed by another teacher (pre-service) on the first day of school was one concern; a larger concern seemed to be the view of some that it was the university's job to teach candidates how to teach before sending them to schools for practice. Most of my colleagues seemed to agree with the latter group of associate teachers: some theory should precede practice. Unfortunately, following a pattern quite familiar in schooling, the views of student teachers counted for very little. Since 1999, 'minor' program modifications have continued to erode the initial premise that learning from experience could and should be a fundamental program goal and method.

The personal experience of seeing a radical change attempted with initial success, only to be abandoned subsequently with virtually no organizational consideration of premises underlying the practicum, compels me to explore those assumptions in the context of ongoing concerns about the inability of universities to achieve reform of their teacher education programs (Goodlad, 1990; Sarason, 1993). The examples used in the following analyses are drawn from my ongoing self-study of my own teaching of preservice teachers and from case studies of events at my own university.

Located in the Canadian province of Ontario, with about one-third of the country's population, Queen's University has experienced annual reductions in government funding for at least 15 years. In the years 1995 to 2003, a conservative provincial government legislated major structural changes to medical, educational and social services funding, along with a general program of tax reduction. In the 2002–2003 school year, the longstanding fifth year of secondary school (long known as Grade 13) was phased out. The teaching profession was branded as a 'special interest group' and a general decline in professional satisfaction and school climate flowed naturally from constant government criticisms. While many Canadian provinces have moved to two-year teacher education programs, those in Ontario remain at eight- to ten-month levels, with a minimum requirement of 40 days of practicum experience.

The Ontario pattern for pre-service teacher education typically involves earning a Bachelor of Education (B.Ed.) degree in a program spanning one academic year following completion of the B.A. or B.Sc. degree. The 2003–2004 pre-service teacher education program at Queen's University began in early September and concluded in late April. More than 700 candidates were about equally divided between elementary and secondary options; about one-third had been enrolled in a concurrent program since beginning undergraduate studies either at Queen's or nearby Trent University. Courses are provided in categories of Curriculum, Focus Track, Foundations, Educational Studies, and Professional Studies. The first of two terms begins in September with three weeks of classes prior to the first five weeks of practicum in an Associate School; two further weeks of classes and five more weeks of practicum in the same Associate School complete the first term. The second term begins with seven weeks of classes and continues with two practicum blocks: an 'alternate practicum,' generally in a non-school educational setting and linked to the Focus Track, and three additional practicum weeks, often in the same Associate School attended in the first term. The program closes with two final weeks of classes, including an 'exit conference' in which a professional development portfolio is shared with others.

The Associate School model, introduced with the radical program restructuring in 1997–1998, calls for assigning candidates in groups rather than individually. Each group is supported during the practicum by a Faculty Liaison, who may be a full-time faculty member but more commonly is a retired teacher or principal or a Ph.D. candidate in Education. Elementary groups include 3 to 8 people, while secondary groups range from 2 to 12 or more. Thus faculty members assigned to secondary schools provide support and supervision across the full range of subjects. Candidates are asked to meet for three hours per week to discuss experiences and issues related to equity, exceptionality, action research and professional development. In the next section I compare the assumptions that underpin both the experience first structure verses the theory first structure.

COMPARING ALTERNATIVE ASSUMPTIONS ABOUT THE PRESERVICE PRACTICUM IN TEACHER EDUCATION

Embedded in the familiar approach of *gradual introduction* to practicum experience are several interrelated assumptions and perspectives that might be expressed in the following terms:

1. Those learning to teach require extensive preparation for assuming the responsibilities of the classroom teacher. Their many years of experiences as students provide little in the way of guidance for the experience of teaching.
2. Those learning to teach can and will be assisted in preparing for teaching responsibilities by observing and assisting in classrooms. Such activities can be made more valuable by the provision of guidelines for observation and structures for reporting on the activities as an observer or assistant.
3. Those learning to teach are able to gain increasing control over their teaching behaviors as they come to see in greater detail, by experiences of observation and assistance, the complexities of individual and group learning processes.

Embedded in the unfamiliar approach of *rapid introduction* to practicum experience are several interrelated assumptions and perspectives that might be expressed in the following terms:

1. Those learning to teach have extensive experience of what happens in classrooms, but little has been done to analyze and interpret that experience. They have had little access to how teachers plan and think about their work.
2. Those learning to teach will make most rapid progress when they begin full-class teaching that enables them to experience how a teacher needs to think about the students being taught and the way they are being taught.
3. Those learning to teach need to see that full-class teaching is dramatically different from observation and tutoring.

For convenience, I label these contrasting sets of assumptions as 'theory first, practice later' (graduation introduction to the practicum) and 'experience first, understand later' (rapid introduction to the practicum) respectively. In the following section I extend this initial account by discussing a range of issues associated with the two approaches to the practicum.

THEORY FIRST, PRACTICE LATER

This section begins with comments about the tradition of gradual introduction to teaching and to practicum experience. It continues with points relevant to the relationship of the practicum to teacher education reform, exploring two issues in particular: Teacher educators are often ambivalent about the schools in which the practicum occurs; teacher educators' assumption that adding reflective practice to a theory-first approach may be self-defeating.

The Tradition of Gradual Introduction

- Gradual introduction is understandably and appropriately used in fields where the beginner is completely inexperienced. A would-be doctor does not step straight into surgery, nor does a future lawyer step straight into a courtroom. In these professions, there is a great deal to learn that is extremely unfamiliar. Education can be argued to be quite different, because all teachers-to-be have more than 15,000 hours of experience observing teachers at work. For most individuals, that experience has never been examined, yet it has led to the development of what Bruner terms 'folk theories' of pedagogy.
- The practice of gradual introduction is questionable in the field of teaching because images (acquired in context) are so much more powerful than *words* (heard out of context). Teacher educators and future educators alike appear not to recognize this as a relevant issue, perhaps because traditional teaching practices place such overwhelming confidence in the power of the spoken word.
- The tradition of gradual introduction to experiences of teaching persists in part because it is familiar and alternatives are unfamiliar and risky. It also continues because those who have already learned how to teach want to be helpful to those just beginning. At the same time, teacher education often houses a complex and unanalyzed fear that new teachers will be 'contaminated' by existing school practices. Thus teacher educators assume, or at least hope, that our words can 'vaccinate' beginning professionals against the diseases of poor practices that persist in schools.

Teacher Educator Ambivalence toward the School Setting for the Practicum

Teacher educators are well known for their criticisms of 'traditional' teaching practices in schools. This is one of many elements that make genuine school-university partnership so difficult to achieve. Teacher educators know that there are calls for schools to change, just as they know that many teacher candidates will not see during the practicum many of the practices that are recommended in education classes. Approaches associated with phrases such as 'constructivism,' 'cooperative small-group learning,' 'balanced literacy,' and 'meeting students' individual needs' are advocated in teacher education institutions. While such practices may be scarce in schools, our universities are not well known for their critique of their own practices. Both schools and universities continue to display extensive reliance on 'transmission' teaching. A gradual introduction to the preservice practicum is consistent with the traditions of transmission-based classroom teaching and learning: First the teacher will tell you, and then you will go and practice for yourself.

Adding 'Reflective Practice' to 'Theory First' May be Misguided

'Give us stuff, not fluff' were the words of one teacher candidate at Queen's University, words spoken to express expectations for formal classes after 14 weeks of an immersion practicum. Practicum experiences had primed the pump and raised expectations; no longer were good words and intentions enough to satisfy expectations. Experience generates more than questions; experience also generates a filter that quickly distinguishes between what is practical and realistic and what is not—between what will work in real classrooms and what will not.

Exhortations about the importance of being a 'critically reflective practitioner' are little more than 'fluff' when expressed by teacher educators who do not appear to be such practitioners themselves. If teacher candidates have seen little evidence that teachers in schools are critically reflective toward their practice, then they need evidence from teacher educators' own actions. *Reflection has a direct relationship to experience, and if education classes are not rich in experience, then where are the possibilities for reflection*? Reflection needs to be taught and modeled. Simply inserting exhortations into a traditional 'theory first' approach does more to call attention to what is missing than to help teacher candidates become critical of practice. Segall (2002) makes a strong case for bridging the theory-practice divide by using the experiences in education classes at the university as the basis for illustration.

EXPERIENCE FIRST, UNDERSTANDING LATER

This section begins with comments about the extent to which teachers at all levels are unfamiliar with learning that is rooted in experience rather than in logically organized accounts of other people's experiences (the school curriculum). It continues with several perspectives on the experience of immersion in the practicum experience.

The Unfamiliar Terrain of Learning from Experience

Providing experience first to those learning to teach does not come easily, and a general reluctance to focus preservice programs on learning from experience comes naturally to all of us. Virtually all teacher educators begin their work by teaching as they themselves were taught. Our reluctance to have the preservice practicum begin a program of teacher education goes far beyond our limited familiarity with learning from experience in an academic or school setting. The predisposition to 'help' and make earliest teaching experiences 'easier' comes naturally to most adults. Our culture has long traditions of trying to make life easier for the next generation, whether in the parent-child relationship or in the teacher-student relationship. This predisposition also continues the teacher educators' overall faith in propositional knowledge, despite decades of evidence that theory does not readily translate into practice.

- Collectively, teacher educators appear to have a fundamental commitment to the importance of bonding first with the teacher education site. Less powerful bonding with the practicum site follows at some later point.
- Even though those learning to teach *always* report that the practicum is *the most important program element*, those practicum experiences rarely become the extended focus of time spent in education classes.
- Teacher educators may hold a subconscious fear that those learning to teach will be so enamored of 'practice' that they will lose all interest in 'theory.'

Comments about a 'Sink or Swim' Approach to the Preservice Practicum

The following comments are selected from those offered by members of a group of preservice candidates at Queen's University in 1996. An arrangement with the University of Waterloo generated the opportunity for a small number of future science teachers to teach for four months before beginning their education courses. While most acknowledged the shock of a rapid immersion in teaching, they also stressed the motivational aspects of the experience, including the generation of questions to which education courses might be expected to provide at least preliminary answers.

> Andrea: I know now of many books that I'll be reading, questions I need to ask, and things I need to learn, but it wasn't until I had been teaching for a week before I really knew what to ask or where I needed help. In this way, the 'sink or swim' method is excellent.... Before I had done some teaching I had no idea of where I needed help. Afterwards I had a list of questions as long as my arm. (Featherstone, Munby, & Russell, pp. 87–88)

> Steph: The key is wanting to learn, and being ready to take risks—and enjoying or suffering the consequences, whatever they may be. Students are generally candid, and they will let you know soon enough how you are doing.... Overall, I think the experience was great. I didn't just get my feet wet, I got drenched! But it was worth it. The best way to learn something is to get right into it. (Featherstone, Munby, & Russell, p. 91)

> Heidi: You can't really teach someone how to teach; you can only guide them.... I have experiences, both good and bad, and I can improve through my learning here. I know what didn't work, and hopefully will gain some knowledge at Queen's to improve or modify situations.... Now I'm ready to learn how to make what I know better—more dynamic. (Featherstone, Munby, & Russell, p. 94)

Strengths and challenges of where to position the practicum in relation to teacher education classes are summarized in Table 8.1. This table is followed by the central pedagogical issue if the practicum comes early in the program: 'What can teacher educators do in their own classes to help teacher education students learn from their experiences?'

Drawing on Practicum Experiences in University Courses

How easily one can write that 'the task of the teacher educator is to help the student teacher explore and refine his or her perceptions.' What might this mean in practice, and how does it relate to assumptions related to a 'practice first, understanding later' perspective? Over the last 10 years, my membership in the Self-Study of Teacher Education Practices (S-STEP) special interest group within the American Educational Research Association has supported and inspired my own efforts to foster learning from experience in my work with preservice teachers. The points that follow attempt to summarize my own professional learning and my efforts to understand the meaning of the points already cited from the work of Kessels and Korthagen (1996). Korthagen et al. (2001) is a fundamental reference for this topic.

Listen to those learning to teach

My own students have helped me learn most of what I understand about incorporating their program experiences into my teaching (Loughran & Russell, 1997). Munby and Russell (1994) cast an argument in terms of recognizing that there is an 'authority of experience' that is new to most preservice teachers and requires appropriate adjustments in preservice classes. Cook-Sather (2002) has provided the most elaborate case to date in favour of listening to those we teach; helping the student teacher explore and refine perceptions certainly requires that their teachers listen to and work with them. From the familiar topics for a methods course in science, my students and I select those

Table 8.1. Comparison of two approaches to the preservice practicum in teacher education.

	Theory first, practice later	Practice first, understanding later
Rationale	• Gradual introduction to practice is understandably used in fields where the beginner is completely inexperienced. A would-be doctor does not step straight into surgery, nor does a future lawyer step straight into a courtroom. • 'Theory first, practice later' is the familiar approach used in most school and university classrooms. • This approach persists in part because teacher educators want to be helpful to those who are assumed to know so little about teaching. • Teacher educators may fear that new teachers will be 'contaminated' by existing school practices. • We assume, or at least hope, that our words can protect beginning professionals from the 'disease' of poor teaching practices.	• Those learning to teach always report that the practicum is the most important program element. • 'Sink or swim' appears drastic, but most who succeed with theory first will also succeed with practice first. • If we wish to prepare new teachers with a predisposition to improve what happens in schools, then beginning with experience sends a strong message that a new type of learning is an important part of learning to teach. • If we wish to help new teachers learn how to learn from experience, then starting with experience may be the best way to initiate and support that goal. • Those learning to teach are very eager to learn the mysteries of the teacher's view of the first day of school: 'How do they manage to get things started?'
Reservations	• Education can be argued to be quite different from all other professions, because all teachers-to-be have more than 15,000 hours of experience observing teachers at work. • 'Theory first' may be questionable in teaching because *images* (in context) are more powerful than *words* (out of context) • The tradition of gradual introduction may actually be a replication of the poor practices we wish to guard against • Adding reflective practice to 'theory first' may be misguided • On a 'theory first' approach, practicum experiences rarely receive detailed attention in university classes.	• There may be a fear that those learning to teach will be so enamoured of 'practice' that they will have no interest in 'theory' if they begin with practice. • Collectively, teacher educators appear to have a fundamental commitment to the idea that their students should bond first with the teacher education site. Less powerful bonding with the practicum site presumably follows at some later point. • Many approach learning to teach with the assumption that they know little and need to be told a lot. • Experienced teachers may be reluctant to have new teachers observe the stressful early days of the school year.
Problems	• The theory-practice problem persists for all teachers. Both theory and research tend to be seen as irrelevant. • Persistent calls for school reform and improvement often look to new teachers, yet new teachers do not see themselves as change agents.	• Beginning with experience is so far removed from traditional practices that it may be impossible for large groups of teacher educators to make a commitment to such a major innovation.

that are most urgent in light of their background and accumulating experiences.

Signal intentions early and often

When a student with extensive experience of self-directed learning (SDL) suggested that experiences with SDL could help support learning from experience, I was determined to try. I located an appropriate textbook (Gibbons, 2002) and announced that we would devote part of our time to an SDL approach after they had gained some teaching experience. By the time we began, people were not surprised; most were pleased with what they learned about themselves, both positively and negatively. At the end of the course they chose to put the letters S D L at the centre of the ceiling tile they decorated in my classroom.

Model and interpret, don't preach

Why is 'actions speak louder than words' so rarely a teaching principle in preservice programs? Why do my students still experience a lecture about why they should not lecture to their students? Perhaps it is because our extensive experiences of being told lead us to teach as we were taught. Segall (2002) argues cogently for creating in preservice education classes experiences that illustrate the principles we wish to 'transmit' to new teachers. Kroll (2004) offers very clear illustration of how a set of fundamental program principles were enacted in her own teaching, writing that 'the case illustrates how the way student-teachers are taught theory can help them integrate their own ideas of learning and teaching with constructivist theory in order to think critically about their own practice in an ongoing developmental manner' (p. 199). Almost subconsciously, I recently found myself 'teaching' the significance of non-verbal behaviour not by telling students that wait-time can make a difference in how students respond to questions but by deliberately waiting much longer than usual and then explaining what I was doing. The impact was dramatically different; they were fascinated to learn that teachers can make productive teaching moves without using words.

Teach reflection indirectly

How often are those learning to teach told that they should be 'critically reflective practitioners'? What meaning can those words possibly have for someone with little or no teaching experience? In 2001, one of my students suggested that I stop 'pushing' reflection and instead teach people how to reflect, and then show them what I had done. I no longer use 'the R-word' [reflection] in my classes. Instead, with little explanation I provide each student with a word-processed file containing five tables in which they are to respond to open-ended questions appropriate to five stages of their progress through our program:

1. After three weeks of classes?
2. After the first five weeks of practicum?
3. After two more weeks of classes and five more weeks of practicum
4. After seven more weeks of classes
5. After six more weeks of practicum and two final weeks of classes

A three-column table format is crucial to help candidates make sense of their experiences as shown in Table 8.2 (used with permission of the author). The

Table 8.2. One row selected from installment 4 of the story assignment.

Question	Teacher candidate response	Teacher educator comments
What new goals and insights have classes in January-February provided for your development as a teacher?	I think that Jan/Feb have in fact shown me *what professional development, and what my development as a teacher, have the potential to be.* I will be the first to admit that I was not a very philosophical person when I came into this program, but I think that I would also be the first to admit that I have changed into one. *I think that a major insight of mine has been to realize that setting goals and developing insight is quite tangible.* I think back to Joseph's 'How I Succeeded at McArthur,' and one of his points was, **'Allow yourself to change.'** That is exactly what you have to do. Don't put effort into this, it just happens. Stop worrying or over analyzing. When you stop doing these things, or putting in too much effort, the change starts. I must say, it feels quite amazing. That is one of the most powerful pieces of advice that I received this year, and if I can send a message to anyone next year, that would be it. I don't want to take any credit for passing it to next year's class, but it's incredible when you realize that it has happened.	You have done this far more rapidly and impressively than anyone I can recall! And it's a delight to watch because I was also able to see how GOOD your teaching practices already are. You have the courage to enact your convictions and then watch to see how students respond—that's what teaching is all about! EXACTLY the right link to be making at this point! (Maybe I should put it up in our classroom with the other little signs already there!?!) GOOD! Any thoughts about how and when to introduce it? If I had spoken it to you in September, you might well have had a very puzzled look on your face!

Note: Bold and italic fonts added as part of the comment process.

second column provides an initially small space that expands to contain as much as they wish to write; the third column provides space for my comments immediately opposite theirs. When they review all their entries as part of the fifth assignment, they realize how much their views have changed as they acquired experience. They also seem to appreciate my extensive comments, an unusual alternative to the brief comments often inserted in the margin of a journal. With all five tables completed, the stage is set to end my classes with them by identifying their writing as 'reflection' and revisiting how such writing enables them to can link their changing perspectives to their teaching actions.

Acknowledge that transmission is very comfortable

Many prospective teachers begin a post-graduate preservice program with the expectation that they will learn to teach just as they learned the subjects they studied as undergraduates. They tend to assume that telling produces professional learning. They tend to assume that they know more of the subjects they will teach than their students will know, and they often assume that they need to be told (1) how to plan a lesson and a unit, and (2) how to manage students' classroom behaviour. They also tend to assume that it the teacher's task of 'covering' a curriculum is supported by knowing the answers to all the questions students might ask. While I try not to criticize these prior views, I work behind the scenes in my teaching to subvert them, always in constructive ways so that the comfort of transmission is replaced not by discomfort but by comfort in learning from experience.

Seek coherence and consistency above all else

All changes to teaching are challenging and difficult; we all have strong tendencies to revert to comfortable and familiar strategies such as telling, especially when time is short and there is much to 'cover.' Nothing interferes with new approaches and messages as strongly as incoherence and inconsistency. Once one begins a series of new practices that imply new perspectives on how people learn to teach (such as exploring the impact of practicum and program experiences), then coherence and consistency in developing those new practices is an essential part of achieving the intended effects.

My learning in the last 10 years has been the most exciting of my 25 years in preservice teacher education. There is a great deal of coherence and consistency in a set of experience-first assumptions, particular if theory-first assumptions are seen as inadequate. There is a great deal of challenge (and uncertainty and confusion) in working to enact a new set of assumptions, just as there is much challenge for those learning to teach who want to improve the quality of their students' learning.

CONCLUSION

Writing about teachers and technical knowledge in 'speculations on change' at the conclusion of his study, Lortie (1975) raised issues about teachers that may well apply to teacher educators' predisposition to avoid considering fundamental assumptions about the preservice practicum:

> The ethos of the occupation is tilted against engagement in pedagogical inquiry. Reflexive conservatism implicitly denies the significance of technical knowledge, assuming that energies should be centered on realizing conventional goals in known ways. Individualism leads to distrust of the concept of shared knowledge [sic]; it portrays teaching as the expression of individual personality. Presentist orientations retard making current sacrifices for later gains; inquiry rests on the opposite value. (Lortie, 1975, p. 240)

Assumptions about the place of the practicum in preservice teacher education programs are closely intertwined both with issues of reform in teacher education and with issues of school improvement. Not surprisingly, issues of the quality of student learning in schools and the quality of professional learning in universities share much common ground. I assert here that assumptions about the timing and structure of the preservice practicum remain unexamined in the context of teacher education reform. A number of questions can be posed for teacher educators:

- Are we prepared to rethink the structure of the preservice practicum in order to reduce the gap new teachers perceive between theory and practice?
- Are we prepared to rethink the relationship of the practicum to the courses we teach?
- Are we prepared to rethink the nature of learning from experience, in order to understand the potential contribution of phronesis to preservice professional learning?
- Are we prepared to rethink our actions, in teacher education classrooms and programs, if our rethinking of the preservice practicum indicates the potential for improvement of the quality of learning in preservice teacher education?

Structural links between theory and practice appear to be missing from many preservice teacher education programs. Explanations may include the following:

- Those learning to teach already have strong views about what would constitute links between theory and practice. Those views tend to be unproductive, and the preservice practicum experience is more likely to reinforce than to challenge those views.

- Teacher educators have similarly strong and unproductive views about links between theory and practice as well as between schools and university. Uncritically and unintentionally, many teacher educators appear to follow the traditional view that theory is first taught and then practiced. This traditional view is firmly embedded both in the epistemology of the university and in the curricular organization of the school.

To sum up, how we learn from experience continues to be a neglected and poorly understood issue, despite its relevance to reform and improvement. In both school and teacher education contexts, research perspectives on conceptual change and self-directed learning have major implications for how we teach. Extending these perspectives into the structure of practicum elements and our assumptions about them could provide invaluable assistance in moving forward concurrently with school and teacher education improvement.

REFERENCES

Bruner, J. S. (1996). *The culture of education.* Cambridge, MA: Harvard University Press.

Cook-Sather, A. (2002). Authorizing students' perspectives: Toward trust, dialogue, and change in education. *Educational Researcher, 31*(4), 3–14.

Featherstone, D., Munby, H., & Russell, T. (Eds.). *Finding a voice while learning to teach.* London: Falmer Press.

Gibbons, M. (2002). *The self-directed learning handbook: Challenging adolescent students to excel.* San Francisco: Jossey-Bass.

Goodlad, J.I. (1990). *Teachers for our nation's schools.* San Francisco: Jossey-Bass.

Kessels, J. P. A. M., & Korthagen, F. A. J. (1996). The relationship between theory and practice: Back to the classics. *Educational Researcher, 25*(3), 17–22.

Korthagen, F. A. J., & Kessels, J. P. A. M. (1998). Linking theory and practice: Changing the pedagogy of teacher education. *Educational Researcher, 28*(4), 4–17.

Korthagen, F. A. J., with Kessels, J., Koster, B., Lagerwerf, B., & Wubbels, T. (2001). *Linking practice and theory: The pedagogy of realistic teacher education.* Mahwah, NJ: Lawrence Erlbaum Associates.

Kroll, L. R. (2004). Constructing constructivism: How student-teachers construct ideas of development, knowledge, learning and teaching. *Teachers and Teaching: Theory and Practice, 10*, 199–221.

Lortie, D. C. (1975). *Schoolteacher: A sociological study.* Chicago: University of Chicago Press.

Loughran, J., & Russell, T. (1997). Meeting student teachers on their own terms: Experience precedes understanding. In V. Richardson (Ed.), *Constructivist teacher education: Building a world of new understandings* (pp. 164–181). London: Falmer Press

MacDonald, B. (1975). Introduction. In J. Elliott & B. MacDonald (Eds.), *People in classrooms* (pp. 2–13). Norwich, UK: Centre for Applied Research in Education, University of East Anglia.

Munby, H., & Russell, T. (1994). The authority of experience in learning to teach: Messages from a physics methods class. *Journal of Teacher Education, 45*, 86–95.

Russell, T. (1999). The challenge of change in teaching and teacher education. In J. R. Baird (Ed.), *Reflecting, teaching, learning: Perspectives on educational improvement* (pp. 219–238). Cheltenham, Victoria: Hawker Brownlow Education.

Russell, T. (2000, July). *Moving beyond 'default' teaching styles and programme structures: The rise, fall, and marginal persistence of reflective practice in preservice teacher education in the period 1984–2000.* Paper presented at the First Carfax International Conference on Reflective Practice, Worcester, England [available at http://educ.queensu.ca/~russellt/papers/marginal.pdf].

Sarason, S. B. (1971). *The culture of the school and the problem of change.* Boston: Allyn & Bacon.

Sarason, S. B. (1993). *The case for change: Rethinking the preparation of educators.* San Francisco: Jossey-Bass.

Sarason, S. B. (1996). *Revisiting 'The culture of the school and the problem of change.'* New York: Teachers College Press.

Segall, A. (2002). *Disturbing practice: Reading teacher education as text.* New York: Peter Lang.

Chapter 9

Who Stays in Teaching and Why?: A Case Study of Graduates from the University of Kansas' 5th-Year Teacher Education Program

Pam Green, Mary Lynn Hamilton, James K. Hampton
and Margie Ridgeway
University of Kansas, USA

CONTEXT OF THE TEACHER EDUCATION PROGRAM

This chapter presents findings from a detailed case study of the University of Kansas extended teacher education program and identifies factors that contribute to retention and attrition in the teaching profession. The main focus of this research project was graduates of the five-year program (KUTeachers) and their relationship with the profession within the statewide context.

Rationale for Study

The topic of teacher retention is one that can be looked upon as being worthy of utmost attention in view of prognostications concerning pending teacher shortages (Riley, 1999) and corresponding predictions of the need to hire more than two million new teachers by 2008 (Hussar, 1999). While statistics indicate that a sufficient number of people are being prepared to teach, only 60–70% actually enter the teaching profession. Rather, they select other career paths because of worries about unpreparedness, discomfort with the work environment, and personal concerns (Darling-Hammond & Sclan, 1996). Even more troubling is the number of teachers who are initially prepared and hired but do not remain in the profession. Darling-Hammond (2000b) noted that the highest rate of teachers leaving the profession (up to 30% of attrition) occurs within the first three years of practice. Of new teachers from urban schools, around half leave the field within their first five years of experience (Haycock, 1998). With more than 50% of the teacher work force above the age of 50 (Darling-Hammond, 1997; Jordan-Irvine, 2001), coupled with the large attrition rate (especially among novice teachers), the teaching profession must find ways to address this issue.

G. Hoban (ed.), The Missing Links in Teacher Education Design, 153–167.

Since the early 1990s, the number of individuals leaving the profession has outpaced the number entering it, with this gap continually widening (Darling-Hammond, 2003). Furthermore, it has been reported that only about one-fifth of these exits can be attributed to retirement (Henke, Chen, & Geis, 2000; Ingersoll, 2001). Thus, when analyzing the issue of teacher supply and demand, the corresponding emphasis commonly given to teacher recruitment oftentimes seems to be misplaced. The true crux of the matter appears to lie not so much in trying to attract more prospective teachers to the field, but rather in retaining those that have already been prepared to teach (Grossman, 2003; Joftus & Maddox-Dolan, 2002; NCTAF, 2003).

Conceivably one of the most problematic issues to be dealt with in addressing the quandary of teacher attrition revolves around discerning what keeps some teachers teaching while others choose to leave the profession. Considerations previously noted as being particularly influential in attracting individuals to the profession include aspirations of working with young people (NEA, 1992), as well as altruistic motives such as the desire to make a difference (Farkas, Johnson, & Foleno, 2000). Other studies have shown that the very factors that initially draw individuals to teaching are among those that likewise cause them to remain. Kozol (2001) stated that if novice teachers remain in the profession, they do so for the love of children. Nieto (2003) reported that reasons given by teachers who have stayed in the field encompassed such facets as their own personal identities, love for their jobs and their students, emotions of hope and possibility/anger and desperation, belief in democratic practice, the opportunity for intellectual work, and the ability to shape the future. Johnson and Birkeland (2002) contended that the ultimate decision as to whether one chooses to remain in teaching often hinges on just such intrinsic work satisfactions which teachers seem to find so personally rewarding.

By contrast, a perusal of past research related to this subject reveals numerous possible reasons for teacher attrition, ranging from inadequate preparation (NCTAF, 2003) to difficult working conditions (Ingersoll, 2001). According to Jordan-Irvine (2001), teachers do not remain in the teaching profession because they cannot accomplish what they want—to be caring, competent teachers. Kozol (2001) claimed that we are not able to keep novice teachers in schools because they are overwhelmed with lists and tests and expected to teach scripted lessons that do not accommodate for creativity. Further exacerbating the situation is the fact that new teachers are frequently given the most challenging placements and class assignments (Jordan-Irvine, 2001; Kozol, 2001). Moreover, the cultural disparity between teachers and students can affect their ability to function successfully in the classroom.

In general, Darling-Hammond and Sclan (1996) denoted the following variables as being potential contributing factors in who leaves teaching: gender, age, ethnicity, academic background, career stages, teaching field/grade level, salary, workplace conditions, attitudes, and experiences in teaching. Among those described as being more likely to quit teaching are the youngest and oldest individuals, minorities, the academically talented, secondary school teachers with majors in an academic discipline, and special educators. These generalizations mirror earlier research which disclosed that the risk of attrition was highest for young women, individuals with high standardized test scores, high school science and math teachers, and those in their first few years of teaching (Murnane, Singer, Willett, Kemple, & Olsen, 1991). Similarly, a study undertaken by Johnson and Birkeland (2002) revealed that characteristics such as prior career experience, gender, and preparation played an instrumental role in whether or not novice teachers decided to remain in the field during their first three years in the profession. Their findings indicated that mid-career teachers, men, and those prepared through alternative certification programs left teaching in higher proportions than did first-career teachers, women, and those prepared through traditional avenues of teacher education.

Furthermore, teacher preparation has been identified as one of four major factors—along with salaries, working conditions, and mentoring support—that have an impact on teacher attrition (Darling-Hammond, 2003). Some work has been done on retention that infers that strong teacher education programs can counteract the high attrition rate (Darling-Hammond, 2000). Past research investigations have tied lower retention rates for new teachers to lack of prior student teaching experience (Henke, Chen, & Geis, 2000) or specific training related to teaching per se (NCTAF, 2003), non-credentialed status (Darling-Hammond, 2002), and alternative certification programs (Fowler, 2002; Raymond, Fletcher, & Luque, 2001). In general, findings such as these imply that those teachers who do not obtain sufficient preparation to begin with tend to be more likely to leave the field (Darling-Hammond, 2003).

Given the probable link between teacher preparation and retention, it seems appropriate that studies also be undertaken to explore the concept of how teachers feel about their teacher education experiences. Lanier and Little (1984) reported that, generally speaking, teachers' perceptions of their own professional preparation have been found to be largely negative. A report by Public Agenda, *A Sense of Calling: Who Teaches and Why*, came to a similar conclusion (Farkas, Johnson, & Foleno, 2000). Even those teachers who gave their teacher preparation programs positive ratings as a whole still offered criticisms related to how they were trained in crucial areas such as classroom management and effectively assisting low-achieving students. Even more disheartening is the fact that almost two-thirds of the study's respondents (63%) indicated that their teacher education programs did only a 'fair' or 'poor' job of preparing them for the realities of teaching.

Still other studies support this presumption of teachers' perceiving a 'lack of readiness' to teach. Based on an analysis of data from the 1999–2000 *Schools and Staffing Survey* (SASS), the Southeast Center for Teaching Quality reported that significantly less than half of beginning teachers from the Southeast gave the response that they felt 'very well prepared' in seven key teaching areas—classroom management, instructional methods, subject matter, computer usage, lesson planning, student assessment, and selection of instructional materials (Berry, Luczak, & Norton, 2003). This particular group of new teachers considered themselves to be most prepared in subject matter (39.8%) and lesson planning (37.2%), and least prepared for classroom management (21.4%) and computer usage (17.4%).

Another area of research interest within this arena concerns extended teacher education programs. Advocated by both the Holmes Group (1986) and Carnegie Task Force on Teaching as a Profession (1986), such programs are designed to provide prospective teachers with more extensive disciplinary, pedagogical, and clinical preparation. Conant (1963) claimed that the primary differentiation between four- and five-year programs was in the amount of available electives, leading him to declare that the fifth year was of "dubious value" (p. 204). Yet Darling-Hammond (1996) asserted that five-year programs better prepare teachers. Findings from other studies have revealed that graduates of extended teacher education programs not only report greater levels of satisfaction in regard to their teacher preparation (Andrew, 1990), but also receive higher ratings from administrators and colleagues as being better prepared and effective than do graduates of four-year programs (Baker, 1993). Although research related to this topic is still somewhat limited, results have tended to be generally positive in favor of longer preparation experiences.

In a similar vein, higher rates of teacher retention have been linked to more extensive teacher preparation efforts (Zeichner & Gore, 1990). Andrew and Schwab (1995) reported that, comparatively speaking, graduates of five-year teacher education programs go into and remain in teaching longer than do their four-year counterparts. Darling-Hammond (2000a) echoed this sentiment and also noted that graduates of the more traditional four- and five-year teacher education programs exhibit less attrition than do those individuals prepared through shorter alternative certification routes. Based on results such as these, the addition of a fifth year seems to be an approach to enhancing teacher education programs that has merit.

Further still, how individuals feel about their teacher preparation experience seems to have an influence on the decision as to whether or not to remain in the profession. In this regard, graduates from traditional teacher education programs have been found to be more likely to indicate that they were well prepared to teach, and expect to continue to do so, than do those without this type of training background (Darling-Hammond, Chung, & Frelow, 2002). Therefore, it is becoming increasingly apparent that high-quality teacher preparation may be a key element in successfully combating the problem of teacher turnover (Berry, Luczak, & Norton, 2003).

Of all of the items delineated herein, a growing body of evidence points to the vital impact that workplace conditions have on teachers' job satisfaction and corresponding plans to remain in the profession. Factors previously identified by teachers as important in this regard include school facilities, bureaucracy, administrative competence, and opportunities for professional development (Johnson & Birkeland, 2002). Prior research has also linked greater levels of teacher attrition to lack of administrative support, discipline issues, minimal faculty input, and insufficient salaries (Ingersoll, 2001).

Additionally, classroom conditions have been found to affect teachers' approaches to and comfort in the profession (Hargreaves, 1988). A recently released report by Public Agenda, *Stand by Me: What Teachers Really Think about Unions, Merit Pay, and Other Professional Matters*, cited teachers' concerns with school atmosphere, administrative favoritism, inadequate parental support, unrealistic expectations, and ill-conceived reform plans (Farkas, Johnson, & Duffett, 2003). Despite these hindrances, 74% of the teachers surveyed indicated that they are strongly committed to the profession as a lifelong career. But an equally large amount (76%) nonetheless felt that they are often made "the scapegoats for all the problems facing education" (p. 12). Given these findings, the call by Johnson et al. (2001) for renewed efforts to improve school culture seems warranted in that such actions may prove to be beneficial in the quest to retain more teachers in the future.

Moreover, it has been pointed out that the issues surrounding the availability of teachers today are much different than was the case in the past. Ingersoll (2001) explained that teaching has exceedingly become a 'revolving door occupation'. In addition, what was once the typical reason behind young women exiting the profession—to raise a family—is presently much less prevalent, with the preponderance of those who now leave doing so to pursue other career paths (Darling-Hammond & Sclan, 1996). Olson (2000) emphasized that the teaching profession is already faced with the fact that the most promising students often choose disciplines other than education, attracted by jobs that are more lucrative in terms of money, power, and prestige. The picture appears even more bleak considering the shrinking job pool caused by increased opportunities for women and minorities in other fields (Johnson & Birkeland, 2002). Based on current circumstances, the need to develop and implement effective strategies to meet the challenge of retaining new teachers—especially in high poverty areas—becomes even more pressing (Joftus & Maddox-Dolan, 2002).

Significance of Study

In the face of national claims of inadequate teacher preparation and a teacher shortage, anecdotal evidence from employers suggests that the University of Kansas School of Education (KUSOE) prepares excellent teachers who become professional leaders. According to administrators around the state (e.g., L. Englebrick, personal communication, 9/21/2000; N. McFraizer, personal communication, 1/14/2001), KUTeachers are some of the finest teachers employed by their districts. They are prepared to teach in their content areas, they are confident about their abilities, and they serve as leaders within their schools.

Yet consistent with the national trend, Kansas is experiencing a crisis in retaining teachers beyond their third year (KSDE, 2001). Assuming KU graduates match national trends, while 85% of the KUTeachers who graduated in academic year 2000 took positions as teachers, many of these people would not be expected to still be teaching in three years. Do KUTeachers reflect current trends? Do they disconfirm these trends? Why do they remain in the profession? What, if anything, can be identified in their teacher preparation program as contributing to decisions to stay in or leave the teaching profession? This case study was undertaken to explore these key questions.

Within the School of Education and the University, attempts have previously been made to document the paths of students in the profession. Prior to 1996, the KUSOE annually carried out a longitudinal evaluative follow-up of students who completed their licensure program. Approximately half an exiting class of teachers who were one, three, and five years removed from the School was sampled to participate in an intensive telephone interview. As part of this self-evaluation activity, the principals of these teachers were surveyed. Their responses indicated that the teachers were doing an excellent job in the classroom and generally had positive things to say about the University, the School, and its programs. However, this survey did not address issues related to retention in the profession nor seek out information from those who were not teaching.

In addition, the Professional Development School (PDS) Alliance obtained a grant from the State to examine the career pathways of the KUTeachers who interned in PDS sites during their fifth year (Tollefson, Hinrichsen, & Peres, 2001). Using data gathered from a sample of PDS graduates between 1993–2001, this research effort explored their placements in the schools as teachers and addressed retention issues. Findings from this investigation advanced the notion that five-year (extended) teacher education programs better prepare their graduates for teaching. Yet little information was revealed about those people no longer in the teaching profession. Hence, the case study of KUTeachers can serve to build upon results of this prior research.

Clearly there has been antecedent exploration of the topic of teacher retention in Kansas, but the work thus far has addressed only an overview of KUTeachers as well as the general population of teachers in the state. One such example is the Emporia survey, which analyzes the supply and demand of teachers within the Kansas Public Schools. In addition, the Kansas State Department of Education has a certification survey that centers on issues of employment including those people not working in the teaching profession after certification and reasons why. Although identifying information about teacher retention in general, specifics regarding how KUTeachers fit into this overall picture cannot be gleaned from these data.

Thus, while prior research does exist that offers suggestions of trends and generalities regarding the issue of teacher retention within the state, more specific information to provide a complete picture is absent. Though the knowledge base regarding teacher attrition and teacher retention is growing, there is still a lack of qualitative case examples that look specifically at how extended teacher education programs prepare teachers for the realities of the classroom and sustain their commitment to the profession. This case study can furnish both undergraduate and graduate teacher education programs with insights into the relationship of initial teacher preparation to teacher retention in the profession of teaching in the state of Kansas and beyond.

STRUCTURE OF THE TEACHER EDUCATION PROGRAM

Within the University of Kansas (KU), a highly respected tertiary institution in the United States, the School of Education (SOE) accepts a small number (approximately 150) of well-prepared students (defined by their grades and writing aptitude illustrated during the application process) each year into its elementary and secondary programs. These students come mostly from the surrounding regions of Kansas. Collaborating with state and federal educators, the SOE faculty seeks to improve education at all levels and strives to provide the best education possible for its students making reflection and change constant in this environment (Hamilton, 2001).

Since the mid-1990s, the KUSOE periodically engaged in its own self-study of teacher education. Charged by the Board of Regents (a state entity that oversees institutions of higher learning) to become an excellent model of how to best address needs of our students in an increasingly complex world, the KUSOE has studied, reorganized, redesigned, and reexamined its teacher education program. With each turn, the faculty sought to design the best possible teacher preparation program.

Currently the KU teacher education program extends to five years. Students graduate with a Bachelor's degree in education in four years and move into a fifth year program that includes 22 weeks of teaching (8 weeks of student teaching in the fall semester and 14 weeks of internship in the spring semester). Students competitively accepted into the KUSOE begin their professional education courses in their third year at the University. Once admitted into the School, students identify content areas along with a grade level focus (e.g., elementary, elementary/middle, middle, middle/secondary, secondary) and take the appropriate coursework. During their fifth year, the students do their student teaching, plus enroll in a series of graduate level courses focused on research, school law, and assessment. At the end of their spring internship, the students have completed 15 hours of graduate work and can be certified to teach.

Perhaps more importantly, the extension of the teacher education program is not simply an issue of quantity. Rather, it is an opportunity for prospective teachers to hone their reflective and pedagogical skills under the watchful eyes of their supervisors and their cooperating teachers. In the initial eight-week period, fifth-year students are guided by their cooperating teachers to implement a variety of unit and lesson plans that allow them to actualize the knowledge about practice that they have developed in their coursework.

Likewise, the graduate-level coursework taken between the student teaching and the internship underscores and emphasizes the learning that occurred during the initial experience. In the spring, the internship allows prospective teachers to take their work to the next level. During this time, they initiate their own lessons and generate their own assessment tools. In these ways, KU's fifth-year students develop their confidence for their initial classroom teaching experiences.

LINKS BETWEEN UNIVERSITY AND SCHOOL EXPERIENCES

Methodology

Inspired by Darling-Hammond and Sclan's (1996) suggestion that "Qualitative studies are needed to explore more fully how teachers make decisions about whether to . . . remain in teaching" (p. 96), this two year case study used qualitative and quantitative research strategies to collect and analyze data that explored teacher retention and the decisions of KUTeachers to stay in or leave the teaching profession. Through this work, we hoped to increase our understanding of retention issues in teacher education and of how to better prepare teachers for the profession. A purposive sample of our graduates was used, namely fifth year students of the KUSOE teacher education program who completed the program between 1990 and 2000 and varied in age, gender and ethnicity to the extent that the KUSOE clientele does.

Initially we conducted and analyzed the Professional Teacher Survey (PTS) of KUTeachers (which we undertook to establish the trends involved in retention of KUTeachers). With a 45% return rate, we felt confident in the trends we identified. Then, drawing pertinent information from those data, we used a focus group to affirm/disaffirm the identified trends. Once those data were collected, we interviewed a selected sample of people to gather qualitative data to provide a richer description of our KUTeachers and their beliefs about teaching and the profession. The final phase of the case study was a follow-up email survey.

All data collected were triangulated to provide the fullest picture of the teaching experiences of KUTeachers. In this way, each piece of information or conclusion was validated by information collected through other means (Borman, LeCompte & Goetz, 1986; Denzin, 1978). By so doing, we insured the best representation of data as well as the strongest interpretation of the information gathered. This project produced a detailed look at some of the factors that contribute to the retention of KUTeachers in the teaching profession.

Research Findings

The Professional Teacher Survey (a four-page document) was sent out in early January 2002 and by late in the month we had obtained a 45% response. As for the demographic characteristics of the 284 individuals who responded to the original survey, 94.4% were White Americans, and 82.7% were female. The majority of the respondents (59.9%) were between the ages of 25–30, while 31.7% were aged 31–35. Representation by grade level was fairly equal, with 46% being elementary teachers and 54% being middle/ secondary teachers. A total of 42.6% obtained their most recent degree within the time span of 1999–2001, 33.5% in 1996–1998, 15.1% in 1993–1995, and 7.4% in 1990–1992. Almost half (47.2%) of the respondents indicated that they had already completed a Master's degree.

In regard to employment status, approximately two-thirds (65.1%) of respondents reported that they were currently teaching. Of the subgroup of individuals that had been teaching for more than five years, reasons given for remaining in the profession most often centered on working with kids, making a difference, the rewarding/challenging nature of the job, the flexible work schedule, and job security. Conversely, those individuals not presently in the profession responded that they had decided to not pursue teaching as a career due to such causes as lack of support, little respect, loss of autonomy, time and stress pressures, low pay, and raising children.

Out of the 284 participants in the survey, 97 respondents indicated that they were not currently teaching. Of this number, 39% (n = 38) noted that they were stay-at-home parents, while another 27% (n = 27) were involved in either graduate studies or in a teaching-related field (e.g., Administrator, Librarian, Counselor). Only 37% (n = 36) reported that they were no longer in a teaching-related field. When this subgroup of respondents were asked why they were not currently teaching, the results were quite varied with fourteen different categories of reasons given. The top three reasons given, which constitute the vast majority of the respondents, were as follows: desiring to stay at home with one's own children, financial considerations, and perceived lack of support within their school and/or district.

For those respondents who choose to stay at home with their kids, the decision to step away from teaching usually took one of two forms. First, many of the respondents indicated a strong desire to be at home and raise their children during their pre-school years. Some respondents indicated that due to the birth of their child(ren), teaching was no longer in their future. However, other respondents were more willing and even eager to return to teaching.

When examining participants' explanations for not teaching, it is easy to assimilate many of those factors (e.g., desire to move to a non-complementary field and failure to finish the fifth year) under the larger umbrella of financial considerations since the interviews indicated that these factors almost always had a financial reason behind them. A total of 29% of participants indicated that finances were an important factor overall in their decision to leave teaching. Their complaints about finances ranged from the lack of salary necessary to pay daycare expenses and remain in teaching, to the inability to raise a family of four on a teacher's salary, to finding a job that paid more, and to not being able to have the lifestyle desired on two teacher's salaries. One important issue that came up regarding finances was the lack of meritocracy when it came to pay raises for experienced teachers.

While not true of all respondents that eventually chose a non-teaching related occupation, finances did serve as the rationale for such a move for many of the respondents. Some subjects experienced either their parents' or their own divorce during their fifth year of the program or shortly after starting teaching and subsequently needed to find a higher paying job. Others simply could not make it financially during the fifth year since they were expected to student teach without pay while also paying for hours at KU and still find the time to work the necessary hours to make ends meet for themselves or their families while avoiding the accumulation of more debt.

Unfortunately, finances are a factor that is beyond the scope of any teacher education program to alleviate. While all programs should ensure that students know the approximate pay scale of education in the area, there is little the program can do to increase the salary levels of teachers. However, the issue related to students being unable to finish their fifth year due to teaching without pay, making it nearly impossible to find a second job, should clearly be evaluated as to its impact on the success of the fifth year.

Lack of support was the third primary reason for leaving. This lack of support was evident from three main sources. First was the lack of support for teachers by the administration. Several subjects cited a lack of support, particularly from principals, at their schools. This lack of support by principals in failing to enforce the rules often made the teacher's job more difficult. Others indicated lack of support from their teacher-mentor during the student teaching experiences. One subject lamented the poor mentorship program for new teachers in her district. Yet another subject voiced a lack of support by the school district to maintain ongoing teacher training as a principal reason for her leaving the teaching profession. Lack of support from parents was the third reason listed by several of the respondents as one of the fundamental factors for leaving the teaching profession.

By and large, respondents seemed able to deal with one major factor, such as lack of support, and still remain in the profession. However, when there were two or more major factors (e.g., school safety, salary, lack of support, apathy of students, stress, and time commitment) listed by the respondents, then the probability was high that these individuals were now involved in either a non-teaching related field or were pursuing further education in a non-education field.

CONCLUSION

Generally speaking, respondents expressed overall high levels of satisfaction with the KU teacher education program as evidenced by their ratings of twelve specific items on the original teacher survey related to professional preparation that were ranked on a Likert-type scale ranging from 1 (not prepared) to 4 (very well prepared). All except three of these particular items had means at 3.0 or above. KU Teachers felt most prepared in their ability to plan successful lessons and in understanding the developmental needs of students (mean = 3.6), followed by content knowledge in their field, ability to reflect and improve instructional practice, and ability to implement varied teaching strategies (means = 3.5). Areas in which respondents felt somewhat less prepared were in the ability to work with parents (mean = 2.62), ability to adapt for students with exceptionalities in general education settings (mean = 2.7), and ability to work with students with special needs (mean = 2.84).

Comments provided to the open-ended questions of the survey concerning the KU teacher preparation program experience were generally very positive as well. Strengths of the program that were most frequently noted included the dual student teaching opportunities, lesson planning/teaching strategies, and content knowledge. The main weaknesses that were mentioned revolved around issues regarding discipline, urban settings, special education, technology, the day-to-day logistics of teaching, and dealing with parents. Suggestions for improvement were that the program incorporate even more practical experiences for students (and early on), plus provide additional occasions for interaction with practicing teachers (e.g., in the form of a mentoring program).

When responding to the survey question "As you consider your teaching experience, in what ways did your teacher education program experience prepare you for your career as a teacher?", respondents often credited the extended field experiences encountered in the fifth-year as being of paramount importance. A few of the more noteworthy remarks in this respect are reflected in the following statements:

> The courses were mostly helpful, especially methods. The year of student teaching, actually the whole 5th year, was the most help. It's hard to teach what really happens in a classroom.
>
> The single most important thing I received from my teacher education program was classroom time. The opportunity for two student teaching experiences was invaluable.
>
> The most relevant would be the student teaching and the internship as this provided long-term, daily interaction with students, other teachers and parents.
>
> The fifth-year program was excellent preparation. The semester I spent as an intern helped me prepare for the demands and the pace of my first job.
>
> The most beneficial aspect of my teacher education program was the internship.
>
> The real classroom experience was very valuable in helping me prepare for my own classroom.

Along these same lines, the major theme that emerged from the focus group was the perception that participants felt they were extremely well prepared by KUSOE's five-year program. Comments made during this session indicated that this realization generally came about once KUTeachers were actually 'out in the field' and compared themselves to other beginning teachers. While acknowledging that the first few years of teaching are far from easy and can at times seem overwhelming, participants stated that they felt their teacher education experience was of high quality and provided them with the type of preparation needed to become successful teachers. The fifth-year was described as being an essential element of the program, with the extra field experience seen as being especially beneficial. Some of the described advantages of the five-year program were that it attracts people with true commitment and is perceived as being prestigious. One participant also postulated that fifth-year students are more apt to finish a Master's degree in education which may in turn result in their being more likely to stay in the profession.

Even though all of the focus group participants were still teaching, one of the posed questions asked them to share information concerning people they knew who were prepared by KU but decided not to teach or started teaching and left the profession. Responses to this inquiry yielded the same type of reasons typically noted in this regard such as not liking the student teaching experience, influences of the working climate, family issues, and salary differentials. However, one other concept did come up in the focus group that did not arise in the original survey—that the school principal might be a key factor in a teacher's decision to quit teaching.

Results of the personal and phone interviews basically corroborated previous findings obtained from the original survey and focus group. Interviewees expressed high opinions of the effectiveness of their teacher preparation experience and were strong advocates of the fifth year. Recommendations for improvement entailed more involvement with 'real' teachers in classroom settings. Explanations given for those who were not teaching covered such aspects as recognizing they did not want to be a teacher after all, job burnout, parental indifference, raising a family, and financial considerations (e.g., concerns over low pay, more attractive job offers in the corporate world). Interestingly, answers to the question as to how much influence a school principal plays in a teacher's decision to stay in or leave teaching did not really reveal this as being much of a potential factor.

Findings from the e-mail follow-up survey further confirmed results from the other components of the case study. The majority of respondents still employed in the field cited love of teaching, love of children, and personal satisfaction as reasons for remaining in the profession. Reasons listed as to why their peers had left teaching included lack of money, childrearing/need for time with children and family, lack of administrative support, lack of respect from parents and community, excessive paperwork, and inability to find a job in a particular subject matter area.

As for KU's extended teacher education program, the response was unanimous in favor of the five-year program. KUTeachers indicated that they felt they were better prepared than colleagues who entered the profession from traditional four-year programs. Overwhelming the reason given for the positive response was the increased time in actual classroom settings due to the dual student teaching experiences inherent in the fifth year. Based on such findings, the fifth-year can be looked upon as serving as an important structural link in efforts to help bridge theory and practice in teacher preparation.

REFERENCES

Andrew, M. D. (1990). Differences between graduates of 4-year and 5-year teacher preparation programs. *Journal of Teacher Education, 41*(2), 45–51.

Andrew, M., & Schwab, R. L. (1995). Has reform in teacher education influenced teacher performance? An outcome assessment of graduates of eleven teacher education programs. *Action in Teacher Education, 17*, 43–53.

Baker, T. (1993). A survey of four-year and five-year program graduates and their principals. *Southeastern Regional Association of Teacher Educators (SRATE), Journal 2*, 28–33.

Berry, B., Luczak, J., & Norton, J. (2003). *The status of teaching in the Southeast: Measuring progress, moving forward.* Chapel Hill, NC: University of North Carolina, The Southeast Center for Teaching Quality.

Borman, K., LeCompte, M., & Goetz, J. (1986). Ethnographic and qualitative research design and why it doesn't work. *American Behavioral Scientist, 30*, 42–57.

Carnegie Task Force on Teaching as a Profession. (1986). *A nation prepared: Teachers for the 21st century*. New York: Carnegie Forum on Education and the Economy.

Conant, J. B. (1963). *The education of American teachers*. New York: McGraw-Hill.

Darling-Hammond, L. (1996). *What matters most: Teaching for America's future*. New York: National Commission on Teaching and America's Future.

Darling-Hammond, L. (1997). *Doing what matters most: Investing in quality teaching*. New York: National Commission on Teaching and America's Future.

Darling-Hammond, L. (2000a). *Solving the dilemmas of teacher supply, demand, and quality*. New York: National Commission on Teaching and America's Future.

Darling-Hammond, L. (2000b). *Solving the dilemmas of teacher supply, demand, and standards: How we can ensure a competent, caring, and qualified teacher for every child.* New York: National Commission on Teaching and America's Future.

Darling-Hammond, L. (2002). *Access to quality teaching: An analysis of inequality in California's public schools.* Stanford, CA: Stanford University.

Darling-Hammond, L. (2003). Keeping good teachers: Why it matters, what leaders can do. *Educational Leadership, 60*(8), 6–13.

Darling-Hammond, L., & Sclan, E. M. (1996). Who teaches and why. In J. Sikula (Ed.), *Handbook of Research on Teaching Education* (2nd ed., pp. 67–101). New York: Macmillan.

Darling-Hammond, L., Chung, R., & Frelow, F. (2002). Variation in teacher preparation: How well do different pathways prepare teachers to teach? *Journal of Teacher Education, 53*(4), 286–302.

Denzin, N. (1978). *The research act*. Chicago: Aldine.

Farkas, S., Johnson, J., & Duffett, A. (2003). *Stand by me: What teachers really think about unions, merit pay, and other professional matters*. New York: Public Agenda.

Farkas, S., Johnson, J., & Foleno, T. (2000). *A sense of calling: Who teaches and why*. New York: Public Agenda.

Fowler, C. (2002). *Fast track... slow going?* Education Policy Clearinghouse Research Brief, Vol. 2, Issue 1 [On-line]. Available: www.edpolicy.org/publications/documents/update v2i1.pdf

Grossman, P. (2003, January/February). Teaching: From *A Nation at Risk* to a profession at risk? *Harvard Education Letter* [On-line serial]. Available: http://www.edletter.org/past/ issues/ 2003-jf/nation.shtml

Hamilton, M. L. (2001). Living our contradictions: Caught between our words and our actions around social justice. *School Field, 12*(3/4), 61–72.
Hargreaves, A. (1988). Teaching quality: A sociological analysis. *Journal of Curriculum Studies, 20*(3), 211–231.
Haycock, K. (1998). No more settling for less. *Thinking 6–16, 4*(1) 3–12.
Henke, R., Chen, X., & Geis, S. (2000). *Progress through the teacher pipeline: 1992–93 college graduates and elementary/secondary school teaching as of 1997*. Washington, DC: National center for Education Statistics, U.S. Department of Education.
Holmes Group. (1986). *Tomorrow's teachers: A report of the Holmes Group*. East Lansing, MI: Author.
Hussar, W. J. (1999). *Predicting the need for newly hired teachers in the United States to 2008–9*. (Publication No. 1999026). Washington, DC: National Center for Education Statistics.
Ingersoll, R. M. (2001). Teacher turnover and teacher shortages: An organizational analysis. *American Educational Research Journal, 38*(3), 499–534.
Joftus, S., & Maddox-Dolan, B. (2002). *New-teacher excellence: Retaining our best*. Washington, DC: Alliance for Excellent Education.
Johnson, S. M., & Birkeland, S. E. (2002). *Pursuing "a sense of success": New teachers explain their career decisions*. Cambridge, MA: Harvard University, Graduate School of Education.
Johnson, S. M., Birkeland, S., Kardos, S. M., Kauffman, D., Liu, E., & Peske, H. G. (2001, July/August). Retaining the next generation of teachers: The importance of school-based support. *Harvard Education Letter* [On-line serial]. Available: http://www.edletter.org/past/issues/2001-ja/support.shtml
Jordan-Irvine, J. (2001, March). *Caring, competent teachers in complex classrooms*. Paper presented at the annual meeting of the American Association of Colleges for Teacher Education, Dallas, TX.
Kansas State Department of Education (KSDE). (2001). March Meeting—Study session of teacher preparation issues. Available on-line: www.ksde/org/commiss/bdmin/mar01mins.html.
Kozol, J. (2001, March). *Opening night lecture—ordinary resurrections*. Paper presented at the annual meeting of the American Association of Colleges for Teacher Education, Dallas, TX.
Lanier, J. E., & Little, J. W. (1984). Research on teacher education. In M. C. Wittrock (Ed.), *Handbook for Research on Teaching*, 3rd ed., (pp. 527–569). New York: Macmillan.
Murnane, R., Singer, J. D., Willett, J. B., Kemple, J. J., & Olsen, R. J. (1991). *Who will teach? Policies that matter*. Cambridge, MA: Harvard University Press.
National Commission on Teaching and America's Future (NCTAF). (2003). *No dream denied: A pledge to America's children*. Washington, DC: Author.
National Education Association (NEA). (1992). *Status of the American public school teacher 1990–91*. Washington, DC: Author.
Nieto, S. M. (2003). What keeps teachers going? *Educational Leadership, 60*(8), 14–18.
Olson, L. (2000). Finding and keeping competent teachers. *Education Week, 13*, 12.
Raymond, M., Fletcher, S., & Luque, J. (2001). *Teach for America: An evaluation of teacher differences and student outcomes in Houston, Texas*. Stanford, CA: Center for Research on Educational Outcomes, The Hoover Institution, Stanford University.
Riley, R. (1999). New challenges, a new resolve: Moving American education into the 21st century. Speech given 2/16/1999 in Long Beach, CA. Available on-line: http://www.ed.gov/Speeches/02-1999/990216.html
Tollefson, N., Hinrichsen, J., & Peres, D. (2001). *Final Report for the professional development school retention study funded by the Kansas State Department of Education through a Title II professional development schools grant for research on the effectiveness of the professional development school model in teacher preparation units in Kansas*. Unpublished manuscript.
Zeichner, K. M., & Gore, J. M. (1990). Teacher socialization. In W. R. Houston (Ed.), *Handbook of research on teacher education* (pp. 329–348). New York: Macmillan.

Part III

Social-Cultural Links amongst Participants in the Program

Introduction by Garry F. Hoban

Part 2 of this book focused on ideas to provide links between theory and practice by considering the relationship between school and university settings. These ideas on theory-practice links together with the ideas from Part 1 on conceptual links across the university curriculum are summarised in Figure B.

Part 3 of this book focuses on ways to develop social-cultural links amongst the participants in the program. These are fundamental because a teacher education program takes a long time to develop and is constantly evolving. For this reason, structures need to be put in place to not only "keep the conversation going" but also to maintain a flow of new ideas into the program design. Interestingly, although most teacher educators realise this, very few programs have structures to accommodate and sustain social interactions of staff and students.

In Chapter 10, Gaalen Erickson, Linda Farr Darling and Anthony Clarke from the University of British Columbia explain how sharing their own beliefs about teaching and learning was fundamental to establishing a community of inquiry. Their community of inquiry is based on three fundamental understandings: (i) learning is social; (ii) learning to teach is a matter of developing dispositions towards others and towards inquiry; and (iii) community of inquiry members are committed to ongoing research, critical reflection and constructive engagement with others. Interestingly, they use an online discussion forum involving past and present students to help maintain their community interactions and to invite a variety of perspectives into their discussions.

Clare Kosnik and Clive Beck in Chapter 12 also reiterated the importance of social interactions claiming that program development and community-building go "hand-in-hand". They used a cohort structure at the University of Toronto/OISE to localise decision making for their large number of teacher education students. This included each cohort of 65 students having two co-ordinators, contact with 12–15 schools and a unique focus for each cohort such as a focus on technology, the arts or science and maths. This selected focus is negotiated between the cohort and schools. The key, therefore, in maintaining such unique structures for each cohort is the social interaction as

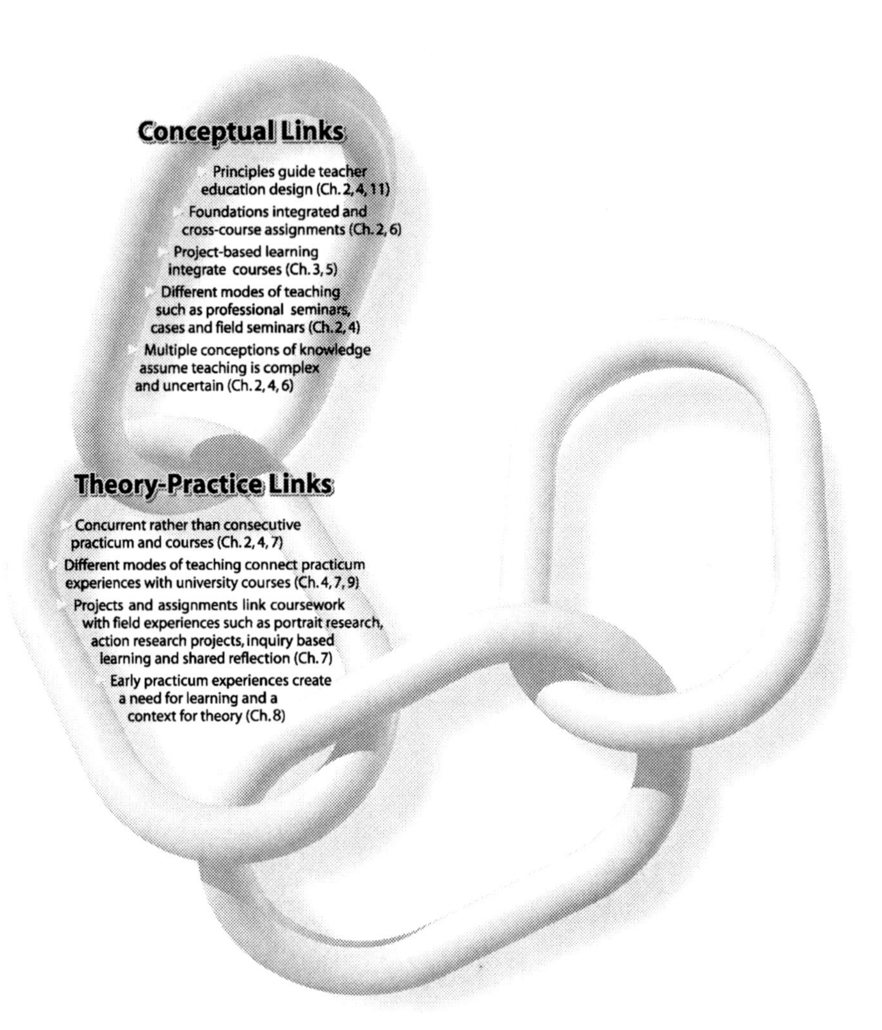

Figure B. Key ideas to promote conceptual and theory-practice Links

"it is the interplay between community, experience and academic and professional learning that so urgently needs to be recognised in teacher education and education generally."

Part 3 includes an interesting chapter from John Loughran, Amanda Berry and Elizabeth Tudball from Monash University who not only promote the importance of social interactions, but invite criticism of their teaching to develop a "culture of critique". They model this process to their student teachers which first involves developing trust and confidence to seek critical feedback on teaching practices. Importantly, they outline the need to foster social interactions because teaching contexts change so much, "we believe that building relationships requires a genuine concern to listen to, and be aware of, the changing nature of the classroom context, and to be interested in, and responsive to, the needs of students." As the contexts of schools and universities increasingly change throughout the 21st Century, the need to establish and maintain social structures for staff and students will become more important.

Chapter 10

Constructing and Sustaining Communities of Inquiry in Teacher Education

Gaalen Erickson, Linda Farr Darling and Anthony Clarke
University of British Columbia, Canada

This chapter explores the notion of missing links in teacher education by examining concepts of community and inquiry as they pertain to the social dimensions of 'learning to teach.' We know that while these are popular notions in educational discourse we believe their philosophical import has been undervalued in designing teacher preparation program. We have an expanded vision of community that includes school personnel, pre-service teachers, campus-based instructors, and graduates of our program. Similarly we have an expanded vision of inquiry that includes collaborative and individual investigations by all members of the community. These investigations are focused on the program itself and give shape to its continual evolution. Hence, while the concepts of community and inquiry remain constant, the program each year is a unique reflection of its participants and their particular concerns.

In 1997, several colleagues with strong commitments to teacher education reform began to share visions for creating a new initiative within the Faculty of Education at the University of British Columbia (UBC). Conceptually speaking, we stood on a big patch of common ground with all of us believing that preparation for teaching should be considered a moral as well as intellectual and even aesthetic endeavor. We shared concerns that much of teacher preparation is regarded in our own institution, as well as others, as a technical enterprise. Programs are often focused on the mechanics of teaching, rather than on the development of dispositions, sensitivities and understandings that guide thoughtful judgments about what to believe or do in the complex world of the classroom (Fenstermacher, 1990; Goodlad, 1994; Schön, 1987; Thomas, Wineburg, Grossman, Myhre, & Woolworth, 1998). We also held common understandings about the social nature of learning in general, and learning to teach in particular. As our conversations unfolded, two concepts became central. The first was community, and the second, inquiry. As we explored possibilities for creating an alternative option within the existing program, these two concepts began to take root.

G. Hoban (ed.), The Missing Links in Teacher Education Design, 173–191.

Community became an umbrella term in those first discussions. Sheltered beneath it were things we believed had been missing in our experiences working in teacher education programs, including coherence, cohesiveness, and the construction and expression of collective understandings. Emphasizing community also pushed us to think about the sorts of connections we wanted with our school partners. The notion of inquiry brought into focus dimensions of the intellectual side of becoming a teacher that can also be underrepresented in programs: critical engagement with theory, robust and continuous synthesis of ideas, and active participation by students in decisions about the substance and nature of their inquiries and how they learn to be teachers.

These initial visions for teacher education reform were created within several contexts that would continue to shape our plans: the one-year post-baccalaureate teacher preparation program at the UBC, and the wider backdrops of teacher education in the Province of British Columbia and in Canada. Before we could consider an alternative to existing practices in teacher education, we needed to take these contexts into account.

CONTEXT OF TEACHER EDUCATION PROGRAMS IN BRITISH COLUMBIA AND CANADA

Each province in Canada has its own Ministry of Education. In several provinces, including British Columbia (BC), there are separate ministries for K-12 education and for tertiary level education, including teacher preparation programs. Fifteen years ago the BC government created a College of Teachers (modeled after Colleges of Physicians and Surgeons that exist in most jurisdictions) which was legislated to be a self-regulating body responsible for establishing standards for the education of public school teachers issuing teaching certificates, conducting certificate reviews and, where necessary, suspending or canceling certificates. The original legislation established a 20 member board, 15 elected teachers representing regions of BC and five government appointments. The College began conducting reviews of the teacher education programs in the Province in 1988. It reviewed both existing and proposed programs until May, 2003. At this time the government substantially amended the legislation of the College. When this legislation is enacted in 2004 there will be 12 elected teachers and eight appointed members[1]. The previous 'program approval process' will be replaced by a system for establishing professional

[1] The Government initially proposed eight elected and 12 appointed Board members, but this legislation was strongly contested by the teachers of B.C., to the point of refusing to pay their yearly fees to the College. In December, 2003 the Ministry of Education agreed to reverse the representation on the Board to 12 elected teacher members and eight Government appointed members.

standards for provincial teacher preparation programs. The degree to which the various institutions in the Province offering teacher education programs meet these standards will now be the focus of the College's evaluation.

THE STRUCTURE OF THE TEACHER EDUCATION PROGRAM AT UBC

Pre-service teacher education at UBC requires that students have a bachelor's degree, English language proficiency, work or voluntary experience with youths, and several prerequisite courses. (Prerequisites vary depending on the program one applies to, elementary or secondary, or the specialization, e.g., Science, English, etc.) The 12-month elementary teacher education program runs from September of each year through the middle of August, and is considered intensive in terms of time and workload. In the first term, students take seven courses (39 hours each) and participate in weekly school visits known as "pre-practicum experiences." These courses aim to build the groundwork for learning about teaching. They include courses on principles and practices of teaching and related communication skills, foundations of literacy, developmental theories in educational psychology, and finally, policy issues and the social and political context of schooling. During the same term students also take a course in the curriculum and instruction of art, and one in music.

In the first two weeks of January, students participate in a two-week school experience in which they observe classrooms and engage in small numbers of teaching and planning activities. Until the 13-week practicum begins in mid-March, students are back on campus taking five curriculum methods courses in elementary school subjects: language arts, mathematics, science, social studies and physical education. Of these, the course in language arts is allotted almost double the hours, reflecting the elementary school emphasis on learning to read and write. Upon successful completion (courses in these two terms are marked pass/fail) students enter the extended practicum of 13 weeks, typically in a single classroom. Those with successful practicum reports return to campus in the summer for four final courses: an administrative course on school organization, two courses from Educational Psychology, (one on measurement and assessment practices and another on teaching children with special needs), and finally a course on either the social foundations of education or the philosophy, history, or anthropology of education. Upon successful completion of these courses, students have fulfilled the requirements for a Bachelor of Education degree, and then are recommended to the BC College of Teachers for elementary teaching certification. If this looks like a demanding, even whirlwind schedule, it is. Recent surveys conducted through the Teacher Education Office at UBC and the BC College of Teachers (1997) have shown that our graduates are fairly united in concluding that although they generally feel sufficiently prepared to teach, their biggest challenge during the program was time management. It has been frequently pointed out by former students that there are too many courses, and too little meaningful integration between them, too many, especially small assignments, and too much content duplication, particularly in the areas of lesson and unit planning, and the ubiquitous, and often less than meaningful, "reflections." Some respondents have noted that they did not have opportunities to develop relationships with their faculty advisors prior to the January field experience, and that they had too little contact with their instructors because they had so many classes. Many graduates have complained about the lack of close connection between campus and the world of practice. They say that most of their learning occurred while they were in their elementary classrooms during the practicum component, not a surprising finding given that 35% of the elementary 12-month program actually takes place as guided apprenticeships in schools.

The survey results and other less formal indicators of student satisfaction with initial teacher preparation are not unfamiliar to teacher educators who have raised similar issues (Sachs, 1997; Tom, 1997; Wideen & Grimmett, 1995). Critics of initial teacher education programs note persistent theory-practice gaps, redundant course content, and insufficient time to engage in careful observation of, and dialogue about, good teaching practices. Others point to insufficient technological preparation, and still others to a lack of agreement between the expectations of teacher preparation held by preservice teachers, faculty, and school-based personnel. These were also some of the reasons that prompted us to explore the possibilities for constructing an alternative within the existing program.

CITE COMES TO LIFE

Our aim was to offer prospective elementary teachers a program that was conceptually and experientially coherent and faithful to ideals of both community and inquiry. Ideally it would integrate two distinct learning contexts. The first context is the campus. Integration here consists of creating a curricular framework to develop themes that can be threaded through all courses, including those courses on the social, historical, and psychological foundations of teaching and those focused on how to teach particular subjects in schools. While there are reports in the literature of cohort-based models (Bullough, Clark, Wentworth, & Hansen, 2001; Koeppen, Huey, & Connor, 2000; Mather & Hanley, 1999; McIntyre & Byrd, 2000; Radencich, Thompson, Anderson, Oropallo, Fleege, Harrison, & Hanley, 1998; Tom,

1997) many of the cohorts described do not encompass the whole program or have little coordination between instructors. By far the most common model is a series of courses accompanied by some combination of field experiences. The complex tasks of understanding, synthesizing and applying knowledge to practice settings is left up to the students themselves, as none of their campus instructors or school advisors have an understanding of the program as a whole.

A second, more complex, context requires a model for integrating the students' school and community-based experiences with the campus-based components of their program (Farr-Darling, 2000; 2001). This requires the development of a common set of values and commitments from three distinct groups: the school-based teacher educators[2], the campus-based teacher educators, and the pre-service teachers. In the regular program it is rare that the faculty advisor who works with the pre-service teachers in the practicum setting has taught any of their campus courses and thus he or she has limited access to the perspectives and content being presented. More importantly, the most critical person in the practicum setting, the "school advisor" (Harlin, Edwards, & Briers, 2003; Montgomery, 2000; Putnam & Borko, 2000) almost never has access to campus course work and frequently harbors the belief that until students "enter the real world" of classroom practice they have little appreciation of what it means to teach. Often students are explicitly or implicitly told to forget all of the stuff done in the "ivory tower" because the only way to learn about teaching is to immerse yourself in the day to day world of the classroom. This kind of fragmentation between academic learning and on-the-job training has been well documented in the literature of other professional fields of practice such as medicine, social work, commerce, law, and engineering and is often described as the "theory-practice gap" (Bernstein, n.d.; Landers, 2000).

If conceptual and practical coherence is to be achieved within a teacher education community, it can only be done through the development of integrative curricular structures, teaching techniques, and evaluative strategies. These integrative approaches must be agreed upon, designed, and then enacted by all members of this community—a very complex and time-consuming agenda. Our teacher education project aimed to establish such a community, and to sustain it over an extended period of time. We hoped to do this with the development of innovative teaching approaches, the production of curricular

[2] These are the classroom teachers and school administrators who work closely with the CITE pre-service teachers for a total period of about 18 weeks over the course of the year. We call them 'school advisors' to mirror the designation of our 'faculty advisors' who also spend considerable time in the schools working with the pre-service teachers. In other jurisdictions they are sometime called 'sponsor teachers' or 'teacher associates'.

materials and approaches that could be used by other instructors and teacher education programs.

We founded our alternative program on the basis of shared beliefs about teaching, learning and what it means to be a member of a community of inquiry. Early on we agreed that the following statements would guide the construction of the program:

- Learning is social; it takes place in a variety of contexts and through different kinds of inquiry. To learn with and from others, is to enter into a community of inquiry.
- Learning to teach is a matter of developing dispositions towards others and towards inquiry, as well as gaining content and pedagogical knowledge. These dispositions can be cultivated within a community of inquiry.
- In a community of inquiry members are committed to ongoing research, critical reflection, and constructive engagement with others. The epistemic and moral virtues developed and expressed in the community include respect, open mindedness, perseverance, integrity, and a sense of justice.

These underlying commitments, or design principles, owe much to our enactment of features that characterize contemporary socio-cultural theories of learning. The perspective which has been most influential in our work has been that associated with learning through the active participation in a "community of practice" (Lave & Wenger, 1991; Lave, 1995; Palincsar, Magnusson, Marano, Ford, & Brown, 1998; Wenger, 1998) or as others have called it, a "community of learners" (Bereiter & Scardamalia, 1993; Brown, 1994). For Bereiter and Scardamalia, a community of learners must be structured so that community members can productively engage in activities to share their knowledge and support one another in knowledge construction. Notions of "progressive discourse" (in which ideas build on one another through dialogue) and "collective expertise" are reflected in the approaches that we use in CITE as we engage in different forms of collaborative inquiry into 'learning to teach.'

Conceptualizing our cohort as a community of inquiry required exploring the nature of such communities, as well as the nature of inquiry into matters of teaching and learning. Although our understandings about communities of inquiry hearken back to C.S. Peirce (Mounce, 1997), Dewey's beliefs have had the most enduring impact on the educational discourse about them. For Dewey (1916), a community is more than an aggregate of persons, even if they happen to possess common goals. In a genuine community people communicate their goals, revise them together, and work collectively to achieve them. They continually engage with each other in a critical process of personal and social reconstruction. They do this by responding to and building on each other's ideas. Inquiry in a community challenges the outer limits of each member's epistemological horizons. This challenge requires vigilant efforts to engage multiple viewpoints in deliberation. Community members come to understand that any "argument is bigger than anyone of us comprehends from our own perspective" (Kennedy, 1998, p. 21). We believed that by bringing students together with instructors, school personnel and other teacher educators we could construct a purposeful community in which no single member would hold the answer key to questions about how to teach. Ours would be a collective pursuit of knowledge and understanding.

PRACTICES OF COMMUNITY, PRACTICES OF INQUIRY: CREATING A COMMUNITY OF INQUIRY IN TEACHER EDUCATION

The conceptual and practical coherence characterizing such a learning community can only be developed through agreement on a shared set of values and beliefs among all community participants on important issues—such issues as the purposes of education, models of teacher preparation, and perspectives on learning (both pupil learning and teacher learning). From a program perspective this coherence is achieved through the development of interdisciplinary curricular structures, innovative teaching techniques, appropriate evaluative strategies, and effective communicative practices. This latter practice is critical if we are to achieve the level of understanding and agreement on values and purposes, such as those outlined above, with all of the program participants. In order to design some of these practices we were mindful of some of the earlier empirical and conceptual work undertaken by two different research groups, whose primary focus was on developing "communities of learners" in school learning situations (Bereiter & Scardamalia, 1993; Brown, 1994).

While both of the above research groups use somewhat different language (e.g. 'knowledge building communities' and 'community of learners' respectively), their underlying design principles for creating an appropriate learning environment to establish and sustain these 'learning communities' are similar. Bereiter and Scardamalia (1993) introduce the notion of a "knowledge-building community" (KBC) as an educational strategy for "producing a school environment that supports development beyond what comes naturally [and] is what we must discover if we are to educate for expertise" (p. 199). They see this approach as an alternative to the two polar instructional approaches of teacher-directed didactic instruction versus student-directed discovery learning. They draw upon other examples of KBCs—most notably the scientific research group and other disciplinary-base communities in the social sciences and the humanities, and industrial firms with their research and development groups for pursuing inquiry. For Bereiter and Scardamalia a community must be structured such that the participants in a KBC are encouraged to engage in activities wherein they:

- share their knowledge;
- support one another in knowledge construction;
- develop and engage in progressive discourse;
- develop a kind of collective expertise that is distinguishable from that of the individual group members; and,
- demonstrate respect and recognition for peers.

Sharing Knowledge

While this feature brings to the fore the important issue regarding the nature of the knowledge that is being generated and shared among the community participants, this knowledge will clearly be very different and dependent upon the setting in which the community is located. The critical design issue for CITE was to create the types of institutional structures and social linkages that would yield common understandings of the nature and kind of knowledge that was considered to be of most value to our own community and the broader teacher education community.

Support in Knowledge Building

Many others (Barth, 1990; Oakes & Quantz, 1995; Sergiovanni, 1994) have documented the important role played by supportive colleagues in community-like settings. However, it is important to try and understand better the nature of how this supportive social environment assists in the construction of a kind of knowledge that would not likely occur in the absence of such a community (Schoenfeld, 1999). This is one of the aims of the CITE project as we examine the efficacy of different communicative strategies using both conventional and computer-mediated models of engagement.

Progressive Discourse

The notion of progressive discourse entails the development of a language and a way of practicing that "motivates inquiry and transforms its results into knowledge" (Bereiter & Scardamalia, 1993, p. 209). It also leads to the awareness on the part of the group members that their current understanding of some phenomena represents an advance over their earlier efforts. We will demonstrate this feature below as we illustrate the potential of a collaborative, web-based, discussion group for engendering this type of progressive discourse.

Collective Expertise

By "collective expertise" Bereiter and Scardamalia (1993) refer to the development of a type of knowledge that is distinguishable from that which is constructed by the individual group members. As Castle, Drake and Boak (1995) pointed out when discussing their experiences with a collaborative professional development group: "We discovered for ourselves that sharing is a powerful strategy for facilitating transformation in perspectives" (p. 259). We think that this transformation in understanding can be best achieved through the creation of particular practices and activities within the CITE community which we will describe in greater detail below.

Respect and Recognition for Peers

This characteristic is one of the primary moral virtues of any effective community, be it an elite scientific research community or a group of pre-service teachers engaging in a discussion about the merits of curriculum integration. We think that this characteristic is a necessary prerequisite for the emergence of many of the other community features described above. As such, it is one of the virtues that we discuss early and explicitly in the program.

As we discuss below some of the particular practices that have characterized the CITE community to date, the relationship between these practices and the above design features should be evident. A second, related conceptual commitment of the CITE program is inquiry.

INQUIRY AS A PROGRAM CHARACTERISTIC

As has been claimed by educators and philosophers, the justification of much educational practice rests or should rest upon the nature and substance of genuine inquiry (Goodlad, Soder, & Sirotnik, 1990; Dewey, 1916; Schon, 1983, 1987). In the context of CITE, inquiry is a central concept in two respects. First, learning to be a teacher can be conceived as cultivating certain dispositions as well as gaining content and pedagogical understandings. Cultivating a habit of inquiry and an inquisitive spirit should begin in a teacher preparation program and carry on throughout one's teaching career. In this way we can productively speak about teacher education as initiation into a community of inquiry. Second, it is of value for a teacher to know how to establish classroom environments that both create and support inquiry among their pupils (Lipman, 1993, Paul, 1994).

Thus we designed CITE with the purpose of encouraging inquiry and in so doing to develop and exhibit those habits of mind and virtues which will move the inquiry forward. These virtues include honesty and integrity, respect for persons and their ideas, a sense of justice, and the disposition to persevere in seeking answers to the inquiries that are entered into by members of the community.

We have designed a number of features or practices that we have incorporated into the program structure of CITE. Some of these practices can be clustered around a particular function or theme. In general these practices can be characterized as follows:

- The use of **collaborative planning** activities with the pre-service teachers and the teachers and administrative officers of six elementary schools, which sponsor the pre-service teachers, to develop a set of campus and school-related experiences to enhance the learning of all participants.
- The introduction of new **communicative strategies**, particularly technology-based tools to ensure shared understandings and open access to all levels of the program.
- The design of a series of **innovative teaching practices** that are consistent with and advance our guiding principles of shared governance, interdisciplinarity, and community.

Collaborative Planning

Given our commitments to shared decision making and inducting our students into those democratic practices that we think ought to characterize educational practices in school settings, we designed a number of planning structures to facilitate collaborative decision making among all of the participants in our community. While we acknowledged that faculty members have both the primary responsibility and the time for developing the basic structure of the program, we introduced a number of practices which enabled both the pre-service teachers and the school-based advisors to participate in making many of the program decisions. These decisions ranged from longer term planning such as the length and sequencing of school experiences, to more immediate decisions regarding the scheduling of particular class curricular activities and assignments, etc. There were several different kinds of structures that we developed for these shared planning/decision-making sessions. The primary structure we used was that of joint meetings. Thus we met about once a month with a group of teacher representatives (school coordinators) from each school to discuss a series of issues related to the school experience component of the program. We met weekly with the instructional team and a representative group from the pre-service teacher cohort, to discuss the weekly activities and plans for the campus-based component of the program. Another venue for participating in community governance decisions was a web-based discussion forum where the minutes of meetings were posted and where community members could post questions or make comments on any aspect of the program.

Communicative Structures

While our primary communicative structure is the face to face discussion situated in the context of class activities or in dedicated program meetings, we have developed a number of other communicative tools designed to promote dialogue and discussion through the use of several, computer-mediated programs. We have used a number of the features embedded in a limited access, web-based programs (such as WebCT and First Class) as well as a open access webpage (http://www.educ.ubc.ca/courses/cite). In the password protected environment we primarily use the discussion forum and calendar functions. On our 'open' webpage, we post the minutes of all of our standing and ad hoc community meetings and inquiry groups for immediate perusal and comment by all community members.

We also use e-mail extensively for straightforward communication of information to community participants. These latter, computer-mediated communicative structures have been very successful with the campus-based members of the community, but initially was less so with the school-based community members. However, in the last few years, as the accessibility to the internet has become much easier in elementary schools and the use of computer-based communication tools becomes more a part of the routines and practices of most school teachers, we have found this to be a valuable communicative tool with our school-based community members.

Innovative Teaching Practices

We have introduced a number of innovative teaching and evaluation practices over the past three years of the CITE program with the intent of enacting our vision of an ideal teacher education program. One of the key content decisions was to explore different curriculum integration models to structure various activities. We anticipated that these curricular integrative approaches would model curricular units being planned by the pre-service teachers for use in their practicum classrooms. For example, we organized curricular activities around powerful, overarching concepts such as 'structure' and 'change' in science, math, art and social studies.

Other innovative teaching practices we have tried include:

- establishing six-person inquiry groups that independently investigate pedagogical matters of interest and concern to the group, and present their findings in a public forum (actual or virtual);
- teaching some of our 'methods courses' in an elementary school context, rather than on campus;
- using an electronic course management tools, such as those located in First Class or WebCT, to post and share student work and resources that have been collected in various curricular areas;
- structuring on-line discussion groups to deliberate on educational policies and practices; and finally,
- all students create an electronic portfolio which serves as a comprehensive and creative documentation of their experiences in the program and of their growth as a professional educator.

Not every innovation has continued over more than one or several years. Some experimental practices have evolved in unexpected ways. All have been subject to public scrutiny and discussion and have been refined on the basis of feedback from students and instructors. We believe that these practices have not only benefited our pre-service teachers, but have encouraged them to experiment with similar innovations in their practicum classrooms. In one chapter it would be impossible to describe all of these or their impact on the CITE community. Instead, we focus on one innovation that continues to change and grow. It is the subject of lively discussion each year, and both its advocates and critics would agree it has sparked the kind of debate that is essential to the vitality of a community of inquiry.

EXAMPLE OF A COMMUNICATIVE PRACTICE USED TO ENHANCE THE COMMUNITY OF INQUIRY

In providing this example of one of the communicative practices that we have incorporated into CITE, we hope to provide an illustration of how we have attempted to encourage and nurture an inquiring disposition among our community participants. It also provides an illustration of how the CITE instructional team is continuing to inquire into our pedagogical practices.

The example is of an on-line discussion forum using a semi-public "discussion board" in a password protected web environment. The very notion of a community of inquiry presupposes a set of standards of practice, which governs the conduct of community members and provides a justification for the knowledge claims generated by that community. One of the important features of these claims is the requirement that they must be open to public scrutiny and criticism. (In this instance we argue that a "limited" public is most appropriate as we introduce beginning teachers to this notion of 'going public' with their ideas.) In most contexts involving a discussion of teaching and learning practices among teacher educators and pre-service teachers, these discussions are essentially private (while they do occur in face to face classroom settings or in small groups, the conversations and any knowledge claims made in these discussions are ephemeral). Furthermore, they are limited in both time and scope to the specific context where this discussion takes place thus constraining the possibility of participation and the creation of further social links between those educators who are campus-based, and those who are school-based. By engaging in a web-based, on-line discussion forum, we were able to overcome these shortcomings of face-to-face discussions. Furthermore, this practice provides the opportunity of forging an important social linkage between current CITE participants and previous graduates of the CITE program who have teaching positions throughout the world in a variety of educational contexts. Given that participation in this type of forum is still relatively unique for both the pre-service teachers and the teacher educators, the standards of practice and the most appropriate structures for this type of collaborative inquiry are still evolving. Our analysis of this type of practice, then, focuses on the nature of the dialogue and the communicative structures that enable the community members to learn more about the complexities of learning and teaching.

Evolving Practices

We began to explore the utility of on-line discussion components in the second year of the program when we introduced the topic of 'curriculum integration as part of a language arts course assignment. Participants were asked to make at least seven contributions over a four-week period.

The guidelines for posting contributions were that they should be thoughtful, succinct, and threaded (referenced to other contributions). In addition to the 36 pre-service teachers, the forum was open to all of the campus-based educators, four teachers from the practicum schools, and a colleague of one of the authors from Australia. We were pleased with the outcomes of this initial effort at on-line, collaborative learning and so we decided that in subsequent years we would explore more systematic and sustained forms of on-line learning. A required course in our program that seemed particularly suitable for this type of inquiry was called Educational Studies—a course devoted to an examination of a series of social and equity issues (such as multiculturalism, poverty, gender and sexuality, aboriginal issues, and language) that influence our practices as educators.

Thus, the following year we organized the Educational Studies course so that half of the classroom time, normally devoted to face to face discussion and lectures, was given over to an on-line component. To expand the community we invited previous CITE participants, as well as a group of pre-service teachers from another university in Eastern Canada, to join in the discussion forum.

Our primary purpose for this practice was to enable the participants, in particular the pre-service teachers, to investigate their own learning and understanding about the topics under discussion and to gain an appreciation of the potential value in using an on-line, collaborative inquiry space. To this end we asked the pre-service teachers to focus on the types of learning using the on-line process, to consider how it was different from other teaching and learning experiences, and to reflect on its value as a tool for collective inquiry. Finally we encouraged them to think about how this form of writing and dialogue could be related to their own teaching practice.

Results

The data available for analysis includes the record of the on-line discussion itself, a set of reflective comments made by the pre-service teachers at the conclusion of the forum, some interviews and group discussions with a focus group of five students who met before and after the forum to discuss in greater depth some of the features of this type of forum (Mitchell, 2001).

Some of the questions that we were interested in exploring included: Would this kind of inquiry lead to the development of a coherent perspective or point of view on a given topic area? What types of reasons would the participants use to justify and support their claims? How would they engage with the ideas of their peers? All of these questions, and more, would seem to be important in creating and sustaining a community of inquiry. Overall it seemed clear that the pre-service teachers found this activity to be both enjoyable and worthwhile. In general we found that the participants used a combination of reasons and sources to support their views. Many of the pre-service teachers' comments included some combination of a general statement or belief about the topic under discussion along with some reference to either personal experience or the literature provided on the topic. A further finding was that most of the comments included some reference to one or more of their peers' comments. Thus it seems that this type of forum not only encourages the participants to provide some justification for their viewpoint, but the 'permanent access' that they had to the ideas of others meant that they explicitly quoted and referenced the contributions of their peers. Many of the pre-service teachers recognized both of these features of this forum. The following comments by three different pre-service teachers on the forum illustrate their insights:

> This type of discussion reflects problem solving, in that we were thinking critically, and questioning the thoughts of one another. This questioning benefits both the outside readers, and the actual participants, because when a participant's idea or point of view is challenged, one of two things happen. The writer either adjusts his or her thinking, or deepens his or her understanding by justifying the point of view to others.
>
> By bringing in the outside communities, the forum became better than talk. Our replies were permanent and hopefully well thought out. We were going public! We had to refine the way we presented our views because we could not always defend them in person or clarify them easily. I found it interesting the way people looked at my responses because sometimes what I meant and what they saw were different things. The way they viewed my ideas gave me a new way of looking at the problem; it also taught me the importance of considering audience.
>
> The responses of others to the question that were posed helped to solidify my own viewpoints, or they served to provide more food for thought. In the past, I have done most of my learning on my own. I have not worked with other people, nor have I bounced ideas off them. Learning has been done solely on my own, in an environment fraught with a competitive edge. What has been encouraged is sharing of ideas. This learning has been about delving into issues, expressing our viewpoints and sharing them with others.

While we accept that these comments are largely of an anecdotal nature and we have no systematic comparative data with other cohorts using these techniques, all of the data available to us indicates that this on-line forum was, for the most part, very effective in establishing a learning environment that promoted collaborative inquiry. There were, and continue to be, a minority of students who would prefer not to participate in this type of electronic forum. Although the on-line forum represents only one of many face-to-face and computer-mediated practices that CITE community members participate in over the course of the program, we think that it captures quite nicely the way in which participants come together as a community of learners. In this brief example it is possible to see elements of the design features that we discussed earlier. It is evident that the participants were encouraged to "share their knowledge" in a public space and were often engaged in the task of "supporting one another in knowledge construction". The design characteristic of "developing a kind of collective expertise that is distinguishable from that of the individual group members" is more difficult to assess but we see glimpses of this feature in all of the participants comments above. Finally the characteristic of "demonstrating respect and recognition for peers" is readily evident in the students' comments as well as their actions and contributions to this particular form of communicative practice.

EMERGING IDEAS: TEACHER EDUCATION AS A 'COMMUNITY OF MEMORY'

In this chapter we have described some of the features of a one-year teacher education program for elementary teachers that we designed and has now been in operation for eight years. This design process was strongly influenced by our view that teaching and learning are co-constitutive activities. While we have been using the phrase, 'the design process', and we have identified design features from the literature on creating 'learning communities', we wish to emphasize the point that the realization of our aims of creating and sustaining a community of inquiry can only be achieved through the thoughtful engagement of the community members in a complex set of social practices. As program designers we can only try to generate supportive program structures and practices that afford and nurture this type of thoughtful engagement. Wenger (1998) makes a similar point when he discusses the notion of designing "communities of practice"—a broader and more generic term for the types of communities that we have been discussing. He claims "Communities of practice are about content—about learning as a living experience of negotiating meaning—not about form. In this sense, they cannot be legislated into existence or defined by decree. They can be recognized, supported, encouraged, and nurtured, but they are not reified, designable units. Practice itself is not amenable to design" (p. 229).

In summary, our view of teaching is that it consists of a complex set of actions structured around sets of relationships and communicative practices that enable others to learn different forms of knowledge and ways of knowing. Learning to teach, therefore, involves the development of understandings about the sorts of relationships and communicative practices that support learning in different contexts and with respect to different subject matter. Further, we are persuaded by the view that much of our learning and knowing occurs as a result of our participation in social communities. From this perspective, learning and teaching are both highly social activities that require the emergence of diverse and rich learning environments for these practices to flourish. The task of educators, then, is to create "inventive ways of engaging students in meaningful practices, of providing access to resources that enhance their participation, of opening their horizons so they can put themselves on learning trajectories they can identify with, and of involving them in actions, discussions, and reflections that make a difference to the communities that they value" (Wenger, 1998, p. 10).

Our eight year history with CITE has led us to a broader place of reflection. We now see ourselves as becoming a kind of "community of memory" (Bellah *et al.*, 1986; Boyer, 1990; Nicholson, 1991). Our current practices are animated by the relationships between our past experiences and our visions for the future. Following Bellah *et al.* (1986), we are looking forward and backward in time (p. 333), to understand our identities as teachers and learners within the CITE community. The community is characterized by dynamic interaction between former students, current students, school advisors, and campus-based instructors. Our graduates, some of whom are now leaders in the field, come back to us at our orientations for new students every year. They share their memories of CITE and their reflections on their own classroom practices. They also keep in touch with us in an expanding circle that now includes individuals who have taught or are teaching in Japan, China, Thailand, England, Australia, and Central America. The sense of collective memory is enhanced by new communicative technologies that allow greater social links than are normally possible in teacher education programs. Our commitment to these technologies as tools for communication about and for learning was articulated in the first year of CITE and continues to evolve.

The concepts of inquiry and community are enriched by the realization that we are becoming a community of memory characterized by common purposes and commitments, and a continual desire to revitalize our practices and reexamine our goals in light of the experiences and traditions that are behind us. We are fortunate that the teacher educators involved in CITE, as well as our students and school partners, have for the past eight years, shared this belief.

REFERENCES

Barth, R.S. (1991). *Improving schools from within*. San Francisco: Jossey-Bass.

Bellah, R.N., Madsen, R., Sullivan, W.M., Swindler, A., & Tipton, S. M. (1986). *Habits of the heart: Individualism and commitment in American life*. Berkeley: University of California Press.

Bereiter, C., & Scardamalia, M. (1993). *Surpassing ourselves. An inquiry into the nature and implications of expertise*. Chicago: Open Court.

Bernstein, D. (n.d.). On bridging the theory/practice gap. Available at http://www.engin.umich.edu/dept/aero/people/faculty/bernstein/gap.pdf (last accessed on March 4, 2004).

Boyer, E. (1990). *Campus life: In search of community*. Princeton: Princeton University Press.

British Columbia College of Teachers. (1997). *Report of the 1997 survey of recent graduates of B.C. teacher education programs*. Vancouver: BC College of Teachers.

Brown, A.L. (1994). The advancement of learning. *Educational Researcher, 23*(8), 4–12.

Bullough, R.V., Jr. Clark, D.C., Wentworth, N., & Hansen, J.M. (2001). Student cohorts, school rhythms, and teacher education. *Teacher Education Quarterly, 28*(2), 97–110.

Castle, J.B., Drake, S.M., & Boak, T. (1995). Collaborative reflection as professional development. *The Review of Higher Education, 18*(3), 243–263.

Dewey, J. (1916). *Democracy and education*. New York: Macmillan.

Farr Darling, L. (2000). Communities, cohorts and contradictions: Some unanswered questions in teacher education. *Journal of Professional Studies, 7*(2), 18–27.

Farr Darling, L. (2001). When conceptions collide: Constructing a community of inquiry for teacher education in British Columbia. *Journal of Education for Teaching, 27*(1), 7–21.

Fenstermacher, G. (1990). Some moral considerations on teaching as a profession. In J. Goodlad, R. Soder, & K. Sirotnik (Eds.), *The moral dimensions of teaching* (pp. 130–151). San Francisco: Jossey-Bass.

Goodlad, J. (1994). *What schools are for?* (2nd ed.). Indiana: Phi Delta Kappa.

Goodlad, J., Soder, R., & Sirotnik, K. (Eds.). (1990). *The moral dimensions of teaching.* San Francisco: Jossey-Bass.

Harlin, J., Edwards, M., & Briers, G. (2003). A comparison of student teachers' perceptions of important elements of the student teaching experience before and after completing an 11-week field experience. *Journal of Agricultural Education, 43*(3), 72–83.

Kennedy, D. (1998). What is a community of inquiry: Consideration on an e-mail discussion list. *Inquiry: Critical Thinking across the disciplines, 17*(1), 21.

Koeppen, K.E., Huey, G.L., & Connor, K.R. (2000). Cohort groups: An effective model in a restructured teacher education program. In D.J. McIntyre & D.M. Boyd (Eds.), *Research on effective models for teacher education* (pp. 136–152). Thousand Oaks, CA: Corwin.

Landers, M.. (2000). The theory-practice gap in nursing: the role of the nurse teacher. Journal of Advanced Nursing, 32(6), p1550. Also available at http://www.blackwell-synergy.com/rd.asp?code=JAN&vol=32&page=1550&goto=abstract (last accessed on March 23, 2004).

Lave, J. (1995). Teaching, as learning, in practice. *Mind, Culture and Activity: An International Journal. 3*(3), 149–164.

Lave, J., & Wenger, E. (1991). *Situated learning: Legitimate peripheral participation.* Cambridge: Cambridge University Press.

Lipman, M. (1993). *Thinking, children and education.* Montclair, N.J.: Dubuque Kendall/Hunt.

Mather, D., & Hanley, B. (1999). The effect of cohort grouping in teacher education. *Canadian Journal of Education, 24*(3), 235–250.

McIntyre, D. J., & Byrd, D. M. (Eds.). (2000). *Research on Effective Models for Teacher Education.* Thousand Oaks, CA: Corwin Press.

Mitchell, J. (2001). *Computer Technology in Teacher Education: Tool for Communication, Medium for Inquiry, Object of Critique.* An unpublished Ph.D. dissertation, University of British Columbia, Vancouver, BC.

Montgomery, B. (2000). The Student teacher and cooperating teacher relationship. *Journal of Family and Consumer Sciences Education, 18*(2), 7–15.

Mounce, H. (1997). *The two pragmatisms: From Peirce to Rorty.* London: Routledge.

Nicholson, C. (1991). Teaching on uncommon ground: The ideal of community in the post-modern era. *Education and Society, 9*(1) 47–53.

Oakes, J. & Quantz, K. (1995). Creating new educational communities. *Ninety-fourth Yearbook of the National Society for the Study of Education Part I.* Chicago: University of Chicago Press.

Palincsar, A., Magnusson, S., Marano, N., Ford, D., & Brown, N. (1998). Designing a community of practice: Principles and practices of the GIsML Community. *Teaching and Teacher Education, 14*(1), 5–19.

Paul, R. (1994). *Critical thinking handbook.* Sonoma, California: Centre for Critical Thinking and Moral Critique.

Putnam, R., & Borko, H. (2000). What do new views of knowledge and thinking have to say about research on teacher learning? *Educational Researcher, 29*(1), 4–15.

Radencich, M.C., Thompson, T., Anderson, N.A., Oropallo, K., Fleege, P., Harrison, M., & Hanley, P. (1998). The culture of cohorts: Preservice teacher education teams at a southeastern university in the United States. *Journal of Education for Teaching, 24*(2), 109–127.

Sachs, J. (1997). Reclaiming the agenda of teacher professionalism: An Australian experience. *Journal of Education for Teaching, 23*(3), 264–277.

Schoenfeld, A. (1999). Looking toward the 21st Century: Challenges of educational theory and practice. *Educational Researcher, 28*(7), 4–14.

Schön, D.A. (1983). *The reflective practitioner: How professionals think in action*. San Francisco: Jossey-Bass.

Schön, D.A. (1987). *Educating the reflective practitioner.* San Francisco. Jossey Bass.

Sergiovanni, T. (1994). *Building community in schools*. San Francisco: Jossey Bass.

Thomas, G., Wineburg, S., Grossman, P., Myhre, O., & Woolworth, S. (1998). In the company of colleagues: An interim report on the development of a community of teacher learners. *Teaching and Teacher Education, 14*(1), 21–32.

Tom, A.R. (1997). *Redesigning teacher education*. New York: State University of New York Press.

Wenger, E. (1998). *Communities of practice: Learning meaning and identity.* Cambridge: Cambridge University Press.

Wideen, M.F., & Grimmett, P.P. (Eds.). (1995). *Changing times in teacher education: Restructuring or reconceptualizing?* London: Falmer Press.

Chapter 11

Developing a Culture of Critique in Teacher Education Classes

John Loughran, Amanda Berry and Elizabeth Tudball
Monash University, Australia

This chapter examines some of the social and cultural aspects that are important in shaping the nature of communication amongst teacher educators and their student teachers when sharing in the process of learning about teaching. The focus of this study is a third year double degree subject "Curriculum & Pedagogy" that we team-teach together. Through developing and teaching this subject we have come to better understand the value of explicitly modelling particular aspects of teaching and how to purposefully 'unpack' such experiences through honest and professional critique. We trust the chapter helps to explicate this work in a meaningful way for the reader to both understand the approach to pedagogy we employ and to offer insights into how others might learn from our experiences and translate such learning into their own practice of teaching about teaching.

CONTEXT OF THE TEACHER EDUCATION PROGRAM

Across Australia, there has been increasing interest amongst students entering tertiary education, in applying for Double Degree programs—as opposed to the more traditional one year, end-on Post-graduate Diploma in Education. In the Faculty of Education at Monash University, one of the teacher preparation pathways is a 4 year Double Degree program, where students have the opportunity to combine studies in areas including arts, music, business, science and information systems, with a teaching qualification in primary or secondary education. Enrolling in an Education Double Degree program, it is often argued, enables students to develop a broad discipline base while at the same time pursuing an understanding of how such 'content' knowledge might be developed in terms of teaching through the involvement in studies in education. The decision to enroll in a Double Degree is often associated with students' making an early career choice to be a teacher as opposed to completing a degree and then choosing to pursue a career in teaching (as is commonly the case the Post-graduate Diploma in Education).

G. Hoban (ed.), The Missing Links in Teacher Education Design, 193–208.

The Double Degree program has an early focus on the 'other' Faculty (e.g., Arts, Science etc.) with, in the first year, only 25% of students' studies being in education. Then there is a gradual shift until by the final year (usually 4th year but it may be later depending on the 'other' Faculty, subject completions etc.), students' (generally) focus solely on education. It is also in this final year that the more traditional school teaching experiences linked to teaching methods are completed (10 weeks). In the early years, school practicum experiences are limited to observations and school studies with minimal opportunity for teaching. Overall then, the non-education degree must be completed before students enter their final year (full Education year).

STRUCTURE OF THE TEACHER EDUCATION PROGRAM

In their two first year education subjects, students begin to develop their theoretical knowledge of teaching and learning. In the second year, the focus is on students developing the skills and confidence to reflect on their own understandings of teachers' lives and work through case studies of varied teachers' experiences represented in film, stories, and through direct experiences of teaching they observe during teaching practicum. Students also develop insights into the attitudes, behaviours and work practices of teachers, as well as the role and status of teachers in contemporary societies. In addition, the students investigate the ways in which historical, social, political and legal factors have shaped the work of teachers. In essence then, this first two years is really about Education as a discipline rather than Education as teaching—this distinction is important when considering the nature and intent of the Double Degree in these first two years when classroom teaching practice is still so far off.

Third year marks the transition from Education as a discipline to Education as preparation for teaching and so it is critical that students have opportunities to apply their theoretical knowledge of education in practical teaching situations. Not surprisingly then, it is in the transitionary period that we see the development of a culture of critique as central to helping student-teachers genuinely learn about teaching in ways that might shape *their* views about, and *their* practice of, teaching. Curriculum and Pedagogy, the subject on which this chapter is based, creates a series of teaching and learning activities designed to encourage student-teachers' critical reflection about teaching.

In final year of the double degree, student-teachers are enrolled in two method subjects (e.g., mathematics and science, or English and History, and so on), two subjects pertaining to studies of professional issues in education and choose two elective subjects. This final year is not all that different to the traditional end-on, one year post-graduate Diploma in Education.

SOCIAL-CULTURAL LINKS: DEVELOPING A CULTURE OF CRITIQUE AMONGST STUDENT TEACHERS

In the third year subject Curriculum and Pedagogy (EDF3002) within the Double Degree program, intensive peer teaching experiences are used as one way of helping student-teachers to focus on and learn about their own teaching. In our conceptualization of Curriculum & Pedagogy, we have organized our teaching with the explicit purpose of modelling particular aspects of pedagogy (Loughran, 1996) for our student-teachers and we 'unpack' these aspects of teaching through honest and professional critique. This purpose carries with it the requirement that we also focus student-teachers' attention on the need to concurrently learn to critique teaching actions, rather than unwittingly engage in personal criticism of individuals. We initiate such learning by creating situations through which professional critique can be modelled; starting with our own practice.

Modelling Critique

In the first two sessions, one of us teaches an example of specific content (for example, using a Predict, Observe, Explain activity—White & Gunstone (1992)—to explore the nature of air pressure). Then the episode is publicly de-briefed in order to highlight particular aspects of the teaching and to model approaches to critiquing practice. This initial foray into critiquing practice is organized as a serious pedagogical experience itself (such that) as we are attempting to illustrate how careful questioning of a teacher's purposes and practices can offer insight into the pedagogical reasoning and the feelings that accompany the decision-making and shaping forces during a teaching and learning episode. Through such a critiquing experience, the colleagues conducting the critique explain the thinking that underpins the questions they ask of the teacher about his/her actions, behaviours, thinking and feelings during the teaching session. They also gradually invite class members into the practice by asking them to raise their own questions and, where appropriate, helping to illustrate ways of re-shaping questions in response to the spirit of critique on practice, as opposed to personal criticism.

Trialling Critique

These initial modeling sessions are followed by a 2:2 teaching experience whereby pairs of student-teachers teach a pair of Year 7 (first year of high school) students. In this situation, one student-teacher teaches while the other observes. After the teaching, the observer interviews the students in an attempt to access their perceptions of the experience. Through this experience, the student-teacher pairs collaborate in planning the teaching and de-briefing, and together engage in a process of critique of their own practice, hopefully reflecting the learning about such critique from the early sessions in the subject. The 2:2 is formally completed through their joint construction of a Reflective Assignment about the experience, highlighting their practice, views on their critique, their feelings and their understanding about their learning (again mirroring the teaching, de-briefing and critiquing of the early sessions).

Following the 2:2, the majority of the subject then proceeds through video-taped peer teaching experiences whereby groups of student-teachers teach their peers. Just as we modelled in the initial stages of the subject, the focus of the peer teaching is on the 'teaching' rather than the 'content' of the session so that a diversity of teaching procedures is encouraged as student-teachers learn to experiment with, and feel what it is like, to teach and learn in different ways. For this peer teaching, student-teachers are organised into small groups (3–4) to prepare their teaching session with their peers (one hour sessions). Each group is responsible for collaborating in the planning, teaching and de-briefing of the experience. As in the 2:2 experience, the group also collaborate in completing their written reflection of the experience. This includes their response to viewing the video-tape and reactions to the verbal and written feedback provided by all students and lecturers. This approach to learning from experience is designed to encourage participants to begin to recognize the value of listening to alternative perspectives on situations and to develop their practice in response to their own and their peers' critique of the teaching and learning experience. It also helps them to access various learners' views and to place an emphasis on their own feelings and actions at different times and in different roles throughout the session.

Implementing Critique

Finally, student-teachers participate in a short school practicum—during which they teach some lessons and attempt to push the boundaries of their learning about teaching through collecting feedback about the effects of their teaching on their students' learning from a variety of perspectives. The practicum is designed to build on the reflective processes modeled in classes at the university, with an explicit emphasis on 'appropriate' post class de-briefing about their teaching actions. The lesson(s) they conduct are, whenever possible, organized around the placement of a peer in the same school, so that again the supportive and collaborative nature of the experience is reinforced. If this is not possible, the supervising teacher is advised of the purpose of the teaching and learning through written and verbal explanation in an attempt to maintain a focus on critique rather than personal criticism (or, in the case of some supervising teachers, the well intentioned and somewhat inevitable 'teach like me' approach to de-briefing—which is counter productive to our intentions for constructive critique). There is a clear intent then for our student-teachers to feel encouraged to 'take risks' with their teaching, and to be prepared to learn from both positive and not so positive experiences. Following the practicum experience, the subject concludes with an emphasis on the 'learning about teaching' that has occurred.

This remainder of this chapter is organized around the use of student-teachers' own writing about Curriculum & Pedagogy (constructed from their reflective reports during the program and presented as vignettes) and from focus group interviews and open-ended questionnaire responses (conducted one year after they had completed the subject) that offer different participants' perspectives on their experiences (i.e. each quote is from a different participant). The chapter, we trust, highlights how the social aspects of learning about teaching through Curriculum & Pedagogy from these student-teachers' perspective is influenced by the nature and development of professional critique.

DEVELOPING TRUST

One aspect of our understanding of learning about teaching hinges on the need to effectively differentiate between 'telling' and 'teaching'. Hand in hand with the need for such differentiation is the view that teaching (as opposed to telling) is based on an understanding of oneself and others (see for example, van Manen, 1991), thus, teaching is about relationships. Building relationships involves both an understanding of individuals and the ways they interact and develop within their group. And just as each individual learns and develops, so too the group develops as the relationships within the group evolve in response to these changes. These relationships clearly involve important social understandings and practices.

From our perspective as teacher educators, we believe that building relationships requires a genuine concern to listen to, and be aware of, the changing nature of the classroom context, and to be interested in, and responsive to, the needs of students (as individuals and as a group). The development of trust, which is so important if learning is to be more than knowing, and if teaching is to be more than telling, therefore becomes a two-way process that is equally important from both the teacher's and learners' perspective. And, just as Mitchell (1992) found through PEEL (Project for the Enhancement of Effective Learning, see Baird & Mitchell, 1986; Baird & Northfield, 1992) that trust is an important factor in shaping changes in students' approaches to their learning, so too we have found that trust is equally important in teaching and learning about teaching as it involves affective aspects of learning that are often overlooked in teacher educators' practice. This is particularly true when the 'script' for social patterns of learning (and teaching) are challenged through an approach to teacher education that confronts existing views of appropriate behaviour in learning to teach as in the case of a focus on professional critique.

Building Confidence

For both student-teachers and teacher educators alike, confidence matters (Loughran, J.J., Berry, A., & Tudball, L., 2002). For example, consider Mandi's response to an opening session where critique of a colleague's teaching was the introduction to the subject.

> Having one of us prepared to demonstrate her vulnerability and show that we genuinely cared about the learners' responses gave students the confidence to engage in honest critique of their experiences of the teaching. An excerpt from my journal illustrates [this point]: What is interesting is that it feels to me like we are exploding the idea that creating a learning community in which students take safe intellectual risks takes a long time. One student commented at the end of the first session, "I felt comfortable enough to say what I thought." The fact that we could create this learning experience together so quickly both surprised and excited me. (Berry & Loughran, 2002, p. 24)

However, this notion of confidence carries different meaning when considered from a student-teacher's perspective because, commonly, many see teaching as an uncomplicated act of telling students what to learn—a consequence of years of uncritical observation of their own teachers at work (Britzman, 1991; Pajares, 1992). Consequently, beginning teachers may enter pre-service programs with an expectation that they can be told how to teach and therefore appear to be in search of a recipe for teaching. This recipe may well comprise a set of practical teaching strategies that will 'ensure their success' in the classroom and they may therefore be critical of their teacher preparation program if this does not occur (Britzman, 1986). Hence, recognizing these perspectives influences our understanding of our student-teachers' particular needs and concerns. We see this as crucial in shaping learning to teach (in ways similar to that which Korthagen et al., 2001 outlined in their Realistic Teacher Education Program).

We extend this point by asserting that in teaching about teaching, being aware of the *feelings and* expectations that student-teachers have about learning to teach is important as it reminds us of the impact that the demands and expectations of the subject will have on them and their practice. Thus, confidence emerges as a search for balance[1] as confronting some of the student-teachers'

[1] This balance is in us being sensitive to the competing demands of these elements as being important for the development of student teachers' confidence and to feel confident they have to trust that it is worthwhile to do.

needs and expectations through the processes and practices of Curriculum & Pedagogy can, if not carefully thought through, shake their confidence. We therefore pay careful attention to finding this balance through the way student-teachers respond to the situations they encounter in the subject. We use a variety of means of keeping in touch with our students' (and our own) responses to the subject[2], both during and after teaching in the subject. The open-ended questionnaire responses, below, were gathered from students in the year following their experiences of Curriculum & Pedagogy, and illustrate their retrospective understanding of the subject.

> Overall, I feel the subject was useful especially for actual confidence building for teaching. (Open-ended questionnaire response)

> When I began the subject, I really needed a confidence boost, just to prove that I was going to be able to stand up in front of a class. This subject gave two memorable opportunities—the peer session and the 2:2—which eased my fears considerably. It provided a non-threatening 'testing-ground' environment. (Open-ended questionnaire response)

The 2:2 experience is one way in which we aim to create a teaching and learning situation that will build confidence while at the same time gently challenge some of the preconceptions our student-teachers hold about the nature of teaching. We offer the following vignette of one student-teacher's response (pseudonyms apply) to the 2:2 experience in order to illustrate what we see as a beginning point in building confidence and creating a 'stepping off point' for further development. It is also an early opportunity for the student-teachers to begin to confront their own views about the relationship between professional critique and learning—and actively link the two.

45 MINUTES IN THE LIFE OF A TEACHER

The students . . .

> While who is in your class cannot be controlled, human nature dictates that in most cases, even trained professionals will inherently favour those whose countenance is more appealing. In the classroom this is a major danger. It would be all too easy to dote on the students who complete your tasks without fuss, the ones who give you the answers you desire and make you feel good as a teacher. Sadly, it

[2] Throughout the semester, we meet a regular basis to discuss the teaching that we plan and the sessions that we have taught. Generally this involves a weekly discussion after class but also includes maintaining journals, electronic communication and our interactions through team teaching. We also maintain close contact with our students through individual and group discussions after their peer teaching sessions, e-mail and the range of reflective papers they develop during the subject. Further to this, much of the data for this paper is drawn from a study of these participants' understanding of the subject one year after they had completed it in order to understand their perspective of the influence of the subject on their developing pedagogy.

is often those students who really need the expertise of their teacher who suffer most from the favouritism of the *brighter* students.

In this particular instance, the students that we happened to choose seemed to fit into the latter category, and while I am loath to affix stereotypical labels, I am well aware from personal experience that often they are correct.

The task and its purpose . . .

Compared to some of the other lessons I suppose mine was up there among the most mundane. However, to put it bluntly, students aren't always going to like what has to be taught in class—it's all in the way that it's approached, that makes it interesting and engaging. (Point in my own defence—while the two students said they had done my task before, they both said that in the end they had enjoyed the lesson).

The task consisted of two choices—the students could either write a brief story about their ideal future, or draw and label a picture of their ideal future. I had hoped that at least one of the two students would choose to do the writing task; however, this did not occur.

In the beginning, they seemed a little apathetic about doing the task, stating that they had done something similar in other classes.

Direction and deviation . . .

As time progressed I got the distinct impression that the boys were becoming bored with the task. In a normal classroom I am well aware that boredom is the mother of chaos and is to be avoided at all possible cost. I hadn't really planned for discussion to take place in the middle of the task, but found it necessary to prompt both boys to continue their drawing by questioning what they had already drawn. As it turned out, Jude wants to build a laserpowered rocket that can travel faster than the speed of light, and wants to work for NASA in order to achieve that goal. Joshua on the other hand had decided that he wanted to conquer Mars and be ruler of a city there. I found that it was he who needed the most prodding and that he was easily distracted by the constant banter.

Speaking to the boys helped me realise another thing about teaching that I, in particular, should pay close mind to. People often talk about things that they no little of, and students are no exception. It is really hard not to correct someone when they voice something incorrect and even more difficult when they defend it to the bitter end.

At one point, I found myself grinding my teeth to prevent myself from rebuking everything Jude said and putting him straight, but realised the only thing that that would achieve would be to put a dent in his self esteem or incite rebellious argument that would detract from the lesson. I also understand that in a classroom environment, telling students that they are wrong flat out is a sure-fire way of putting them off offering opinions in the future.

The De-briefing . . .

Between Emma and myself the de-briefing was short and sweet. I was very much relieved to hear that Joshua and Jude had deemed me to be a half-decent teacher, as far as one can conclude after so brief a relationship.

> Another point of contention with me is that I sometimes come across a little intimidating. I was pleased to be informed that not only did my conscious effort to be less intimidating pay off in that both boys were not intimidated, but that they thought that it was good that I talked about things that they were interested in.
>
> Emily and I agreed in the end that the lesson had been a success despite the deviation from the actual task in favour of conversation. This illustrates that the set task need not be followed to the letter order for the purpose of the lesson to be fulfilled, and that a teacher needs to be prepared to accept this, and sometimes abandon their plans in favour of something that the students are more likely to be engaged in.

In the end...

> Overall I feel good about the experience, good because everything went smoothly despite the slight deviation from my lesson plan, good because the students finished with a reasonable opinion of me, and good because I still want to be a teacher. Sounds all rather selfish doesn't it? Well, I guess I wouldn't be doing teaching if I didn't think I would get anything out of it. I'm not sure that I learned anything about teaching that I did not already know, however, this exercise brought them sharply to my attention, and now gives me a great many things to consider when planning my next lesson.

The last paragraph of this vignette is important. The student-teacher felt good about herself and although she was, "not sure that she learned anything new", she had come to see some aspects of practice that she *now* understood differently. For us, this is an important 'stepping-off point' in learning to teach because the recognition of a need to see the 'taken-for-granted' differently is an important catalyst for reframing (Schön, 1983) and is an intended outcome of our approach to teaching about teaching; yet requires a confidence to do so. In this case (above), the student is illustrating an ability to professionally critique her own practice. She appears open to alternative perspectives and is critical in a constructive manner of her own practice whilst also drawing parallels between her 2:2 experience and the realities of teaching generally. This aspect of coming to appreciate learning to teach is important to us and is illustrative of the feelings derived from directly experiencing the role of teacher and genuinely seeing into the experience in ways that enhance learning from experience.

As noted earlier, we take seriously the differentiation between telling and teaching. Teaching leads to a greater likelihood that student-teachers will learn about themselves and their practice in meaningful ways so that they see value in their own learning. The 2:2 experience is purposefully designed to offer an invitation to reframe instances of learning about teaching so that personal development will be initiated; based on the notion of personal professional critique as an important starting point. As we trust we have made clear, we are intent on building student-teachers' confidence in what they are doing as well as aiming to extend their view of practice so that their growing confidence encourages them to push ahead, not simply remain comfortable with their existing practice. Inevitably then, such an approach must be embedded in personal experience and as such, the manner of the experiences created through the subject needs to change in light of the learning outcomes. Hence, the transition into another feature of the program, extended peer teaching.

CREATING A 'SAFE' ENVIRONMENT

> I think it [2:2] definitely helped me with confidence. I was so nervous about doing peer teaching ... [but] nobody laughed, nobody did anything crazy. My peers have watched me teach. That was OK, it wasn't a disaster ... [but] it is an environment where you feel safe in class. I think we did have that in our tute group. We were fairly open with each other. (Focus group interview)

The extended peer teaching (micro-teaching) is structured in such a way as to create an environment in which 'intellectual challenge' through engaging in teaching and experiencing professional critique become important factors in student-teachers' development of their own teaching whilst being ever conscious of not stripping away the confidence necessary for them to engage in risk-taking in teaching and learning experiences. This is a crucial time and professional critique needs to be carefully monitored by us as teacher educators and we are exceptionally conscious of it, perhaps never more so that in the early sessions of extended peer teaching. The development of trust is ongoing, it is not something able to be 'front loaded' and then forgotten. Trust is crucial in helping student-teachers recognize that as a result of their growing confidence, that which they are comfortable with in their teaching can also be a powerful support in taking risks in order to grow through learning in new and different situations.

The first few extended peer teaching sessions can create the most anxiety for all of us (teacher educators and student-teachers). Naturally, student teachers approach the task trying to do a good job in their teaching and wanting to be seen as able and capable teachers. Accompanying this is their peer's implicit sense of a need to be supportive; not making the teaching experience more difficult or uncomfortable than it already is. Our concern, as teacher educators, is that we want substantive issues to be raised in ways that cause all of us to confront particular situations as they are occurring, so that we can all 'feel' what it is like and thus, through appropriate intervention, learn together about teaching and learning through these experiences. As teacher educators we are therefore very conscious of the need to continue to develop trust as an overt feature of practice, as we simultaneously model and encourage professional critique of the teaching and learning we all experience in these sessions.

In order to help create a sense of these peer teaching experiences we offer the following vignette constructed from one group's Peer Teaching Report (pseudonyms apply) which highlights some of the issues they recognized through being involved in teaching the rest of the class. The vignette is also a form of backtalk (as described by Russell, 1997) that offers access to the thoughts and feelings of participants through their own teaching and learning experiences and therefore helps us to see into their understanding of the experience of teaching their peers and being submitted to the professional critique of their practice.

Our Peer Teaching Report

Krista, Edith, Beth & Lidia

> *What we planned:* It didn't take long before we realized that although we knew what we expected, it was far from clear to our students . . . and that is where our lesson really started to create challenges for us as the teachers.
>
> *What happened:* We were confronted by off-task students and we started to wonder what this would mean in the de-brief [critique]. Questions arose at almost every turn. "What should we do with students who did not contribute?" "What about groups that were unwilling to devise their own tower and just wanted to copy others?" "What about the groups that used up all their material, finished quickly and then sat around with nothing to do?" This was not as easy as it seemed when we were planning the lesson.
>
> *The de-brief:* During the de-brief, and later when we were going through the written feedback, it became clear that several members of the class had viewed our lesson as having no clear purpose. People were left wondering about the point of the activity. We quickly realized—well we certainly had it pointed out—that in a school classroom, this lack of direction would've caused many problems. Another point discussed was our role—or lack thereof—as teachers. . . It was hard to find a balance between being in the way and directing everything and hanging back and letting the learners take control.
>
> *Our perspective:* At the time, we actually thought the lesson was quite productive. There was much disagreement about what we did and a question was raised, "As teachers, do we encourage students to learn for the sake of learning: or think for the sake of thinking?" that was very interesting. It seems many students do not see the value of this type of lesson; they want a concrete skill or outcome . . . we also ran out of time and so became quite defensive about what we were doing and why and tried to justify why the lesson was valuable and tell them what they should've learnt. We weren't scarred by the experience, but watching it on video was hard. You see so much that you do that you don't realize you are doing at the time. Why is it that we do some things when we don't mean to and we do others things that we mean to happen but they don't come out the way we planned? This was an interesting lesson for us but we're not so sure about the students!

From a learner's perspective, we believe that trust involves knowing and believing that individuals' ideas, thoughts and views can be offered and explored in challenging ways but that such challenge must be professional not personal (building up, not breaking down relationships—a focal point in giving and accepting critique). This requires a trust in the care for others as persons, and it has as its basis a need to maintain and develop one's self-esteem through the challenges presented in the de-brief that comprises the professional critique. The learner also has a need to trust that the teaching and learning environment is a 'safe' place to raise and pursue issues, concerns and the development of understanding. This calls for a genuine commitment to the notion that 'challenge' is not a personal attack but a search for clarification and understanding.

> The way in which they [tutors] created a safe risk taking environment really promoted our learning. The atmosphere of the class was extremely positive, which has a lot to do with its teaching/teacher. Feedback and interactions were helpful. (Open-ended questionnaire response)

The clear purpose for working to develop a safe environment is to enhance learning about teaching therefore it is important to focus on how participants view the value of exploring teaching and learning in an environment created for experimenting with their teaching. If experimenting with teaching is to be encouraged, the value of learning through the subsequent professional critique must be clear and explicit.

> To effectively debrief it is important to pay close attention to practice—or what actually happens—I think this has helped reinforce the importance of thinking a teaching strategy through to the end. (Open-ended questionnaire response)

Encouraging risk-taking

Trust is something that is developed within, and supports, a safe environment. However, in paying attention to social aspects of learning about teaching there is a need for all involved (teacher educators and student-teachers) to trust that learning through experience is valuable and "worth the effort". It seems to us, that this is not really possible though if the teacher educator assumes a role of 'expert' in total control of the direction of inquiry, losing sight of, or not acknowledging individuals' needs. For participants to be able to genuinely raise issues or concerns, they must be able to trust that in so doing their queries will be fairly addressed. They must trust in a number of features of their learning environment in ways that impact on their preparedness to be involved.

> *Brenda:* If we had lecturers or tutors that weren't very focussed on the reflection and their self-reflection then it [Curriculum & Pedagogy] wouldn't be as useful.
>
> *Angie:* I think one of the most important things is the debriefing sessions and discussions that weren't cut short. We were allowed to toss ideas around with [tutors] and with ourselves. They were the places where we learnt the most. So

> you have to find staff who are open to that style I guess... [maybe] it was just the class dynamics that we had... and our groups that it was really open and it was OK to talk and toss open.
>
> *Interviewer:* Anything else?
>
> *Brenda:* Well, you couldn't stand up and say that is wrong, you shouldn't do it like that, the lecturer couldn't do that because there is no one-way to teach. I mean that if we had a lecturer telling us there was only one way to do something then it wouldn't work. There are so many different ways of doing something in a classroom that subject [Developing Pedagogy] wouldn't work if there was a lecturer dead-set on there is only one way to go about things. Do you know what I mean? (Focus group interview)

Without such a trust, there is little incentive to take the risk to speak up. This trust is particularly important in the de-brief sessions whereby alternative perspectives are constantly being sought in order to shed light on different viewpoints rather than simply highlight that which the teacher educator regards as the 'essential learning'.

> Without EDF3002 I doubt whether I would have purposely critically reflected and looked for evidence that my teaching practices were achieving what I thought [my] teaching practices were achieving. I also did this with more understanding. (Open-ended questionnaire response)
>
> I think if there wasn't any debriefing the subject would not have had the depth it did. It certainly helped me in learning to debrief my own teaching in an analytical way, which is essential to becoming an effective teacher. (Open-ended questionnaire response)

Accompanying the development of trust is the need for 'critics' (student-teachers and teacher educators) to withhold judgment—and that can be a difficult task; it is a skill to actively be developed. Learners are less likely to pursue their own understanding or to reconsider others' views if they have a sense of being judged, or if they are responding to questions or situations by trying to "guess what is in the teacher's head". The need to withhold judgment, to be conscious of one's own wait-time and to *want to hear* from others is a key to building relationships that enhance a diversity of learning outcomes and reinforces the value of teaching as opposed to telling (Loughran, 2003).

> The way in which the debriefing was approached never made me feel I was being "attacked". It allowed constructive criticism in a positive learning environment. Taught me not to take things too literally and to not be too critical on others or myself. (Open-ended questionnaire response)

Through our shared adventures in planning, teaching and reviewing Curriculum and Pedagogy, we have come to better understand what it really means to develop trust (and its many forms) in a classroom—especially when student-teachers are being encouraged to be risk-takers in their own learning about teaching. The extended peer teaching calls on approaches to teacher education that are different and demanding to that which is associated with what Korthagen et al. (2001) describe as traditional teacher preparation programs. For example, knowing when or how to *intervene* in a session in order create a situation that might help to make explicit for all what we (as their teachers) might want participants to 'see' or 'feel' in a situation is not something that can be easily planned or scripted in advance. Therefore, appropriate intervention is an important and considered aspect of our pedagogy. It is one that demands a trusting environment so that the confidence necessary for risk-taking might be developed and is crucial to teaching as opposed to telling. Therefore, how one feels about a situation influences how one acts (or does not act) in that situation, hence a careful consideration of all of the issues raised so far in this chapter come into sharp focus when considering how they all interact in a teachable moment.

CONCLUSION

This chapter has attempted to offer insights into ways in which student-teachers experiences of learning to teach might be enhanced through purposeful interventions and approaches to pedagogy that are responsive to their needs and concerns by challenging traditional approaches to, and practices of, teacher preparation. However, simply creating intellectual challenge, encouraging risk-taking and introducing pedagogy that creates a 'feel' for what it is like to be in problematic teaching and learning situations are, of themselves, not sufficient. There is a genuine need for a commitment to the development of trust, confidence and relationships that explicitly support such approaches. The alternative is that,

> ...teacher educators who lecture about the importance of group learning; who espouse the importance of reflection while presenting teaching as a technical act; or, who assert the need for establishing caring relationships while at the same time maintaining emotional detachment from their students, undermine the very ideas they wish their student teachers to learn because they are not seen to be practicing them themselves. (Berry, 2004)

Through the approaches to teaching about teaching that we employ, we purposefully expose practice (ours and our student-teachers') to scrutiny through honest but professional critique through an appreciation of, and sensitivity to, important social aspects of teaching and learning. There is little doubt that such an approach confronts the normal rules of teaching and learning about teaching that shape the ways in which student-teachers and teacher educators discuss one another's practice. Such an approach to honest critique requires an appreciation for the thoughts, feelings and perspectives of others and therefore demands a commitment to caring in accord with the sentiments espoused by Noddings (2001). Being concerned to care, we would argue, is important to pedagogy generally, but, the need for caring is further enhanced through our approach to teaching about teaching. We are constantly aware of the need to explicitly demonstrate our care for our students and not assume that it will simply be taken-for-granted.

Through a focus on the social aspects of teaching and learning about teaching that we have outlined in this chapter, we hope that it has been made clear that our student-teachers do learn to look into their own thoughts and actions in honest and open ways as they learn to respond to the problematic nature of teaching in positive ways. We hope that such learning is then translated into their own practice when they are teaching in ways commensurate with exactly the same feelings and expectations we have for our practice. This further highlights the complexity of teaching and the feelings of uncertainty and discomfort that are a normal part of such important work.

> You know the teaching round activity we had to do where whoever else was at your school had to watch your lesson. I think that was good because I sort of kept that in mind when I was doing my teaching round. I was more aware of how I was coming across because of the activities we had done, because of all that peer feedback. I was aware of how my supervisor might see me . . . suddenly understanding what it is like to be an observer of the teacher because you have done that . . . and that becomes part of your teaching. (Focus group interview)

REFERENCES

Baird, J.R., & Mitchell, I.J. (1986). *Improving the quality of teaching and learning: An Australian case-study—The PEEL project.* Melbourne: Monash University Printing.

Baird, J.R., & Northfield, J.R. (1992). *Learning from the PEEL experience.* Melbourne: Monash University Printing.

Berry, A. (2004). Self-study in Teaching about Teaching. In John Loughran, MaryLynn Hamilton, Vicki LaBoskey & Tom Russell (Eds.) *International Handbook of Self-study of Teaching and Teacher Education Practices,* (pp. 1295–1332) Dordrecht: Kluwer Academic Publishers.

Berry, A., & Loughran, J.J. (2002). Developing an Understanding of Learning to Teach in Teacher Education. In J. Loughran and T. Russell (Eds.) *Improving Teacher Education Practices Through Self-study.* (pp. 13–29). London: RoutledgeFalmer.

Britzman, D. P. (1986). Cultural myths in the making of a teacher: Biography and social structure in teacher education. *Harvard Educational Review, 56,* 442–456.

Britzman, D. P. (1991). *Practice makes practice: A critical study of learning to teach.* New York: New York Press.

Korthagen, F. J., Koster, B., Lagerwerf, B., & Wubbels, T. (2001). *Linking Practice and Theory. The Pedagogy of Realistic Teacher Education.* New Jersey, Erlbaum.

Loughran, J.J. (1996). *Developing Reflective Practitioners: Learning about teaching and learning through modelling.* London: Falmer Press.

Loughran, J.J. (2003). Pursuing Scholarship in Teacher Education. In Deborah Fraser and Roger Openshaw (Eds.), *Informing our Practice.* Special Volume. Selections from the Teacher

Education Forum of Aotearoa New Zealand 2002. (pp. 141–155). Palmerston North, N.Z.: Kanuka Grove Press.

Loughran, J.J., Berry, A., & Tudball, L. (2002). Teaching about Teaching: Learning to help student-teachers learn about their practice. In Kosnik, Freese & Samaras (Eds.). *Making a Difference in Teacher Education through Self-study. Herstmonceux IV: The Fourth International Conference on Self-Study of Teacher Education Practices (Volumes 1 & 2)* (Vol. 2, pp. 67–71). Herstmonceux Castle, East Sussex, U.K. Toronto, Ontario: OISE, Toronto University.

Noddings, N. (2001). The Caring Teacher. In V. Richardson (Ed.), *Handbook of Research on Teaching* (pp. 99–105). Washington, D.C.: American Education Research Association.

Pajares, M. (1992). Teachers' beliefs and educational research: Cleaning up a messy construct. *Review of Educational Research. 62*, 307–332.

Russell, T.L. (1997). Teaching Teachers: How I Teach IS the Message, in Loughran and Russell (Eds.), *Teaching about Teaching: Purpose, Passion and Pedagogy in Teacher Education*. (pp. 32–47). London: Falmer Press.

Schön, D.A. (1983). *The Reflective Practitioner: How professionals think in action*. New York: Basic Books.

Van Manen, M. (1991). *The Tact of Teaching: The meaning of pedagogical thoughtfulness*. Albany, N.Y: State University of New New York Press.

White, R.T., & Gunstone, R.F. (1992). *Probing Understanding*. London: Falmer Press.

Chapter 12

Community-Building and Program Development go Hand-in-Hand: Teachers Educators Working Collaboratively

Clare Kosnik[1] and Clive Beck[2]
Stanford University[1]
OISE/University of Toronto[2], *Canada*

The research on teacher education is surprisingly consistent in identifying the perennial problems of teacher certification programs. Darling-Hammond and Sykes (1999) succinctly list five basic critiques: inadequate time; fragmentation of the program; uninspired teaching methods; superficial curriculum; and traditional views of schools (p. 23). Lortie's (1975) observation that teacher education without substantial teacher induction programs leaves beginning teachers with too heavy a load to be successful still applies. Goodlad (1994) contends that both the structure and the content of teacher education programs need to be reconceptualized and reformed, adding that teacher education and school renewal must occur simultaneously and in collaboration (p. 1).

Addressing these serious shortcomings will require a complex solution, one that must involve the teacher educators. Who are the teacher educators? What are their issues? What are their suggestions for reform? How can they be part of the solution? Most teacher educators have a deep understanding of the issues and excellent suggestions on how to improve teacher education. Yet they are often absent from the decision-making table, which we believe is a *missing link* in teacher education renewal. Wide-scale solutions with far-reaching impact will remain elusive until teacher educators are more fully and respectfully involved in the discourse.

This chapter focuses on the work of teacher educators in the elementary preservice program at the Ontario Institute for Studies in Education, University of Toronto (OISE/UT). We begin with a brief description of the difficult times those of us in education have endured as our provincial government implemented radical "reforms" to all aspects of education. Although conditions were difficult, a group of teacher educators—Coordinators of the cohort program at OISE/UT—came together to address some of the concerns listed above. We provide some information about the

G. Hoban (ed.), *The Missing Links in Teacher Education Design*, 209–230.

context and then describe in detail four initiatives—practice teaching, special education instruction, mathematics instruction, and research on academic assignments—aimed at helping to actualize our program principles. We conclude with some reflections and suggestions for next steps. We believe that the strong community we were able to develop among the Coordinators led to substantial improvements in the program, and as we jointly implemented our initiatives the community in turn was strengthened. This interplay between the community and program development is central to our story.

CONTEXT OF THE TEACHER EDUCATION PROGRAM

In general, education in Ontario has had a tumultuous eight years. Our extreme right-wing Progressive Conservative government had a low view of teachers and teaching, leading them to centralize many decision-making processes and implement a number of negative measures. For example, education budgets were centralized then dramatically reduced (in the first year of their term $500 million was slashed from education and more cuts followed); punitive measures were taken towards teachers (implementation of a forced professional learning program); and school districts lost their autonomy (local school boards were dismantled and schools trustees were stripped of their power). This "war on education" hurt teacher morale and job action (strikes, walk-outs, lock-outs) became part of the yearly school experience for most students in the Greater Toronto Area. Universities were not spared the wrath of the government as our budgets were steadily decreased and we were openly criticized by our provincially-elected leaders. Schools of education were put under the microscope of the government and found lacking. To show their might, a teacher certification test was quickly developed with limited pilot testing and imposed on new teachers.

Despite the negativity surrounding education, applications to schools of education in Ontario remained strong. On average OISE/UT receives 6,000 applications for the 1,300 places. All students granted admission to the program have a minimum GPA of B (2.75) and most have experience working with children and youth. When a retirement window was opened to teachers who had approximately 30 years of service, a large proportion of those eligible to retire took the package. This resulted in a teacher shortage that has now abated. In Ontario, the vast majority of the 6,000 new teachers who graduate each year from the 10 faculties of education have completed a one-year post-baccalaureate program. By contrast with practices in many American universities, the one-year program in Ontario leads to a Bachelor of Education (B. Ed.) rather than a master's degree.

STRUCTURE OF THE PROGRAM

OISE/UT is a very large school of education with more than 10,000 students enrolling annually: 7,000 continuing education students; 1,300 teacher education students; and 2,100 graduate students. At the University of Toronto for three decades there were two entirely separate schools of education: one for teacher certification (B. Ed.) and continuing education (non-degree inservice courses) and one for graduate studies (master and doctoral level programs). In 1996 the two schools were forced to merge; not surprisingly, given the distinct cultures of the two schools the period since 1996 has seen a series of challenges. The elementary preservice program was seriously affected by the merger because there was an exodus of tenured/tenure-stream faculty resulting in a dramatic increase in the number of contract instructors. The heavy workload and low recognition of preservice work made it undesirable for many tenure-stream faculty; further compounding the difficulties, the new institution did not include a department of teacher education. The new OISE/UT chose a “matrix model,” with preservice diffused throughout the institution, without its own budget, democratic governance processes, or control over staffing. The lofty goal of the merger was to involve all graduate-level departments in preservice, yet this has not happened. In 2002–2003 only 10% of the elementary preservice faculty were tenure-stream/tenured, the remainder being contract or “seconded” instructors—educators on leave from their school board for a given period of time. (In the remainder of this chapter we use the term contract instructor to include both contract and seconded instructors.) An Associate Dean was ultimately responsible for teacher education, with a Director for each of the Elementary and Secondary preservice programs. One of the authors of this chapter was the Director of the elementary program for three years. This particular model is one that Tom (1997) describes as highly problematic, because the locus of control is too far removed from the teacher educators who actually deliver the program (p. 40).

At OISE/UT there has been a cohort-based preservice program at the elementary level since the mid 1980s. The 585 student teachers in the one-year post-baccalaureate elementary program are placed in nine cohorts, where they have almost all of their classes. Students choose their cohort based on program focus and location of practice teaching schools. In addition, there are also two small two-year programs, a Master of Teaching (M.T.) which admits approximately 25 students each year and a Master of Arts (M.A.) with an annual intake of approximately 40 students.

Each Cohort has:

- two Coordinators who teach courses and arrange the program, timetable, and practice teaching placements for student teachers in their cohort;

- a small team of faculty (including the Coordinators) who work together to deliver the program teaching almost all the courses;
- a small number of partner schools (approximately 12–15) where student teachers are placed for practice teaching;
- approximately 65 students (except for the Masters' level cohorts); and
- a focus to the program (e.g. the Central cohort focuses on technology, Campus cohort focuses on the arts).

Although each cohort has a distinct focus and set of schools, there is a core program to be delivered.

In each cohort the faculty team addresses the mandatory courses yet each has a particular "flavour" or focus. For example, in the Mid-Town cohort our goals for the cohort are inquiry, community, and integration. Since we have control of the timetable we can spend a significant amount of time planning to realize these goals. The first week of classes focuses on community building culminating in a two-day retreat for all faculty and students. To integrate the program many of the assignments cross course lines. The action research project spans four courses: curriculum and instruction, education psychology, teacher education seminar, and school and society. As a team we jointly develop the action research assignment having individual "steps" of the process part of different courses. With the cohort faculty responsible for practicum supervision each instructor works with his/her practice teaching schools to ensure student teachers have ample opportunity to implement their action research project. To realize the inquiry theme each instructor has elements of reflection and a theory-practice link in his/her courses and assignments. Our goal is to immerse students in a coherent program, with sequenced-activities, and all instructors working towards the same goals. Other cohorts have a different approach. The Doncrest cohort spends the first two weeks of the program doing Tribes training for all students and working on Instructional Strategies. These are the conceptual framework for the program and all courses/instructors root their work in Tribes philosophy and practices. All Associate Teachers must be Tribes-trained teachers and must use the Instructional Strategies approach in their classes. The cohort model gives the faculty team a tremendous amount of latitude yet it is accompanied with significant responsibility: the team is fully responsible for organizing both the academic program and all aspects of the practicum.

Post-merger, the 22 cohort Coordinators (18 B. Ed. and 4 M.T./M.A.) quickly became "invisible" because they did not fit into a department and no department was responsible for preservice teacher education. As a result, while the Coordinators were a very talented group they were not present at the decision-making tables. In 2002–2003 seven of the Coordinators had doctorates and another six were working on their doctorates; four had recently been principals; five had been consultants; many had done research; most had published curriculum texts or programs; and all had had leadership experience in their school districts. Some had been with the program for more than 5 years while most were fairly new to teacher education.

PROGRAM PRINCIPLES

As our cohort-based elementary preservice program evolved, we developed a set of principles which reflected our work and helped guide decisions about the program. We relied heavily on the work of Darling-Hammond, especially *Studies in Excellence in Teacher Preparation* (2000) which enunciated principles such as: valuing teaching and research on teaching; connections with schools that match the program's view of teaching; and tight definition of the program experience. Howey's (1996) emphasis on the need for a conceptual framework and attention to preservice pedagogy also influenced our work (p. 145).

Cohort-Based Programming

As noted, each of our elementary cohorts has a distinct program focus. Some are housed in a local elementary school. The cohort structure allows for program coherence, supports the development of community, and allows instructors to be responsive to student teacher needs and interests. Meier (1995), Wasley (1994), and Wasley, Hampel, and Clark (1997), in line with the principles of the Coalition of Essential Schools, stress the need to create smaller schools (or schools-within-a-school) so teachers can work together and teachers and students can get to know each other and share a common school culture. Meier (1995) claims that fostering both intellectual and social values "requires joint membership in an attractive community" (p. 113). Cohort-based programs present some challenges, such as the power of the peer group to lead in unfortunate directions (Tom, 1997); however, the research literature on teacher education repeatedly calls for this type of grouping. "When community exists, learning is strengthened—everyone is smarter, more ambitious, and productive" (Peterson, 1992, p. 2). It is the interplay between community, experience, and academic and professional learning that so urgently needs to be recognized in teacher education and education generally.

Coherent Cohort Programs

Much of our attention in recent years has focused on program coherence within a conceptual framework. For example, the Mid-Town cohort framework includes the principles of inquiry, community, and integration. Howey and Zimpher "found that when there was an explicit and thoughtful conceptual framework, there was also likely to be a reasonable number of core teaching abilities or teacher qualities derived from this framework that were addressed thematically over time in a variety of program activities" (Howey, 1996, p. 147). While all cohorts address the core components of the program, a particular theme is emphasized in each, allowing faculty and students to explore specific topics in greater detail. The cohort faculty team plans the program, rather than simply teaching a disconnected series of individual courses. For example, the faculty team decides who will introduce certain topics (such as teachers-as-researchers), builds on the work done in other courses, interconnects assignments, designs cohort-wide assignments or activities, and plans events such as *Integrating the Arts* or *Science Olympics*.

Effective, Collaborative Faculty

We believe our instructors must be exemplary practitioners, using effective instructional strategies and being thoughtful about their work. As Griffin (1999) argues, "teacher educators should model the teaching they hope their students will enact" (p.15). Given our program structure and small faculty teams, there is an opportunity to teach collaboratively. Instructors new to teacher education are mentored by experienced faculty, instructors team-teach, and an instructor's personal interests and strengths are utilized. Mutual support and professional growth are often a direct result of this collaboration.

Strong School-University Partnerships

The practicum component of preservice programs is widely acknowledged both to be critically important and yet to present a number of challenges (Goodlad, 1994; Knowles & Cole, 1996). Many researchers have stated that the campus program and the practicum should be closely integrated, with various types of connection and constant interchange and collaboration (Bullough & Gitlin, 1995; Fosnot, 1996; Goodlad, 1990; Howey, 1996). OISE/UT has made the development of strong school-university partnerships a major priority. We try to connect the two aspects of the program—academic courses and the practicum—in a logical, natural way, each supporting the other. All the cohorts work with a small number of schools as sites for practice teaching; students are clustered in practice teaching schools for mutual support; assignments require students to attend to both the theoretical and the practical; associate teachers often give classes/workshops in the academic program; new associate teachers are mentored and supported; liaison committees with representatives from the practice teaching schools and university staff are formed; and professional development sessions are offered for associate teachers.

Research-Based Programs

Working within a university strongly committed to research has impacted on our program in a variety of ways. Ken Zeichner, in his 1998 vice presidential address at the American Educational Research Association, implored schools of education to use the research on teacher education to guide policy decisions. At OISE/UT, research on our programs and those of other universities has had a major influence on policy and practice. Our commitment to research carries into the curriculum of our teacher education program. An inquiry focus is the conceptual framework for many of our cohorts, with students conducting small action research projects, using the internship to study a topic in depth, and participating in professors' research on the program.

LIVING OUR PRINCIPLES: PROGRAM DEVELOPMENT AND COMMUNITY BUILDING

Articulating the principles for our program was a challenge, yet living them was substantially more difficult. Richardson (1999) wisely notes that "the complex and competing goals are difficult to negotiate, particularly within boundaries that are created by educational institutions as they are structured today" (p. 152).

Social Connectedness

In the merged institution, the cohort Coordinators found themselves very isolated not only from the graduate school faculty but also from each other because they rarely met as a group. Four years into the merged institution when Clare assumed the role of Director of Elementary Preservice, the program was in some disarray and the faculty were demoralized. Clive was heavily involved in preservice teaching, research, and practicum supervision. Together, we actively worked in and on the program engaging in planning and research on the program.

One of Clare's first initiatives as Director was to bring the cohort Coordinators together to help them develop a sense of belonging. It was important for us to know each other as individuals; to see each other as colleagues; and to jointly develop priorities. The first meeting of the group was characterized by great nervousness on the part of everyone. The situation was so extreme we felt it required a dramatic initiative; we took the radical step of having a party for all the elementary preservice staff (approximately 55 instructors). Clare invited the entire faculty including administrative staff to her house for a barbecue. About 40 staff attended, the noise level rose steadily as individuals introduced each other, and the party extended far into the evening as little groups were huddled together deep in conversation. Peterson notes, "Life in a learning community is helped along by the interests, ideas, and support of others. Social life is not snuffed out; it is nurtured and used to advance learning in the best way possible" (1992, p. 3). This was the first of many social events that occurred over the next three years. The sense of connectedness with others laid the foundation for us to work together on program development.

To further community building we set meeting dates for monthly Coordinators meetings; established an email folder/line for the Coordinators with messages posted every day; and set up a second email folder for sharing materials. Recognizing that publicly posting your work could be frightening, Clare regularly shared course outlines, evaluation rubrics, letters to associate teachers, activities for teaching classroom management, and so on which led the way for others to follow her example. To recognize each person's talents and interests one Coordinator was invited to do a short opening—a reading or poem or song or activity—at each monthly meeting. As the meetings became "safe," Coordinators shared more of themselves leading to a wide range of activities including chanting a Latin verse in the stairwell of the building to create a musical round, or creating a group poem based on our individual interests. Meetings were characterized by hard work, laughter, and a place to ask about the unspoken.

As our comfort level increased, we began to post on the Coordinators' email conference information beyond the official program. We sent words of congratulations when Judy was recognized by her university alma mater as an exemplary teacher who has made a strong contribution to education; we posted the news that Larry's new book on drama was soon to be published; and we announced that Ivor was granted admission to the doctoral program. Peterson (1992) notes that celebration is key to community. "The social life of the learning community is incomplete if it doesn't include celebration, festivity, and fantasy. All these are integral parts of the human experience" (p. 39).

These community-building strategies led to strong bonds within the group, a sense of belonging, and ultimately a distinct elementary preservice culture. When we wrestled some of the control for staffing our program from senior administrative staff, we involved the Coordinators in the interviews for new instructors. Interestingly, after each interview we would ask, Would this person fit into our Coordinators' group? We knew who we were and how we wanted to act—collaboratively and collegially. We have found at the individual cohort level that if the team involved in the program is itself a community, this facilitates program integration and serves as a support for faculty and a model and support for the cohort community as a whole. We were now experiencing this across the total elementary program. This social connectedness, beyond providing a positive feeling, has had a substantial impact on all our activities.

Program Initiatives

The sense of belonging and the high comfort level the Coordinators developed amongst themselves was only partly a result of the social activities. We were simultaneously developing the preservice program, thus nurturing our professional interests. The principles of constructivist teaching and learning apply equally well to our Coordinators: "learning cannot be separated from action: perception and action work together in a dialogic manner. ... Within this framework, the development of an individual relies on social interactions. It is within this social interaction that cultural meanings are shared within the group, and then internalized by the individual" (Richardson, 1997, p. 8). As Director of the program, Clare felt it important for the Coordinators to work together on the program because it would focus our efforts, address various needs in the programs, and develop group norms. We were heavily influenced by Judith Warren Little's definition of collegiality: adults frequently, concretely and precisely talking about practice; observing each other and reflecting and talking about the observations; and working together on all aspects of curriculum design, implementation, and evaluation. She believed adults need to teach each other about teaching, learning, and leading (Barth, 1990, p. 31). At each Coordinators' meeting we ensured that the Chairs of the subcommittees (described below) had a place on the agenda. This simple action validated their efforts, showed our support for their work, and allowed for active involvement of many. As Coordinators got to know each other through the socials and curriculum development projects it seemed that individuals with similar interests and styles gravitated towards each other.

If we were going to move beyond simple congeniality to collegiality, we had to get involved in the often messy work of program development. "We must engage one another intellectually and collectively design new and more vigorous programs. Part of the need for this common ground approach is pragmatic—we are politically vulnerable in our current fragmented and institutionally weak condition..." (Tom, 1997, p. 90). Beyond teaching and service, the Coordinators had to be involved in research, the currency valued at OISE/UT. We worked on a variety of projects, some more successfully than others, yet in each venture our community was strengthened and our program improved. We have chosen to discuss four program development activities, two large-scale and two much smaller.

The practicum subcommittee felt that supervision was absolutely essential for a successful practicum (or to work through an unsuccessful one), yet they astutely realized that part of the problem with supervision was confusion about processes. Not all instructors know *how to supervise*; granted there is not one "correct" way, there are some basic principles. The subcommittee decided as their first action to offer a workshop on supervision, immediately preceding our first practicum session. This workshop, well attended by both new and experienced supervisors, included role-playing, commonly asked questions, expectations, and procedures. The subcommittee has continued to offer workshops on supervision with each session delving deeper into the issue. The subcommittee eventually wrote the invaluable document *Guidelines for Practicum Supervision* which outlines all aspects of the supervision process.

As comfort levels increased on this topic, the Coordinators began to openly share other concerns about the practicum. Supervision loads were unevenly distributed, with some instructors having minimal supervisions and others labouring under unmanageable loads. In the OISE/UT model, course instructors do supervision; unlike many other programs, we do not hire external faculty such as retired teachers and graduate students. We worked with the Associate Dean to assign a fair and equitable supervision load to each instructor, eventually producing a chart showing everyone's supervision allocation.

Through the subcommittees and Coordinators' meetings we were able to address a variety of other issues related to the practicum. Part of the reason for such active involvement was our commitment to acting quickly to capitalize on efforts or to respond to concerns. As the group evolved support was always available; at least one fellow Coordinator (or Clive or Clare) would always volunteer to help out by either joining a subcommittee or meeting informally to explore a topic. No one was ever left alone to deal with an issue. A subcommittee chaired by Louise developed guidelines for dealing with a student experiencing harassment (sexual, racial, ethnic . . .). We drew on John's revisions to the formative/interim evaluation form which led to each cohort faculty team shaping it to reflect their program. Susan's work on lesson plan formats were widely shared and used. In short, reflection, inquiry, and action were all occurring simultaneously.

To further our school-university partnership the elementary preservice Coordinators wanted to move to the next level: professional development. Such an initiative would be unmanageable for one cohort team to organize on its own, but our combined efforts allowed us to offer in-depth and frequent sessions. For example, we organized a breakfast for the principals of all our practicum schools (approximately 90 of our 120 principals attended) which included a talk by our then Dean, Michael Fullan, on large-scale literacy reform. A second event for our approximate 800 associate teachers included a keynote address by David Booth on technology and literacy, a publishers' display, and discussion about the role of an associate teacher. Both events were done on a shoestring budget, involved all 11 cohorts, and were highly successful. The incredible energy of the group was very productive because we focused our efforts on actualizing the program principles described earlier. As a community we were extremely proud of our accomplishments, which led to us developing a shared history. Often conversations began with, "Remember when we did . . . ". Our shared history gave credence to our past efforts and provided a foundation for future endeavours.

Math Activity Day—MAD

We have found that mathematics is a challenging preservice course to teach because instructors often have to teach both pedagogy (e.g. authentic assessment and evaluation) and content (Kosnik et al., 2002a). A subcommittee which included both Coordinators and mathematics instructors was formed to address these issues. This group led by Lucy, Coordinator of the Crosstown cohort, was extremely committed, innovative, hardworking, and realistic. In the subcommittee meetings, the group shared resources for teaching, mentored new math instructors, and decided on common course activities. The math instruction in our program is outstanding in large part because of the collective efforts of the math instructors.

One of this committee's initiatives was Math Activity Day, a day for the entire elementary preservice program (over 600 students) which focused on various strands of the math curriculum. The committee felt this day would be useful in providing instruction, would maximize expertise among the instructors, and would demonstrate the program's commitment to mathematics education. To make linkages with the local school districts, the subcommittee invited local school district mathematics consultants to offer workshops. At each Coordinators' meeting the logistics for the day were discussed; all Coordinators had to agree to "give up" a day in their regular program for MAD; and commit to helping organize their cohorts. All readily agreed and were incredibly supportive, in part because they recognized the problems faced by both students and math instructors. On a minimal budget the day included a keynote speaker, a huge range of workshops, and a publishers' display. Math Activity Day, now in its third year, is enshrined in the program and has had an impact on students and instructors alike.

Special Education Subcommittee

One of the peculiarities of the OISE/UT preservice program is the absence of a formal course on special education. Although many instructors feel a course is necessary, the convoluted governance structure makes it impossible for us, the preservice faculty, to alter the program. The senior administration is committed to special education being "infused" into all courses, which has had the unfortunate result that attention to special education varies dramatically from cohort to cohort. For example, Jackie the Coordinator of the Doncrest cohort, an expert in special education, is able to integrate special education naturally into the program. However, all cohorts unfortunately do not have a team member with Jackie's level of expertise. The instructors for the Educational Psychology course formed a subcommittee and decided to focus their efforts initially on special education. They became involved in a range of activities. For example, Lucy and Hazel conducted formal focus groups with instructors, students, and graduates of the program to study the needs of beginning teachers regarding special education. Kath and Jackie took the lead on organizing a packet of readings on special education to be used in all cohorts: they developed a glossary of terms and practice exercises for students to use to prepare for the teacher certification test. This subcommittee has had a tremendous impact on the program, with the quality of instruction for special education improving dramatically, relieving the pressure on Coordinators to find ways to deliver the information to students, and ensuring that all cohorts receive similar information.

Research on Assignments

In terms of work on the academic program, we took a rather unusual approach. At the *Fourth international conference on self-study of teacher education practices* in 2002, Holt-Reynolds and Johnson presented a paper describing their research on the assignments for their program (Kosnik et al., 2002b, p. 14). This inspiring paper led us (Clive and Clare) to rethink our assignments in our particular courses, which in turn led Clare to suggest that the initiative for the Coordinators for the 2002–2003 academic year be a self-study of our assignments. This suggestion was well received and, over the year half of each monthly Coordinators' meeting was devoted to this research. We worked through a five-step process:

Session 1—Working in small groups (4–6 Coordinators) we all addressed the question, Why do you require students to complete assignments?

Session 2—Each group addressed a distinct question e.g. How do you know when an assignment is not working?

Session 3—As a whole group we decided on a research methodology (survey rather than individual interviews) and a specific focus (the structure of assignments). We generated specific questions or categories to be investigated.

Session 4—As a group we reviewed and modified the questions. In addition, each pair of Coordinators tailored one part of the survey for the assignments specific to their cohort.

Session 5—Each pair of Coordinators brought the tabulated data to a meeting where we talked about our findings.

The instrument we developed had 45 questions (including 9 open-ended questions). The categories were: background information, course work, feedback, practicum, and other comments. Questions included:

- To what extent was each of the following assignments effective/valuablein preparing you to be a teaching professional? (each assignment for the particular cohort was listed)
- To what extent should there be a self-evaluation component to all assignments?
- To what extent did your assignments help you be successful in the practicum/internship?
- To what extent do you like assignments interconnecting across courses?
- To what extent is it important to you that you have a choice in topic for assignments?
- What motivates you to work diligently/fully on an assignment?
- What advice would you give your instructors regarding assignments?

Throughout the process there was lively discussion about the goals of the program and strategies for developing assignments. Because of the strong sense of community among the Coordinators and the high trust level, there was extremely honest discussion. When analyzing and discussing the findings, some described responses that surprised and even upset them. There was no denying, sugar-coating, or blaming, only true inquiry into the effectiveness of our assignments. After our general meeting, each pair of Coordinators took their individual cohort results to their faculty team for use in program development for the 2003–2004 academic year. Two further benefits of the collaborative research were that it allowed us to take some of our Coordinators who are novice researchers through an entire research cycle, and it actualized our program principle of using research to inform our practice.

CONCLUSION

We accomplished a great deal in the past three years, but it would be misleading to suggest that all our initiatives moved forward smoothly and collaboratively. There were definitely "bumps" as we moved into program development. For example, there was some variability in the amount of effort Coordinators were willing to contribute. As we became more public in our work, we opened ourselves up for scrutiny and criticism. Others beyond elementary preservice were sometimes quick to criticize us, perhaps precisely because of our enthusiasm, community, and success.

In addition to all the regular tasks required of Coordinators, our initiatives increased workload. It was extraordinarily heavy and at times we felt we were being exploited. We wished we had argued more vigorously for course release for the chairs of the subcommittees. As we worked to renew our program, we could not accept or act on every proposal brought forward. Some were wrongheaded and some would have been too difficult to implement. We needed to be diplomatic when a Coordinator enthusiastically brought forward an inappropriate suggestion, especially in the early stages when our community was fragile. The pressure on Clare as Director of the program was tremendous. Working through the multiple governance layers within the institution was draining, and being one of the few tenured faculty at the decision-making tables was a weighty responsibility.

Community building and program development went hand-in-hand. As we bravely undertook some initiatives we developed processes for others to present their suggestions. As we got to know each other as individuals and colleagues we learned about each other's working styles. This was especially helpful for Clare when working with the Associate Dean on staffing the cohorts. We were able to create teams that had the potential to be collaborative, with members having complementary styles or interests. As a team of Coordinators we were able to maximize our efforts, which led to substantial cross-cohort sharing. The old barter system was enacted regularly: "You do a session on learning styles with my students and I'll do a session on drama with your students." This led to our students having the benefit of many instructors, not simply those on their team. Our open dialogue helped Coordinators learn from each other and examine their own cohort program, leading to more consistency across cohorts. We did not strive for duplication; rather, similar expectations and programs. By sharing so generously with each other we could mentor new Coordinators, capitalize on each other's strengths, model our way of being, and develop our distinctive elementary preservice culture.

As we move forward, our next steps are both large and small. We would like to develop goals for each course, with exit outcomes, accompanied by a conceptual framework for our program. Given the teacher certification test and increased accountability measures we need to be more explicit about our work. And we need more involvement of full-time tenured faculty and senior administration, because we need many voices at the decision-making tables. Our recently elected Liberal government promises to be more teacher-friendly. We hope for an era of support for all involved in education, including a place for teacher educators so they will no longer be a *missing link.*

REFERENCES

Barth, R. (1990). *Improving schools from within: Teachers, parents, and principals can make the difference.* San Francisco: Jossey-Bass.

Bullough, R. & Gitlin, A. (1995). *Becoming a student of teaching: Methodologies for exploring self and school context.* New York: Garland.

Darling-Hammond, L. (1997). *The right to learn: A blueprint for creating schools that work.* San Francisco: Jossey-Bass.

Darling-Hammond, L. (2000). *Studies of excellence in teacher education: Preparation in a five-year program.* American Association of colleges of Teacher Education.

Darling-Hammond, L., & Sykes, G. (Eds.). (1999). *Teaching as the learning profession: Handbook of policy and practice.* San Francisco: Jossey Bass.

Fosnot, C. (Ed.). (1996). *Constructivism: Theory, perspectives, and practice.* New York: Teachers College Press.

Goodlad, J. (1990). Connecting the present to the past. In J. Goodlad, R. Soder, & K. Sirotnik (Eds.), *Places where teachers are taught* (pp. 3–39). San Francisco: Jossey-Bass.

Goodlad, J. (1994). *Educational renewal: Better teachers, better schools.* San Francisco: Jossey-Bass.

Griffin, G. (1999). Changes in teacher education: Looking to the future. In G. Griffin, (Ed.), *The education of teachers: Ninety-eighth yearbook of the national society for the study of education, Part One.* (pp. 1–18). Chicago: University of Chicago Press.

Holt-Reynolds, D., & Johnson, S. (2002). Revising the task: The genre of assignment making. In C. Kosnik, A. Freese, and A. Samaras, (Eds.). *The fourth international conference on self-study of teacher education practices: Making a difference in teacher education through self-study.* (pp. 14–17). East Sussex, England.

Howey, K. (1996). Designing coherent and effective teacher education programs. In J. Sikula, *et al.* (Eds.), *Handbook of research on teacher education* (2nd ed., pp. 143–170). New York: Macmillan.

Knowles, G. & Cole, A. (1996). Developing practice through field experiences. In F. Murray (Ed.), *The teacher educator's handbook: Building a knowledge base for the preparation of teachers* (pp. 648–688). San Francisco: Jossey-Bass.

Kosnik, C., Beck, C., Diamond, P., Kooy, M., & Rowsell, J. (2002a). *Preservice teacher education in Ontario: Trends and best practices in an era of curriculum reform.* Report for the Ontario Ministry of Education.

Kosnik, C., Freese, A., & Samaras, A. (Eds.). (2002b). *Proceedings: Fourth international conference of the self-study of teacher education practices* East Sussex, England.

Lortie, D. (1975). *Schoolteacher: A sociological study.* Chicago: The University of Chicago Press.

Meier, D. (1995). *The power of their ideas.* Boston: Beacon.

Peterson, R. (1992). *Life in a crowded place: Making a learning community.* Richmond Hill, Ontario: Scholastic.

Richardson, V. (Ed.). (1997). *Constructivist teacher education: Building a world of new understandings.* Philadelphia: RoutledgeFalmer, Taylor & Francis Inc.

Richardson, V. (1999). Teacher education and the construction of meaning. In G. Griffin, (Ed.), *The education of teachers: Ninety-eighth yearbook of the national society for the study of education, Part One.* (pp. 145–166). Chicago, University of Chicago Press.
Tom, A. (1997). *Redesigning teacher education*. Albany: State University of New York Press.
Wasley, P. (1994). *Stirring the chalkdust: Tales of teachers changing classroom practice*. New York: Teachers College Press.
Wasley, P., Hampel, R., & Clark, R. (1997). *Kids and school reform*. San Francisco: Jossey-Bass.

Elementary Preservice
Survey of Assignments
2002–2003

Thank you so much for agreeing to complete this anonymous survey. We think it will take 30 minutes, including the open-ended final section. When completing the survey please include all components of the program (e.g. Related Studies, J/I Teaching Subject, Arts), not simply your core Option subjects.

Purpose

- To develop a better sense of the effectiveness/value of assignments in the program
- To develop a better sense of the rhythm and challenges of the workload
- To develop a better sense of the requirements in the preservice program
- To model for our student teachers being a responsive teacher/teacher researcher/thoughtful practitioner

Option Name: Mid-Town

A. Background Information

1. Program: Circle One
Primary/Junior Junior/Intermediate
J/I Teaching Subject ________
2. Related Studies: Fall or Winter Term, Name of Course ________
3. Do you have a computer at home? Yes No
4. Do you have internet access from home? Yes No
5. Do you have a quiet place at home where you can study? Yes No
6. Do you have a part-time job? Yes No
6a. If yes, approximately how many hours did you work a week? _______
7. How many years since your completed your B.A. or B.Sc.? 1, 2, 3, 4, 5+
8. Do you have additional responsibilities? (e.g. childcare) Yes No

B. Course Work

9. To what extent was the course work in the **entire** preservice program manageable?
A great deal, quite a lot, a fair amount, a little, not at all, not sure

10. Before you began the preservice program, to what extent were you familiar with the number of in-class hours?
(approximately 9:00–3:30 every day)
A great deal, quite a lot, a fair amount, a little, not at all, not sure

11. To what extent were the responsibilities (readings, in-class activities, course hours, attendance . . . .) for each of the following courses **appropriate**? (at this point do NOT consider assignments—see question # 15 re: assignments)

Course	**A great deal**	**Quite a Lot**	**A Fair Amount**	**A little**	**Not at all**
T.E.S.					
Psychological Foundations					
School and Society					
Curriculum and Instruction • Language Arts • Mathematics • Social Studies • Science/Technology					
Visual Arts					
Music					
Physical and Health Education					
Related Studies					
J/I Teaching Subject					
Religious Education					

12. To what extent were you given the course requirements in September?
A great deal, quite a lot, a fair amount, a little, not at all, not sure

13. Were there any courses where the requirements changed? Yes No
13 a. If yes, which courses ___________________________________

14. To what extent were you given adequate time to complete your assignments?
A great deal, quite a lot, a fair amount, a little, not at all, not sure

15. To what extent were each of the following assignments **effective/valuable** in preparing you to be a teaching professional?

Course	A great deal	Quite a Lot	A Fair Amount	A little	Not at all
TES Experience/Mentor/Metaphor Paper					
Prep Steps for Action Research					
Resource Kit					
Psych Foundations Research Paper and Presentation					
Observation Profile of a child (TES)					
School and Society Draft Philosophy					
Final Philosophy					
Curriculum and Instruction Action Research					
Language Arts Sharing Outstanding Activity					
Mathematics Sharing Outstanding Activity					
Social Studies Field Trip Project					
Science/Technology Science Activity Hand Out					
Visual Arts •					
Music •					
Physical and Health Education •					
Related Studies Please list number of assignments and rank each • __ • __ • __					
J/I Teaching Subject Please list number of assignments and rank each					

16. To what extent were the due dates of assignments spaced appropriately?
A great deal, quite a lot, a fair amount, a little, not at all, not sure

17. To what extent did the Option assignments match the philosophy of the Option?
A great deal, quite a lot, a fair amount, a little, not at all, not sure

18. To what extent is it important to you that you have a **choice in topic** for assignments (e.g. choose a topic to investigate)?
A great deal, quite a lot, a fair amount, a little, not at all, not sure

19. To what extent were the assignments in the entire program repetitive?
A great deal, quite a lot, a fair amount, a little, not at all, not sure
19a. What assignments were repetitive?
19 b.Which courses?

20. To what extent did the completion of assignments prepare you to write the OTQT?
A great deal, quite a lot, a fair amount, a little, not at all, not sure

C. Feedback

21. To what extent was the feedback on course assignments appropriate?
A great deal, quite a lot, a fair amount, a little, not at all, not sure
21 a. If an assignment did not have appropriate feedback, what was not appropriate?

____

22. To what extent were you clear about the expectations for each assignment?
A great deal, quite a lot, a fair amount, a little, not at all, not sure
22 a. If an assignment did not have clear expectations, what was unclear?

____

23. To what extent **should** instructors be flexible with due dates?
A great deal, quite a lot, a fair amount, a little, not at all, not sure

24. To what extent do you like group assignments?
A great deal, quite a lot, a fair amount, a little, not at all, not sure

25. To what extent were the number of group assignments appropriate?
A great deal, quite a lot, a fair amount, a little, not at all, not sure

26. To what extent should instructors allow students to resubmit an assignment (after making modifications) and then receive a higher mark?
A great deal, quite a lot, a fair amount, a little, not at all, not sure

27. To what extent do you like a self-evaluation component to an assignment?
A great deal, quite a lot, a fair amount, a little, not at all, not sure

28. To what extent **should** there be a self-evaluation component to all assignments?
A great deal, quite a lot, a fair amount, a little, not at all, not sure

29. To what extent do you like a peer-evaluation component to an assignment?
A great deal, quite a lot, a fair amount, a little, not at all, not sure

30. To what extent do you like Pass/Fail assignments? (rather than an A, B, C...)
A great deal, quite a lot, a fair amount, a little, not at all, not sure

31. To what extent do you like assignments interconnecting across courses? (one large assignment includes marks for a number of courses)
A great deal, quite a lot, a fair amount, a little, not at all, not sure

32. To what extent do you think the grades on your assignments reflected your learning?
A great deal, quite a lot, a fair amount, a little, not at all, not sure

C. Practicum

33. To what extent did your assignments help you be successful in the practicum/internship?
A great deal, quite a lot, a fair amount, a little, not at all, not sure

34. To what extent did you have to complete assignments for your academic courses during the practicum?
A great deal, quite a lot, a fair amount, a little, not at all, not sure

35. To what extent did having to complete academic assignments during the practicum **limit** your success in the practicum?
A great deal, quite a lot, a fair amount, a little, not at all, not sure

36. To what extent was your work during the practicum (lesson planning, marking, locating resources....) appropriate?
A great deal, quite a lot, a fair amount, a little, not at all, not sure

37. To what extent do you like having assignments that require you to link the topic with your work in the practicum?
A great deal, quite a lot, a fair amount, a little, not at all, not sure

38. To what extent are assignments that are linked to the practicum effective/valuable for your learning?
A great deal, quite a lot, a fair amount, a little, not at all, not sure

D. Other Comments

39. What assignments do you feel helped you prepare to be a successful beginning teacher?
40. What motivates you to work diligently/fully on an assignment?
41. What made an assignment difficult to complete?
42. What assignment(s) should be deleted from the program? Briefly explain why.
43. Were there any assignments that you felt helped you be successful in the practicum? If yes, please name the assignment and give a brief reason why.
44. Given the length of the program and university requirements (must have assignments) what advice would you give your instructors regarding assignments?
45. Other comments regarding assignments . . . .

Part IV

Personal Links that Shape the Identity of Teacher Educators

Introduction by Fred A.J. Korthagen

This book is built around four important links that are fundamental to the quality of teacher education. The previous chapters dealt with the first three of these links: conceptual links across the university curriculum, theory-practice links between university and schools settings, and social-cultural links amongst participants in the program. These chapters can help educators in the process of designing teacher education programs and can have a substantial impact on student teachers' professional development. The key ideas developed so far in this book in relation to these three links are summarised in Figure C.

However, we have to be careful. We may easily develop the misconception that it is sufficient to only change a few principles underlying the design in order to improve teacher education. Even paying careful attention to each of the three important links discussed in the previous three parts of this book may not be sufficient.

If we carefully analyse the previous chapters, we can see a fourth and pivotal link surface, although it is easily overlooked. It is the link with the teacher educator as a person. It is often the human factor that determines how program principles really work out in practice. As Tickle (1999, p. 136) says: "The teacher as a person is the core by which education itself takes place", and this is no less true for teacher educators. For this reason, I strongly believe that the wish to change something outside ourselves, for instance our program or the way our students are inclined to teach, requires the willingness to look at our own identities as teacher educators and to change ourselves. Let me give a few examples from the previous chapters to illustrate the central role of the personal factor in teacher education.

In chapter 7, Anne Freese describes how an attempt to change a transmission-driven curriculum into one that is more inquiry-oriented, implies a focus on both personal and professional growth. She shows that if one strives for collaborative learning communities in teacher education, this means that personal relationships become much more important and require a different kind of investment from the teacher educators. In chapter 8, one of

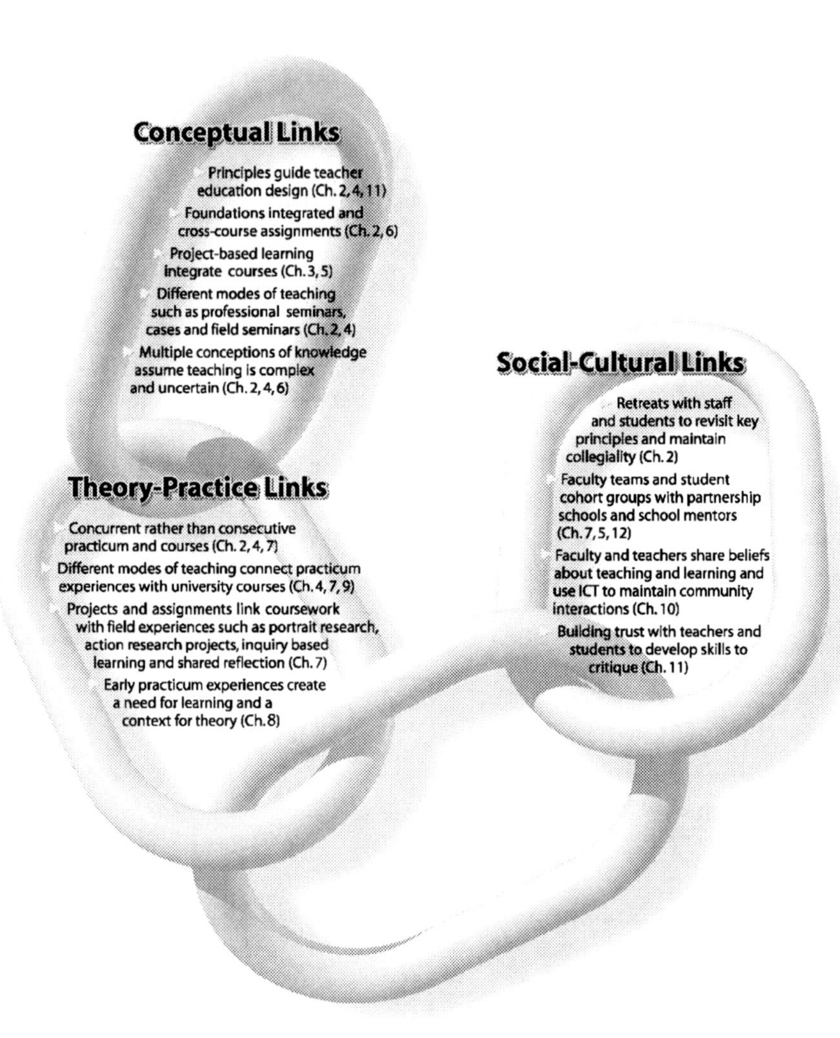

Figure C. Key ideas to promote conceptual, theory-practice and social-cultural links

Tom Russell's student teachers states: "The key is wanting to learn, and being ready to take risks—and enjoying or suffering the consequences, whatever they may be." This student teacher is talking about teaching children, but if he is so clear about his role as a teacher, shouldn't we as teacher educators set the example and show the courage that this student teacher is talking about? In chapter 11, Loughran, Berry, and Tudball explain how they do this, and how much their approach involves such courage. They also discuss that one needs to be very clear about what is needed from the part of the teacher educator. They write: "(. . . .) simply creating intellectual challenge, encouraging risk-taking and introducing pedagogy that creates a 'feel' for what it is like to be in problematic teaching and learning situations are, of themselves, not sufficient. There is a genuine need for a commitment to the development of trust, confidence and relationships that explicitly support such approaches." Loughran and his colleagues emphasize that this requires from us as teacher educators "to explicitly demonstrate our care for our students and not assume that it will simply be taken-for-granted." It is precisely this that points towards the central role of the teacher educator as a person.

The examples support Palmer's (1998) statement that "good teaching cannot be reduced to technique; good teaching comes from the identity and integrity of the teacher", something that is certainly true for the teaching of teacher educators as well. It focuses our attention to the basic requirements for building relationships that are beneficial to growth. In chapter 14, Stefinee Pinnegar will further discuss this issue. Through her personal narrative on her professional experiences, she reveals how her own identity formation has been and still is the key factor in promoting the student teachers' identity formation as teachers. And, as Pinnegar will explain, there is always a third level involved: that of the children in the schools. Indeed, if we consider helping pupils develop their identities an important goal of education, we will have to start in teacher education and, as teacher educators, serve as role models to our students (Korthagen, 2004). Identity formation then becomes a central issue at the levels of children, student teachers, and teacher educators. But firstly, Bob Bullough will, in the next chapter, lay out the landscape of what it takes to develop one's identity as a teacher educator, and especially on the struggle that is always involved in the process of finding our own professional identity, in becoming who we are. He, too, shows that the degree to which we as educators have a sound relationship with our own identities, may determine the way we build relationships with our students, and the degree to which we can help them further develop their identities as teachers.

In sum, if we really wish to make a contribution to the improvement of teacher education, we have to be prepared to look at ourselves, at our own role and identity, and accept that any educational change "must occur parallel for students and teachers", as Tom Russell says in chapter 8. This means that we have to face our own vulnerability, for as Pinnegar will show in chapter 14, we will certainly also meet frustrations when we try to bring our own professional identity in line with new views of program design and when we strive for a non-technical approach to the relationships with our students. To use Tom Russells' words: Are we prepared? All the time we ask from our student teachers to take risks, to expand their comfort zones. Are we willing to expand our own comfort zones? If we accept that education is basically a human enterprise that is grounded in the personal encounter between the teacher and the learner, we may have no choice. The only way in which the other three links discussed in this book may become strong and supportive to our goals is through realizing that in whatever we do as professionals, there is always the "I" that determines what will finally happen. So, are we as teacher educators prepared for accepting the challenge to face ourselves if we wish to change teacher education? This may evoke a life-long quest, for aligning our professional behavior with what Bullough calls "the core self", is not something one realizes overnight. As Palmer (in press) emphasizes, we are talking about the journey towards integrity. He says:

> "(. . .) that word means much more than adherence to a moral code: it means "the state or quality of being entire, complete, and unbroken," as in *integer or integral.* Deeper still, integrity refers to something (. . . .) in its unimpaired, unadulterated, or genuine state, corresponding to its original condition."

Elsewhere I have elaborated how *core reflection* can help in this process, both for teacher educators and teachers (Korthagen, 2004). It is an approach to reflection in which one takes one's inner core and personal qualities, one's ideals and personal missions seriously, but also the requirements from the environment, and deliberately tries to deal with the inner limitations involved in expressing one's inner core in one's professional life. Core reflection requires the conscious decision to strive for integration of the personal and professional dimensions of one's behaviour, to go for "the journey toward an undivided life" as Palmer (in press) calls it. In my view, it is the educator who knows how to align the personal and the professional dimension in teaching, who makes the difference.

In the next two chapters, two excellent educators show how they deal with this challenge. Their contributions fit into the self-study approach to research by teacher educators, an approach in which it is considered essential that teacher educators study their own practice and especially their own role in creating that practice (Loughran, Hamilton, Kubler LaBoskey, & Russell, 2004). Through these final chapters, Bullough and Pinnegar clarify how establishing a climate of professionalism in teacher educator requires an investment in the personal dimension. In this way they elaborate the last of the four links around which this book is built.

REFERENCES

Korthagen, F.A.J. (2004). In search of the essence of a good teacher: Towards a more holistic approach in teacher education. *Teaching and Teacher Education, 20*(1), 77–97.

Loughran, J.J., Hamilton, M.L., Kubler LaBoskey, V., & Russell, T. (Eds.) (2004). *International handbook of self-study of teaching and teacher education practices.* Dordrecht: Kluwer Academic Publishers.

Palmer, P.J. (1998). *The courage to teach.* San Francisco: Jossey-Bass.
Palmer, P.J. (in press). *A hidden wholeness: The journey toward an undivided life.* San Francisco: Jossey-Bass.
Tickle, L. (1999). Teacher self-appraisal and appraisal of self. In R.P. Lipka & T.M. Brinthaupt (Eds.), *The role of self in teacher development* (pp. 121–141). Albany, N.Y.: State University of New York Press.

Chapter 13

The Quest for Identity in Teaching and Teacher Education

Robert V. Bullough, Jr.
Brigham Young University, USA

For us to change how we teach requires us to change who we are as teachers.
(Feldman, 2003, p. 27)

Certainly since Decartes famously asserted, "Cogito ergo sum," questions of identity have been at the center of the Western quest for meaning. What and who is the "I" that thinks and therefore is? While in college in the late 1960s, the stream of the Western tradition continued to flow as my generation sought to discover and then express our true selves, an indubitable but original grounding that echoed a Platonic ideal. By breaking one's chains, chains of illusion, then turning and facing the light emanating from the mouth of the cave, a true self could be found. But how does one know that the self found is the "true" self? Does rebellion against parents and other bearers of "the establishment" necessarily result in self-discovery? I recall participating in protests that were publicly principled but privately just good excuses to party. Yet phoniness was high treason, an affront to the self and to the sincerity of others' quests for authenticity. True to Enlightenment traditions, and despite a growing presence of Eastern thought via the likes of Alan Watts and other cultural translators, the myth of self-creation first so powerfully portrayed by Henry David Thoreau in *Walden*, endured. One could not only find oneself, but, in an act of autogenesis, like Jay Gatsby actually create oneself.

One wonders, as John Murphy quarried, "is this search for an identity proof that a self exists?" (Murphy, 1989, p. 116). Does a generation seeking authentic expressions of the self mean there is a self to seek? No, Murphy argues: The self is a fragile fiction. Identity is merely linguistic, an expression of using a first-person singular pronoun, a habit of speech and of behavior, a performance that ultimately cannot be sustained. Indeed, he suggests, we are inevitably multiple selves depending on the range and variety of contexts we inhabit, each of which calls forth a different self. For some (Gergen, 1991), the discovery of multiplicity is cause for celebration. For others, at its extreme, it is a source of crisis, of severe disorientation and confusion (see Glass, 1993).

G. Hoban (ed.), The Missing Links in Teacher Education Design, 237–258.

What is one to make of this situation? And why are questions of identity and selfhood of such consequence to teachers and to teacher educators?

FROM A STUDENT'S POSITION: A STEP BACKWARD

To begin to answer these questions it is first necessary to step out of the teacher and teacher educator position and into the student position where we confront full-faced the weight of our moral responsibilities as educators. When asked why they decided to teach and to be a teacher (a statement about identity), teachers give a range of responses. Typically they recall their own experience as students and speak of their teachers. For those teachers I have spoken with, content area backgrounds are seldom mentioned. Rather, mention is made of the teacher as a person who, for good or ill, deeply touched their students' lives. Qualities, both positive and sometimes negative, are listed: caring, interested, passionate, curious, engaged, involved, humorous or, alternatively, disorganized, mean-spirited, disengaged. From my own schooling experience I can put human faces to these qualities and in doing so my judgment says something profound about my teachers as persons, about how I interacted with their self-presentation and they with mine and how together we engaged in a process of mutual self-definition.

To my great benefit, some of my teachers were *fully present* to me in the classroom. But each and every one of my teachers' lives presented an argument for a way of being with and in the world and for others. Some of these ways of being influenced my conception of who I was, how I should and could live, and what I might become. It was a teacher, Michael Arvanitas, whose passion for history helped turn me toward imagining myself as a historian. David Patterson (1991) nicely makes the point: "those of us who are teachers cannot stand before a class without standing for something . . . teaching is testimony" (p. 16). This is true whether one is a first grade public school teacher or a teacher educator in a distinguished private university. Parker Palmer extends and deepens the point: "Teaching, like any truly human activity, emerges from one's inwardness, for better or worse. As I teach, I project the condition of my soul onto my students, my subject, and our way of being together. The entanglements I experience in the classroom are often no more or less than the convolutions of my inner life. Viewed from this angle, teaching holds a mirror to the soul [or the condition of one's inner self] (1998, p. 2). Parents certainly are wise to ask of their children's teachers, "What sort of person is he?"

Stepping back into the teacher educator position, questions of identity have profound importance for the kind and quality of professional communities that we form as well as the programs we develop. As will be discussed shortly, the subject positions opened to us by the institutions we serve and the duties we perform shape the kind of lives we live and in turn the kind of lives we live shape the kind of persons we become and the institutions we serve. Thus, program decisions not only have to do with what students learn and do but how we live and whether or not we are able to live undividedly. In turn, the lives we live and the subject positions we occupy and play out define for our colleagues, particularly our younger colleagues, models of professional being and provide conditions of membership. If they are to join with us, beginners must find acceptable and recognized subject positions which may require that they conceal conflicting aspirations. Having long histories, subject positions appear natural, but they are not. They are human creations sustained in multiple and often unrecognized ways through various forms of institutional labor including simply going about our daily business and doing our jobs. And so, a genuine concern with teacher educator identity and identity formation necessarily leads to both self and institutional criticism and perhaps to change and renewal.

MEANING, SELF AND IDENTITY

Already I have used two very slippery terms, "self" and "identity" which require definition and grounding if I am to say anything of value about teacher education and the quest for identity. As a point of departure I draw on the work of Harre and van Langenhove who helpfully distinguish between two senses of self: "There is the self of personal identity, which is experienced as the continuity of one's point of view in the world of objects in space and time. This is usually coupled with one's sense of personal agency, in that one takes oneself as acting from that very same point. Then there are selves that are publicly presented in the episodes of interpersonal interaction in the everyday world, the coherent clusters of traits we sometimes call 'personas'... One's personal identity persists 'behind' the publicly presented repertoire of one's personae" (1999, p. 7). Often these two senses of self are confused. In my own work I have found it helpful to distinguish between "core" and "situational" selves (Bullough, Knowles & Crow, 1991). The result of this view is that under "normal circumstances each human being is the seat of just one person, but of many personas. The same individual can manifest any one of their repertoire of personas in clusters of behaviour displayed in the appropriate social context. Taken over a period of time it becomes clear that each person has many personas, any one of which can be dominant in one's mode of self-presentation in a particular context" (Harre & van Langenhove, 1999, p. 7). This said, the extent of any one individual's repertoire will vary, sometimes dramatically.

It is within interaction that personas reveal themselves, are or are not recognized by others, and are judged as fitting–contextually appropriate or inappropriate to the rules, duties and meanings of an established storyline. Thus, through interaction speakers constitute and reconstitute one another in a kind of moving symbolic dance with contextually set rules and established but ever shifting boundaries. For instance, teachers and students position one another, often oppositionally. To be a good student or a poor one is to act and speak in certain ways which are recognized and confirmed or disconfirmed by teachers. When a young person judged to be a good student fails to act in accord with expectations and challenges a teacher's authority the teacher responds in a way very different from when the disruptive student is judged to be failing. But in both instances, the teacher asserts the rules and duties that bind teachers to students and that make their interactions congruent. Students may resist, but resistance comes at a cost. Conversely, if a teacher fails to act teacherly students will subtly press the teacher to a return to the *proper* teacher position, to the teacher subject position made available by the specific cultural and institutional context of schooling.

THE QUEST

Whether identity is real or imagined, the quest for it is experienced as real. We recognize the quest as simultaneously constructive and destructive both personally and socially and that it takes inclusive and exclusive forms. "I am this sort of person but not this sort." On their part, institutions favor and support some forms of identity and some personas over others. One cannot, then, simply chose oneself–we are all caught, trapped by the limitations and possibilities of the human networks within which and through which we live, the "Das Man" self as Heidegger characterized it, but we are not wholly determined by our location within those networks. We are tugged in multiple directions and are sites of clashing possibilities and conflicting impulses and social demands. As Thoreau argued: There is always the possibility of disobedience, of imagining things not as they are, not as given. This said, social networks and institutions both limit and enable identity formation, and in the limiting and enabling there is the possibility of severe and serious personal and social dislocation as well as of self-discovery and of rebirth.

Locating the self of personal identity as the experience of continuity of a point of view and as a source of agency and embracing self-as-multiplicity-of-personas, quasi-role enactments and self-presentations, brings two very distinct but related sets of problems. Problems of origin, content, and form, come with the first. Problems of consistency and congruence come with the second. Both sets of questions point toward the need to explore biography and moral position, the history of interaction and of the contexts within which interaction takes place and by which rules are and have been set, and the rules and skills of interaction located in episodes, "structures of social encounters" (Harre & van Langenhove, 1999, p. 5) or sequences of "happenings in which human beings engage which have some principle of unity" (p. 4). Episodes "include thoughts, feelings, intentions, plans ... of those who participate. As such, episodes are defined by their participants but at the same time they also shape what participants do and say" (p. 5).

The stories we tell of ourselves are spoken to specific persons, to an audience, and shifts in audience and of place result in changed stories each of which might be recognized as true and as belonging to a single, whole, embodied, life—stories that speak of identity not merely of one's passing personae. When written, however, the narrative is frozen and becomes a thing, reified and resistant to change. Textual coherence reduces multiplicity and "conflates the self as perceiver with the self as perceived" (p. 69). In effect, the order imposed by writing a story of self, a linear unfolding, stands in for the self itself. This is important for how I will compose the body of this chapter. To avoid the reification that comes with the written story form, narratives that have beginnings, middles, and endings, in what follows I will present and reflect upon several episodes that illuminate the challenges of teacher and teacher-educator self-formation and point toward the importance of attending to identity formation when thinking about teaching and learning to teach and of being with children. On the surface, the episodes will seem to be distinct but what binds them together is their place in the unwritten storyline of becoming a teacher educator. Drawing on C. Wright Mills' (1959) insight, I will seek to join biography and history.

EPISODES, IDENTITY AND PERSONAE

This section presents seven episodes, organized under three headings which represent different, but closely related, aspects of identity formation, social processes that shape who and what we are. I should mention up front that there are other fruitful ways of parcing the quest for identity. I have settled on these because they resonate with my experience and seem to be shared. They certainly are not comprehensive although I hope they may prove to be useful and perhaps provocative. The headings are: 1) *Identification and Membership*; 2) *Subject location: Rules and Duties*; and, 3) *Self-Expression and Enactment*. Each of these points toward questions useful for thinking about one's own identity and for considering how one might assist another to better understand what he or she has become or is becoming and why. *Identification and Membership* leads to these sorts of questions: With whom and with what do I identify? To what do I belong? Who or what claims me as a member? *Subject location: Rules and Duty* points toward these questions: Where do I fit, what institutional spaces are open to me? What rules do I follow and duties do I perform and how is my performance connected to and recognized by others? *Self-Expression and Enactment* raises questions related authenticity, to how I feel when I play my part and whether or not the part I play is found to be life affirming and enabling of a sense of self coherence, as well as to whether or not I possess the skills needed for self-enactment. Before proceeding, I must mention that I will have little to say about temperament, which nevertheless has an important place in identity formation. Institutions favor some temperaments over others and temperament has a dramatic influence on recognition and membership. It also has a great deal to do with our ability to tolerate ambiguity and manage contradiction and incoherence, a point nicely illustrated by the life of the philosopher David Hume, for example. While this is an extremely important topic, I can only touch on it very briefly in this essay.

While the seven episodes presented overlap in various and multiple ways across the three headings, they are intended to emphasize one or another point about the teacher and teacher educator quest for identity. I explore the quest itself when I reflect upon each of the episodes.

Identification and Membership

We know who we are in part by who and with what we identify and to whom and to what we belong. Through identification with other teachers and with teaching we take on teacher-like qualities and speak in teacher-like voices and with teacher-like authority when with children and sometimes with parents, particularly less well educated parents. When we see teachers we simultaneously see ourselves. We recognize one another as belonging. Formally, teacher education is charged with facilitating the process of identification through socialization, particularly through field experience. But not all intending teachers need help seeing themselves as teachers, some, particularly young women who "played" school when small, already think of themselves as teachers; they are "called" to teach. A calling is a "form of public service to others that at the same time provides the individual a sense of identity and personal fulfillment" (Hansen, 1995, p. 2). For these persons, teaching is the avenue through which they find the fullest, deepest, and richest expression of their identities. They literally *are* teachers, they are not playing at teaching, even though they never have taught.

I was not called to teach. Nor was I called to teacher education. In some respects I fell into teaching and teacher education as a response to the political and socio-economic period within which I was born and matured. My father was a junior high school art teacher who made a point of telling me that of all things I should avoid teaching as a career. I was acutely aware of the financial struggles of my parents and often resented the fact that my father, a Phi Beta Kappa university graduate, had to work multiple, and what seemed to me demeaning, night jobs to make ends meet. Still, I became a teacher, sensing in it hope for the future and a place within which a moral impulse for social betterment could be expressed. A professor, Florence Krall, helped me to see these possibilities by opening an avenue into alternative education.

As an alternative educator, I had great difficulty identifying with "regular" teachers and with the institutionalized practice of teaching. What I did with my classes probably would not have been recognized widely by others as teaching. I developed a school recycle center. My "students" and I studied the court system. We organized an anti-Olympic protest. We made movies. We wrote lousy poetry. Made pots. Played football. Grew a garden. Visited the state penitentiary. And we argued over issues under a widely spread parachute that draped over the classroom and produced a sense of intimacy and encouraged feelings of belonging. For me, teaching was a form of social action which was central to my identity formation, of finding my own place and way of being with others. Because I worked with young people who would not have attended school without the existence of the program and the program more than paid for itself since student attendance was the basis for funding, I was given remarkable leeway by school administrators to experiment and to explore and build a shared world.

Episode 1

During fall term of my first year of teaching a faculty dinner was planned. I attended knowing that some members of the faculty doubted that an alternative program should exist within what historically had been an elite, but, because of shifting demographics, a rapidly changing school. At the dinner, others were polite but only the special education teacher, Fern Register, spoke openly and was warmly friendly toward me. She recognized and responded to me as a fellow teacher. Fern's program and mine occupied the same floor of the building along with the lunchroom and auditorium. The serious academic programs occupied the top floor, far removed from us and our students. Auto mechanics occupied the basement. Despite dressing up and wearing for the one and only time my Phi Beta Kappa Key, I sensed my place: I was and would continue to be on the fringes of the faculty, which I thought was all right. I was an outsider, one whose position was determined by the limited value placed on my students by other faculty members (but not, I should mention, Principal Joe Richards or especially Vice Principal Mary Caffey).

I found freedom on the fringes. That I taught students who were of so little concern to so many faculty members produced a liberating benign neglect. That established institutional teacher subject positions were not fitting or did not exist for me proved exhilarating. That I was outside of the boundaries and was seen as not belonging meant that I was often criticized, but because of the protection offered by the two building administrators, the net effect of the criticism was only to increase the distance separating me from other teachers and to remove even the faint possibility that I would identify with them as teachers. Instead, I affiliated with other alternative educators who saw themselves as being counter-cultural and looked toward the university and toward my students' well-being for confirmation of myself and of my teaching personae, such as it was. That university faculty members were intimately involved in the program and in the school made identification with them easy. Naively, I dismissed other teachers as "traditional" and their work as morally lacking as I formed my teaching personae in opposition to the institutionally preferred patterns.

Reflection

Stepping into a rapidly changing and dynamic teaching situation profoundly influenced my development as a teacher (or non-teacher). I recall only an occasional tension between my deeper, biographical, sense of self, my identity, and the school personae I developed. I came to appreciate being seen by others in the building as odd, as belonging elsewhere. That many (not all) of the faculty did not understand nor seem to value what I did confirmed the worth of the work; had they embraced me, had they recognized me as one of them, I suspect I would have had to reject their association in order to have maintained my identity. In opposition, I found self-confirmation and strength. Yet, paradoxically, by defining myself and being defined as "not-teacher" the institutionalized position of "teacher" defined me. I played a counter melody to the melody of schooling, and counter melodies exist only in relationship to melodies.

Our patterns of identification and affiliation reveal a great deal about who we are, at base. We do not seek out others whose lives call forth from us an uncomfortable personae or whose expressions of self shake our own, at least not frequently. Yet, we do not only seek confirmation of our identities and the personas we have assumed; we are also animated by other motives, the desire to understand and be understood, for example, as Habermas has argued in his discussion of the conditions for communication. In desiring to understand others, including our students, we may discover ourselves to be a location of distorted meanings. We might even find that we are oppressors, that our identities and the personas we project have been constructed in such a way that to confirm our worth requires the negation of someone else's sense of worth. In any case, if we attend carefully to those whose call we hear and to which we resonate, we learn a great deal about who we are and about the moral space we occupy. Later, I will have something to say about the seduction of teacher educators by the call of the arts and sciences and about the educational and personal cost of this identification.

Episode 2

A few months ago, a colleague who needed to speak with me left his card tacked to my door. It read, Professor so and so, "Professor of Children's Literature." It did not read, "Professor so and so, Professor of Teacher Education." Several years ago I read the obituary of a friend who suddenly died. For years he had taught methods courses in a teacher education faculty but in his obituary, which he wrote, he described himself as a "Professor of Child Development."

Reflection

I understand the desire to distance oneself from teacher education which even in colleges of education remains low status, labor intensive, and unappreciated. Identifying with work and with others judged second rate comes at a cost to self. What sort of person wants membership of this kind? Teacher education is not judged to be serious intellectual work, as John Goodlad concluded from his study of teacher education: "The preeminence of scholarly work and the faculty prerequisites that go with it are pronounced on the campuses of the major public and private universities. It does not take long even for the previously uninitiated to pick up on some of the subtleties of prestige differentiating fields of study, kinds of publications, awards, and the like. And it does not take much probing to find that gaining campus wide recognition as a scholar is exceedingly difficult if one is connected with a school, college, or department of education" (1990, pp. 192). I felt these pressures and recognized the status system even as a graduate student in education and I too distanced myself from teacher education although I knew that if I was to find employment in higher education it would be in a teacher education faculty. I thought of myself as a curriculum and foundations person and not a teacher educator. My dissertation was a historical and theoretical work, a portion of which later became a book on Boyd H. Bode, an important American pragmatist who moved to education from academic philosophy in the hope of strengthening the cause of democracy.

Following graduation I obtained a one year appointment at the University of Utah. During the year I supervised student teachers and taught methods courses tolerably but not exceptionally well and looked forward to a time when

I might have secure employment, which required publication, and teach foundations courses. As a beginning faculty member, I felt deeply divided. Despite my best efforts, I had not escaped the demands of teacher education even as I felt distanced from them. In 1982 I published an article on "professional schizophrenia." The opening few sentences of that piece read: "In schools and colleges of education there are surprisingly few individuals who claim to be teacher educators. They are almost everything but. They are psychologists–'educational psychologists'–or evaluators, historians or whatever. In any case, it is difficult to find anyone who claims to be a teacher educator. For most of these individuals it just happens that education is a vehicle for pursuit of their academic interests; when this vehicle does not serve these interests, it is easily abandoned" (Bullough, 1982, p. 207).

Despite my best efforts at distancing myself from teacher education, I could not fully. For one thing, on campus I was recognized as a member of the education faculty, and this meant I was treated as though I was a teacher educator. One response to such situations is to seek to have others recognize us as the sort of person we think we are. But, this was impossible. I was deeply and profoundly conflicted. I felt disconnected from the courses I taught, alienated. My identity, partially grounded in the experience of having worked in alternative education, insisted that I be engaged with students and committed to their development but I could see little of worth in the content of my courses and in my practice. I knew I had to spend more time publishing if I was to survive, and this seemed to require a reduced investment in teaching and in students.

Episode 3

Human Interests in the Curriculum (Bullough, Goldstein & Holt, 1984) was published at the end of 1983. *Human Interests* was the result of an ongoing study of critical theory with Stan Goldstein and Ladd Holt and of a fellowship spent sitting in on foundations courses with Walter Feinberg, Paul Violas and Harry Broudy at the University of Illinois. In the book Stan, Ladd, and I critically analyzed a range of school programs and did so with a sledge hammer. For a short time following the book's publication I felt very good about my work and my place in the department. My place in foundations and my personae as a foundations person seemed to solidify somewhat. But then one afternoon, Florence Krall, who was now a colleague, stopped me in the hallway near my office to talk. In her inimitable and always straightforward manner she said that she found the book "disappointing" and then remarked, as I recall her words, "there isn't any 'you' in it." I was stunned. I could not help but think carefully about what she had said and why she might have said it. She knew me and my history. Gradually, I came to realize that she was right. In many ways the critic's role well suits me, but what she sensed was that I was hiding in the role and behind a borrowed ideology. Criticism was a form of disengagement, in this case a form of disassociation from parts of myself that she knew. Recalling my past, she invited me to engage in an act of self-recovery. I was in bad faith, as Sarte would way. One cannot simply escape history by denying it.

Reflection

Life as a teacher educator in a university requires a double-identification and membership, one with teachers and schools and one with the academy. Teacher educators stand between two "communities of practice" (Wenger, 1999). To describe this divide as merely a matter of an inevitable tension between theory and practice, as is so commonly done, is to miss the real point. The struggle is over membership and identity—indeed, "formation of a community of practice is also the negotiation of identities" (Wenger, 1999, p. 149). Sometimes schizophrenia results—in asserting oneself, one denies oneself. One lives incoherently. Various attempts have been made to create institutional contexts within which resolution is more rather than less likely. The Holmes Group (1995), for example, championed professional development schools as a way of "forming a tighter bond between scholarship and practice" (p. 60). The promise was that stable, satisfying, and consistently principled professional personas could be formed and that better teachers and schools would result once the divided loyalties of teacher educators were resolved. New loyalties and by inference new identities, members of the Holmes Group seemed to have realized, required new institutional commitments. But the divide continues and in some respects deepens. As the attack on teachers and teacher education grows increasingly shrill and irrational the temptation to withdrawal grows apace.

Affiliation with teachers assures low status within the academy. Strong identification with the academy and with the arts and sciences produces a crisis of authority with school teachers who often and not wholly inaccurately see academics as foreign invaders. In the teacher education classroom, strong identification with teachers, seeing oneself first and foremost as a teacher and being recognized by teachers as part of their world, leads to telling stories about teachers and teaching from one's own experience as a way of establishing authority claims. In contrast, identification with the academy leads to lists of disembodied and decontextualized generalizations and principles and, inevitably, to charges from students of irrelevance. Charges of irrelevance may prove hurtful, but identification with the academy and with the work of the academy is the only road to tenure. It is deeply ironic that even as teacher educators mimic the arts and sciences and seek a strong identification with the academy, the academy consistently refuses to recognize teacher educators as legitimate members. Still, we seek membership and to get it many of us distance ourselves from students and teaching. It is little wonder, as Robert Boice (1991; 1996) has noted, that resentment of the demands of teaching is common among beginning professors across university campuses even as one's greatest professional pleasure may come from teaching.

Episode 4

In the spring of 1984 I found myself sitting in the Trustee Room of Teachers College, Columbia University, surrounded by a collection of deans that comprised the Holmes Group writing committee. In the first Holmes Group Report, *Tomorrow's Teachers* (1986), I am listed as a "participant in the development of the reform agenda" (p. 79). I was to present my view of the state of teacher education and teacher education research in America. Across from me sat Dean Judy Lanier, the force behind the Holmes Group, and above me hung beautifully framed portraits of T.C. notables of the past. With interest I read the nameplates. As I spoke I pulled no punches. What I said reflected my view, an admittedly conflicted non-member's view, of the state of the field. Had a young intending-teacher-educator been present I suspect he would have wondered, "Why would anyone want to affiliate with this field?"

Reflection

At the time I presented, this question was also my question. It was only while doing the research that resulted in *First Year Teacher: A Case Study* (1989) that I came publicly to refer to myself as a teacher educator and to understand the complexity and richness of teacher education problems and issues. I decided to conduct the research for *First Year Teacher* while driving to West Yellowstone for a brief family vacation. When back home I told a senior faculty member I highly respected of my plans. He was surprised and queried, "Why would anyone be interested in a book about an individual teacher?" He could see no possible value in the project, yet I persisted with it. I had come to realize that I could no longer continue to work in teacher education courses and with teacher education students and not try to do a better job for them. Despite consistently positive teacher evaluations, I was unhappy with much of my work and my teaching. To improve the situation, I had to embrace it, fully, and in doing so I found that almost despite myself I had left foundations and curriculum theory and moved into teacher education as an arena of action and of self-definition. I sought membership in the community of teacher educators. In retrospect, I believe the move was only possible because I could, in Parker Palmer's terms, "live divided no more" (1998, p. 168). To be sure, my foundations work had lead to tenure, to institutional survival, and tenure opened the possibility of risking myself and seeking new membership and new forms of recognition.

Subject Location, Rules and Duties

What if, institutional membership brings with it rules and duties that are destructive to self and not just contrary to it?

Episode 5
Before leaving for Columbus, Ohio in the fall of 1973 for graduate study, I received a phone call informing me that I should plan on attending a meeting once I arrived that would signal the beginning of an effort to redesign the undergraduate teacher education program around specific competencies. I was stunned. My heart sank. I knew something about the competency movement in teacher education and I did not like it. Especially I did not like its underpinnings in behavioral psychology, its ontology or its simplistic epistemology. I had accepted a teaching assistantship and my duties included working in the undergraduate program. I was awarded a University Fellowship that would pay me to work full time on my dissertation when the time came. So, I left for Columbus feeling disheartened and, in some ways, trapped by the commitment I had made and duties I had accepted. Thus began my work with Professor Donald Cruickshank. One afternoon during our weekly seminar Professor Cruickshank and I had a disagreement. Over time we had many disagreements. He made a point that there was a need to measure outcomes in teacher education, and that, drawing on words he attributed to Edward Thorndike, he said, "Whatever exists at all, exists in some amount and can be measured." Immediately, without stopping to weigh my words, I corrected him. "No, it was William McCall (1922) who added the phrased 'can be measured' to Thorndike's statement." Then, to trump Professor Cruickshank, I added, drawing on John Dewey's Kappa Delta Pi lecture of 1929, *The Sources of a Science of Education*, that what is important in education cannot be measured.1 Professor Cruickshank ignored my insubordination, after all, I was merely a graduate student. On my part, I found myself increasingly feeling disconnected from the program, the direction being taken and the expectations I was to meet. I considered transferring universities, an action made unnecessary when Professor Paul R. Klohr took me under wing, but that is a story for another time.

Reflection
Peter Taubman (1992) writes of the subject positions open within teacher discourse, the dominate being what he characterizes as the position of the

"master" (p. 229). What if a teacher does not want and is not well suited to be a master or, in my case as a graduate student, a teacher trainer? What if the positions available do violence to one's identity? If the subject positions of a context are few and highly constrained by the distribution of rewards and punishments and one does not and cannot find place, what does one do? Clearly, as a graduate student, I was highly vulnerable. A sensible strategic move would have been for me to have kept quiet, done my duty, obeyed the rules, and engaged in strategic compliance until graduation. Through strategic compliance, I might have been recognized by my professors as belonging to them, as having a legitimate claim on them. I might have muttered to my fellow graduate students from a student personae even while presenting to my professors another, more compliant, personae, that of the eager and willing junior colleague. Or, I could have closed my classroom door and out of sight enacted a subject position more to my liking, more consistent with how I understood and presented myself. Each of these responses were then possible. I had genuine choices before me.

Now, it is much more difficult to hide behind a closed classroom door than it used to be. The greater emphasis on accountability in education generally and high stakes testing specifically has opened wide the classroom door and severely reduced the range of available teacher subject positions as well as tightened work rules. It is increasingly difficult to engage in role play and not be caught and judged deviant. Similar efforts are afoot in higher education, of which more will be said shortly. When outcomes are externally imposed and consistently enforced, when aims and means are kept separate and rules and duties carefully prescribed, it is very difficult to express oneself fully in teaching, to be passionate about one's work, and for many educators the distance between professional personae and identity likely widens as a result. I suspect it is for this reason that teaching is losing much of its appeal even to those initially called to teach. As a technology, teaching requires little investment of identity compared to teaching as an expressive art form. Narrowly prescribed outcomes stand between teachers and students and sunder many teachers' sense of coherence as their practice contradicts their moral commitments and identities.

Episode 6

Shortly after *First Year Teacher* was published it happened that David Berliner visited campus and met with my department chair. During the meeting, Professor Berliner, a former president of the American Educational Research Association and a quantitative researcher with sparkling credentials, mentioned that he had read and much admired the book. My chair, whose own scholarly tradition had led him to conclude that it was a soft study, not research at all, was amazed, so surprised that he could not help but mention the meeting to me. It was as though he had been taken into space on an extraterrestrial vessel and just returned.

Reflection

This chance event proved to have an important influence on how my chair subsequently viewed my work, place, and status in the department. He reassessed me (he reassessed my work and therefore reassessed me), recognized me as a scholar who simply played by a different set of rules than his own, and, because of David Berliner's recognition, reassigned me to a higher status subject position. Suddenly, my institutional life was transformed and not because of any action of my own.

This event followed on the heels of what has sometimes been called the "quantitative/qualitative wars" that came somewhat late to my institution but came with vengeance. The central question was: What counts as research? The subtext was far from subtle which was the question of academic cachet and of what sort of work, or put differently, what sort of persons and identities, would be rewarded within the university and judged authoritative. Part of finding place within a field is finding place within the established modes of inquiry and then of following the rules of scholarship and doing one's duty as a scholar. As William James so well understood, questions of temperament are very important here. There is a close connection between temperament, identity, and scholarship—we study what strikes us, which is part of the "inner drama" of research, the "giving of one's self into the research undertaking" (Mooney, 1957, p. 155). We study best when we use methods that get at the full complexity of the questions that grab us. It was the failure of quantitative methods to do this, to get at the complexity of experience and to allow expression of the temperament of large numbers of educators who wished to better understand the nature of educational experience and not merely of human behavior, that led to the rise to prominence of qualitative methodologies. With the broadening acceptance of qualitative methods came new forms of recognition and new ways of being a professor. As an aside, it is this same uneasiness and lack of place that has led to the growing interest in "self study" in teacher education.

Since the late 1980s, there has been a dramatic expansion of the research subject positions of teacher education. A sea change. But, there are signs of a vigorous and growing backlash. Among the signs is the remarkably narrow definition of "scientific research" championed by the U.S. National Reading Panel and supported by the American president's education policy makers (Darling-Hammond & Youngs, 2002). In policy debates—now increasingly more like friendly insider chats than open debates—constricted definitions of what counts as "data" are winning the day. Rules are tightening. Other signs of constriction include the shift of the National Council for the Accreditation of Teacher Education (NCATE) toward performance outcomes as the basis for making accreditation decisions (Bullough, Clark, & Patterson, 2003). Seemingly unaware of the failures of the earlier competency movement that I first encountered at Ohio State, in the U.S. the Association of Teacher Educators has established standards for "master teacher educators" complete with an assessment model that includes portfolios, "Assessment Center Exercises" including written examinations and simulations, and interviews (see www.ate1.org). It is likely that one result of these developments, each grounded in an abiding distrust of teachers and teachers educators and deep doubt about the value of our work and therefore of us, will be growing pressure from a variety of sources internal and external to teacher education to reduce the range of available subject positions and to reorder the status of those positions that remain.

The implications of these developments for identity formation are far reaching. It appears that the institutional subject positions encouraged by these developments will have little if any connection whatsoever to the well-being of intending teachers or children and much to do with generating an inflationary political currency tied to standardized test scores. Finding place in these positions will take teacher educators away from their central moral responsibility to better serve children. But, we have choices about how we respond; and much is at stake for the well-being of children and of those who work most closely with them in how we respond (Bullough, 2001). Unfortunately, the present mood among the leaders of the various teacher education organizations is defensive and reactive, which does not bode well for teacher education or for children. Courageous responses can only come from strength of identity and clarity of commitment. Too many of us are, using the phrase C.S. Lewis used to criticize intellectuals, "men without chests" (1944/1996, p. 36). Such persons take established institutional practices as given, almost natural, not as historical and changing human creations.

Self-Expression and Enactment

Years ago I conducted a study of a beginning teacher who was uncertain about what sort of teacher she wanted to be and responded in chameleon-like fashion to the institutional demands of teaching, allowing the context to fully dictate her actions (Bullough, 1992). Since teaching is fraught with contradictions and paradox is the stuff of a teacher's life, she found herself facing the consequences of inconsistency. When grading, for example, teachers weigh quality of work against quantity and effort. What does one do when a high achieving student puts forth little effort but produces an outstanding product? Conversely, what does one do when a less able student works diligently and invests extraordinary amounts of energy and time in a product that is good but not great? For this teacher, as I recall, what might be considered the normal paradoxes of teaching were debilitating. She spoke with many voices and stood for nothing. Many of her students, who expected consistency of thought and action from their teachers, were frustrated and occasionally angered by her actions. A strong sense of self, an established but not wholly rigid, identity, is the basis for moral action. Lacking stable identity, a strong personae may produce what appears to be moral action, but to call such action "moral" requires that it be more than a result of a person playing a temporary role—to be moral, action must be committed. As I sat in this beginning teacher's classroom, she lacked classroom presence, seemed timid, insecure and insincere, and uncertain. She waffled. Within the classroom, she could not enact a teacher personae.

Finding that students did not respond to him as he hoped and facing serious discipline problems, another beginning teacher (Bullough & Knowles, 1990) chose to adopt and enact the dominate subject position presented by his school and became a "policeman." To do this he had to set aside his sense of himself as a scientist born of years of experience working in a lab. When he did this, he temporarily lost his bearings, just as he lost himself. He was not a very good policeman, and did not enjoy the part at all. Still, he played it and became better at being a policeman over time because within the school both students and teachers understood and recognized as legitimate this subject position. But the policeman personae was ill fitting.

The first beginning teacher lacked a clear sense of herself as teacher. The second had a sense of himself as teacher but it was not one that he could enact in the classroom. In the urban school culture within which he taught, he could not be who he thought he was as teacher. Perhaps more importantly, he did not possess the skills requisite for enactment of his sense of self as teacher. For each, teacher education failed to address questions of self-as-teacher. A programmatic emphasis on teaching skills had not prepared them to confront the most fundamental problem of teaching–finding and making place and expressing self in teaching.

Episode 7

Sitting in a colleague's office chatting, she suddenly realized that class was about to begin. After glancing at her watch, she looked up, smiled, and said to me, "time to put on my teaching mask." I asked: "You put on a mask?" "Yes, it's like playing a part. I have a teacher's face that I wear when teaching." She left, and I began to ponder what teaching was like for me and what sort of teacher I was.

Reflection

Over years of teaching, my friend had developed a studied professional personae that she easily moved in and out of. She knew her part and knew it and played it well, sometimes brilliantly. She also knew the other players. When teaching she had a teacher's voice; and a teacher's look. Having observed her teach on numerous occasions, I noticed the difference between when she was "on" and when she was "off" stage. Within the classroom she employed a wide range of instructional strategies. Sometimes she modeled what she would refer to as "best practice." She would tell stories, have students engage in group work, work on projects, read research, and arrange then process field trips. As teacher, I realized she played many parts. As I came to know and appreciate her, I realized that her teaching personae reflected a committed point of view, an identity through which was woven a set of fundamental principles. She knew who she was and how she wanted to be with others which was a source of power and influence. Other's responded to her as she wished them to; they recognized her as professor. She had developed a variety of skills to support her effort to be. She was one person but she had multiple personas into which she invested herself fully. Each personae that I knew was an expression of the underlying unity of self, a life's trajectory and moral force.

As I have thought about my colleague and friend and compared my experience with her's I have realized that only when I am uncomfortable and uncertain do I grab hold of a mask and then my self-expression is stilted and my humor strained. The quality of a laugh is the best witness of the authenticity of an expression. Perhaps because I am older than she, and age matters, I seem to have fewer personas, fewer parts to play. After years of professing, I am what I do. Perhaps my habit of self is stiffer and less pliable than her's, less open to surprise and less likely to change. One result is that I am quite resistant to institutional demands and related subject positions that feel snug, tight fitting. For good or ill, having a point of view and a sense of agency, an identity, makes resistance possible; but it also, I am well aware, presents the danger of fundamentalism, of being closed to contrary experience and unable to grasp opportunities to unlearn the world.

CONCLUSION

> This then is our liberation from objectivism: to realize that we can voice our ultimate convictions only from within our convictions–from within the whole system of acceptances that are logically prior to any particular assertion of our

> own, prior to the holding of any particular piece of knowledge. If an ultimate logical level is to be attained and made explicit, this must be a declaration of my personal beliefs. I believe that the function of philosophic reflection consists in bringing to light, and affirming as my own, the beliefs implied in such of my thoughts and practices as I believe to be valid; that I must aim at discovering what I truly believe in and at formulating the convictions which I find myself holding; that I must conquer my self-doubt, so as to retain a firm hold on this program of self-identification. (Polanyi, 1958, p. 267)

Six years ago I had occasion to make a portion of my principles public (Bullough, 1997), the "convictions," as Polanyi states, "which I find myself holding." They represent a piece of my quest for identity as I journeyed from being an alternative educator and reluctant "teacher" to becoming a teacher educator. I shall not repeat what I wrote, but I recommend the practice of going public with one's principles and of systematically putting them to the test which is what Polanyi means by his phrase, a "program of self-identification." Polanyi's warning about the danger of self-doubt to self-discovery is crucially important here. In our time, self-doubt expresses itself in many forms including in the inability to make commitments–and the commitments we make, how we are invested and in what we invest our lives, as I have suggested earlier, are good measures of the persons we are and of our moral standing. Indeed, one manifestation of postmodernism is the ability to shift commitments quickly and to hold multiple and sometimes contradictory commitments and none too deeply. This is one reason why I find inspiring many of the teachers I know: They overcome self-doubt by reaffirming each day their central commitment to children; through their practice, they utter the holy words, "I am."

Often teacher educators ask beginning teachers to write a personal philosophy. The assignment produces flights of fantasy but the real task at hand, as I have suggested, is to consider questions of identification and membership, subject location, rules and duties, and forms of self-expression and enactment. One must dig for data into the ground of one's being and to consider the life lived, the commitments made, the forms and expressions of personal identification and recognition employed—including those that produce anger and disappointment, and inspire joy—and the beliefs that animate and give direction to action. One also must consider one's desired way of being in the world that seeks full expression and invites but never compels bold action. For beginning and experienced teachers alike this is a critical but risky practice; still it ought to be a central concern of both preservice and inservice teacher education and, importantly, of teacher educators. We must not excuse ourselves. Whatever the arena, in teaching and in teacher education the medium is the message and the message is the teacher's life and being, how the teacher makes sense of the world and stands within it. Oddly, this is one focus for reflection that often has been ignored in the teacher education literature and practice yet it is the grounding of all that is important within the practice of teacher education. Perhaps this is so because inevitably to ask questions of this kind leads to sacred soil. In this chapter I have focused on three aspects of identity formation, *Identification and membership*, *Subject location with rules and duties*, and *Self-expression and enactment* and reflected on my own quest for identity as a teacher educator. The episodes are mine, as is the meaning I make of them. But I recognize that other meanings are also possible, other conclusions.

A warning is in order, however. Rather than lead to increasing moral action and greater courage of conviction, the habit of self-criticism can, like Jean-Baptiste Clamence in Camus' *The Fall*, leave behind a person frozen in inaction, lost to self and to others. In contrast, Polanyi's call is to act on the world, to be willing to put oneself at risk for the sake of the self and of the world. Such acts, usually based on only partial information or mere hunches and sometimes only on the judgements embedded in our emotions, point toward the heroic nature of the quest for identity.

A final thought. In some respects, identity might be thought of as a tendency toward the good, a quiet desire. In teaching, personal tendencies dress up and masquerade as authorized conceptions of the good, including judgements about the nature of those we teach. Discovering one's tendencies and uncovering one's pretenses is serious and humbling educational work. We recognize ourselves as deeply and inevitably contradictory creatures. Humility restrains our reproductive urge, the temptation to try and impose our identities on others, to colonize unto death another's personhood. Yet, we know, deep down, that colonization is not even possible let alone desirable and inevitably confront a simple truth: Education is always indirect and its results unpredictable. But in unpredictability resides hope—the possibility that something impossibly wonderful might happen, the miracle of learning, of a student accepting our invitation to engagement and becoming over time more interesting, more centered, better grounded, and more able than are we. There is also opportunity—new subject positions can be created, ones that invite communion inside of the academy and ever fuller expressions of human excellence. Facing my limitations draws me further inward to a deep desire, a longing widely shared by teachers—to enable for others what I seek most for myself: to discover and fully express what the ancient Greeks described as arete, one's particular and peculiar form of virtue or excellence, to be one's own best, that so concerned Socrates. To discover the virtue of self we need to witness virtue in others and in its many and various expressions. This is the teacher's testimony. Through such encounters we come to see that arete is possible, that there is a point to the quest for meaning even as there may not be a fully satisfying conclusion—a fully stable identity. Through identification with questing others, through being allowed—or insisting that we be allowed (and allowing our students)—to occupy subject positions that sustain the quest, and through courageously expressing, investing in, and testing our sense of ourselves, we achieve ourselves for ourselves and for others. The challenge is to remain teachable, open, but not too open, to contrary data, and to stay in touch with the world, and to stay in touch requires staying deeply invested in those we teach and with those with whom we live and work.

1. The full Dewey quote follows: 'That which can be measured is the specific, and that which is specific is that which can be isolated. The prestige of measurements in physical science should not be permitted to blind us to a fundamental educational issue: How far is education a matter of forming specific skills and acquiring special bodies of informatino which are capable of isolated treatment? It is no answer to say that a human being is always occupied in acquring a special skill or a special body of facts, if he is learning anything at all. This is true. But the *educational* issue is what *other* things in the way of desires, tasts, aversions, abilities and disabilities he is learning along with his specific acquisitions' (1929, pp. 64–65).

REFERENCES

Boice, R. (1991). New faculty as teachers. *Journal of Higher Education, 62*(2), 149–173.

Boice, R. (1996). *First-order principles for college teachers*. Bolton, MA: Anker Publishing Company, Inc.

Bullough, R.V., Jr. (1982). Professional schizophrenia: Teacher education in confusion. *Contemporary Education, 53*(4), 207–212.

Bullough, R.V., Jr. (1989). *First year teacher: A case study.* New York: Teachers College Press.

Bullough, R.V., Jr. (1992). Beginning teacher curriculum decision making, personal teaching metaphors, and teacher education. *Teaching and Teacher Education, 8*(3), 239–252.

Bullough, R.V., Jr. (1997). Practicing theory and theorizing practice in teacher education. In J. Loughran and T. Russell (Eds.). *Teaching about teaching: Purpose, passion and pedagogy in teacher education*, (pp. 13–31). Washington, D.C.: The Falmer Press.

Bullough, R.V., Jr. (2001). *Uncertain lives: Children of promise, teachers of hope.* New York: Teachers College Press.

Bullough, R.V., Jr., & Knowles, J.G. (1990). Becoming a teacher: The struggles of a second-career beginnng teacher. *International Journal of Qualitative Studies in Education, 3*(2), 101–112.

Bullough, R.V., Jr., Goldstein, S.L., & Holt, L. (1984). *Human interests and the curriculum: Teaching and learning in a technological society*. New York: Teachers College Press.

Bullough, R.V., Jr., Knowles, J.G., & Crow, N.A. (1991). *Emerging as a teacher*. New York and London: Routledge.

Bullough, R.V., Jr., Clark, D.C., & Patterson, R.S. (2003). Getting in step: Accountability, accreditation and the standardization of teacher education in the United States. *Journal of Education for Teaching, 29*(1), 35–52.

Darling-Hammond, L., & Youngs, P. (2002). Defining "highly qualified teachers": What does "scientifically-based research" actually tell us? *Educational Researcher, 31*(9), 13–25.

Dewey, J. (1929). The sources of a science of education. New York: Macmillan.
Feldman, A. (2003). Validity and quality in self-study. *Educational Researcher, 32*(3), 26–28.
Gergen, K.J. (1991). *The saturated self: Dilemmas of identity in contemporary life.* New York: Basic Books.
Glass, J.M. (1993). *Shattered selves: Multiple personality in a postmodern world.* Ithaca, NY: Cornell University Press.
Goodlad, J.I. (1990). *Teachers for our nation's schools.* San Francisco: Jossey-Bass.
Hansen, D.T. (1995). *The call to teach.* New York: Teachers College Press.
Harre, R., & van Langenhove, L. (Eds.). (1999). *Positioning theory.* Oxford: Blackwell Publishers.
Holmes Group. (1995). *Tomorrow's schools of education.* East Lansing: Author.
Lewis, C. S. (1944/1996). *The abolition of man.* New York: Touchstone.
McCall, W.A. (1922). *How to measure in education.* New York: Macmillan.
Mills, C.W. (1959). *The sociological imagination.* New York: Oxford University Press.
Mooney, R.L. (1957). The researcher himself. *Research for curriculum development*, (pp. 154–186). Washington, D.C.: Association for Supervision and Curriculum Development.
Murphy, J.W. (1989). *Postmodern social analysis and criticism.* New York: Greenwood Press.
Palmer, P. (1998). *The courage to teach: Exploring the inner landscape of a teacher's life.* San Francisco: Jossey-Bass Publishers.
Patterson, D. (1991). The eclipse of the highest in higher education. *The Main Scholar: A Journal of Ideas and Public Affairs, 4*, 7–20.
Polanyi, M. (1958). *Personal knowledge: Towards a post-critical philosophy.* Chicago: University of Chicago Press.
Taubman, P.M. (1992). Achieving the right distance. In W.F. Pinar and W.M. Reynolds (Eds.), *Understanding curriculum as phenomenological and deconstructed text*, (pp. 216–236). New York: Teachers College Press.
Wenger, E. (1999). *Communities of practice: Learning, meaning, and identity.* New York: Cambridge University Press.

Chapter 14

Identity Development, Moral Authority and the Teacher Educator

Stefinee Pinnegar
Brigham Young University, USA

The other parts of this book have spoken to the tangible issues of assessing the quality of a teacher education program. This chapter now speaks to the issues of the teacher educator's identity development. In this chapter I will consider the context where I teach and the impact this has on my own identity as a teacher educator; then, I will consider the ways in which attention to my moral authority as a teacher educator enables me to support the development of the identity of preservice teachers, and finally I will consider the potential confounding relationships of reciprocal identity development for adolescent public school students, teachers, and teacher educators. Key to the awareness of my own identity development is the process of self-study as a recommended professional practice for teacher educators and preservice students.

Aubusson (Chapter 3) not only captures well the issues of secondary teacher education in his context, his account articulates the issues at Brigham Young University where I have been a teacher educator since 1992. During that time, my own identity as a teacher educator has been influenced by three reform efforts in secondary education. We are currently in the third. Having spent three years away from campus working on a special project, my own voice in the current reform effort is minimal and my connection is distant. Aubusson outlines a program similar to ours with similar concerns and disconnects. In his context, I would be one of those generic teacher educators that "deliver" bits and pieces of teacher education preparation, such as educational psychology, school and society, or diversity courses rather than the methods for teaching the discipline that seem more central in his account. As I discuss teacher education at my institution, I will analyze the implications for my own role and its implications for my identity as a teacher educator.

G. Hoban (ed.), The Missing Links in Teacher Education Design, 259–279.

MY OWN IDENTITY DEVELOPMENT AS A GENERIC TEACHER EDUCATOR

Being a "generic" teacher educator means that I am assigned within a department of teacher education to teach courses that secondary preservice teachers must complete for graduation and certification. I am not currently part of designing or implementing any of the larger frames of the program, nor do I participate in student teaching supervision or cross disciplinary groups that have a say over the organization and content of the entire program.

Haare and van Langehoven (1999) argue that roles are not fixed but fluid, and that we negotiate the roles we assume. They suggest that in interaction with others, individuals and institutions, certain roles are made available for us to take up. In forming our identity, we respond to the space available by accepting, rejecting, or negotiating that role through the way we position ourselves in the space or shape the space to reflect our identity. MacIntyre (1997) claims that the way in which we individually make sense of who we are is through our ability to create a coherent narrative of self. This account connects the fluid and divergent positions we assume. It establishes connection and coherence in tracing the history that brought us to this place. Importantly for this account, it also honors and makes sense of the contradictory and contrasting obligations, rights, and duties of these fluid positions, roles, or identities. This narrative is a lived as well as a spoken one. It is the lived aspect of the narrative based in our negotiations in our current positioning efforts that undergirds these negotiations and makes them feel coherent to us as we take up or reject various positions available.

Our narrative reveals not only our identity formation but also its coherence. Bullough (Chapter 13) creates an account of his own identity formation that makes visible the ways in which he positioned himself as an individual across his career (from preservice teacher to teacher educator) to shape and form his fluid yet current identity as teacher educator. Tidwell (Tidwell & Fitzgerald, 2004) provides an account of the role of her students in shaping and forming her identity as a teacher within her role as a teacher educator. Schulte (2002) in examining interactions with her students and how they led her to establish a relationship in which she revealed her own vulnerability provides another such example. Richardson (1998) in using the tool of self-portrait creates an account that reveals the irony and ambiguity of her identity in relationship with her preservice teachers that mirrors what her students' self-portraits reveal about their own identity formation. Oda (1998) articulates the tension in accounting for identity across her childhood experience as an Asian-American and her experience as a multicultural teacher educator. What makes these studies resonate and establishes them as authentic to us is the familiar tension in accounting for and acting on the network of values, beliefs, epistemology and ontology that is the essence of self called "identity."

Repositioning in an Analysis of Context

In this account, I examine my analysis and negotiations with institutional constraints and reveal how this influences my identity formation as well as the identity formation of the preservice teachers I am educating. Thinking of my return to daily work at the university as a repositioning has given me a tool for considering my identity as a teacher educator and how to respond to enact the identity I claim as mine.

With this tool, I can consider what position has been made available, how I will take up that position, given the obligations, rights and duties and thus the role and identity I want to have. In an analysis of this context, I focus on three issues: faculty member's pedagogical understanding, the institutional organization and the role of the school of education.

University Faculty Understanding of Pedagogy

Like other students at the university, secondary preservice teachers start with general education requirements, followed usually by discipline specific coursework intended to deliver content expertise intermingled with or followed by teacher education coursework. Thus, the overwhelming weight of coursework in the university experience of preservice secondary teachers does not occur in interaction with me. In fact, I have direct control over the quality and content of about 1% of the experience. Yet, I have moral obligations concerning the quality and content of their education (for example see Holt-Reynolds 1994, to see the impact of content on the ability of preservice students ability to construct curriculum for their students). I feel a duty to try to impact decisions about the curriculum and experiences offered to and required of preservice teachers. I sense that it is my right to be engaged and involved in decisions about courses required, content provided, and the ordering of the curriculum experiences of preservice teachers from the beginning of their university experience.

Beyond giving me direct control of this 1% of coursework, the institution does not provide space for my voice to be heard or to influence curricular decisions and assessment in either general education or specific subject matters. Attempts on my part to simply take up such a position would seem presumptuous to most other faculty. It would appear to be a denial and constriction of their own identity as an administrator or faculty member and an infringement on their obligations, duties, and rights. It also seems to me to be an act of hubris to attempt to enact such control (Boote, 2003). Yet such a situation provides clear difficulties for my identity formation and honest enactment.

For example, when I first began here, I worked mostly with preservice English teachers. One of their English courses taught them a series of five to ten different theoretical perspectives and engaged them in using the perspectives to analyze texts. The text was written by BYU English faculty members and was one of the best critical theory summary texts available. This course gave preservice English teachers tools for considering how they would teach particular texts, the interpretive skills their students could learn, and the kind of curricular activities that would inform their students. It provided a rich basis for developing depth, variety, and purpose in their curricular planning as they considered whether to take a New Historicism, Postmodern, Formalist, Reader Response, Archetypal, or Feminist approach to a text. The English department deleted this course from the curriculum without requiring or providing options for something similar assuming it would be "covered" in the literature survey courses. The change became obvious to me only when I realized through curricular planning experiences with them that preservice English teachers no longer held those theoretical lenses that had been so valuable and useful to students who had taken the course. My dilemma was that while I felt an obligation to public school students to provide them with teachers who could consider curricular decisions using these lenses; yet the content needed for preservice teachers to function at that level was no longer available to them. Indeed, I thought I had the right to expect that the preservice teachers would come with such knowledge; yet I wondered if providing such discipline based knowledge could be defended as content in a general theory and methods course. I have similar quandries concerning the theoretical tools of interpretation, criticism, and problem solving analysis that I desire preservice teachers from history, fine arts, and the sciences to bring. Part of helping preservice teachers enact in curriculum and practice their obligations, assume their duties and demand their rights in meeting the needs of culturally, linguistically and learning diverse students requires such knowledge. When specific disciplines change the academic knowledge base of the students entering secondary teaching by changing course requirements or faculty teaching assignments, I wonder: what is my duty in providing such content knowledge clearly outside my immediate expertise and beyond the scope of my course? I wonder what recourse I as a single faculty member have to demand that the entire institution change the curriculum of preservice secondary teachers to enable me to fulfill my perceived and individual sense of moral obligation to preservice teachers and their students (Arizona Group, 1997, 1995).

A central feature of my identity as a teacher educator requires that I engage preservice teachers in the pedagogic practices that I want them to enact with their students. This includes the commitment I have made not to ask preservice teachers to teach in ways I do not practice. Another aspect is my belief that experiencing appropriate pedagogy during learning is the best way for preservice teachers to learn how to teach (Loughran, 1996). Yet, other university faculty control the pedagogic experience of the majority of the content provided those preparing to be teachers. The teacher education department provides less than 10% of the total content knowledge contributing to the education of a secondary teacher. Teacher education faculty in the specific departments usually have an even smaller share (usually less than 5%). In every case, cooperating teachers in public schools are responsible for a greater share of the pedagogic content of a future teacher's degree (about 8 or 9%). In the best situation, 80% or greater of a secondary preservice teacher's experience is controlled by people who have a minimal understanding of the coursework and content provided by education departments to prepare future teachers. Perhaps one or two students in one or two majors will be taught by university faculty who have knowledge of, or respect for, the importance of teacher education coursework as a component of their education to be teachers. Further, when a faculty member in biology feels their own children are not getting a good education in biology, they usually feel the fault lies with teacher education or the teacher, rather than their department or the university as a whole. Secondary preservice teachers' experience in content coursework can, indeed, be hostile territory for their education as teachers.

Within my identity as a teacher educator, I feel a duty to lead future teachers to embrace more constructivist models of teaching. Yet, most of the coursework preservice teachers take uses a transmission rather than a constructivist teaching model. As a result, the transmission model of teaching has a bright future in the classrooms of the secondary preservice teachers I prepare. Not only experience but their identity as a teacher is bound up in identification with their discipline. The majority of the content they learn will be delivered from this model. Further, they often choose teaching because a fundamental part of their identity is connected to a conception of themselves as a "history," "English," or "math" teacher. They love their subject and they want to work in it for the rest of their lives. They see teaching that subject in secondary schools as a sure way to do this and their conception of being a secondary teacher contains an image of themselves as the "sage on the stage" discussed so powerfully by Russell in his accounts of learning to teach as a teacher educator (e.g., Russell, 1995).

While elementary education majors may identity themselves as teachers, generically, secondary preservice teachers invariably modify "teacher" with the title of the subject matter they will teach. Because they spend so much time in courses taught from the transmission model, that pedagogic stance becomes a fundamental part of their identity and image of themselves as teacher. Bullough, Knowles, and Crow (1991) have clearly demonstrated the impact of metaphors and images of teaching on the practice of teachers. In fact, if I am honest, one of the difficulties I continually confront in my own teaching is a sense that if my Educational Psychology professors could see me teach in teacher education (since I seldom enact the sage on the stage stance), they would not consider me a "professor of educational psychology". More than once each semester, I am overcome with feelings that I am not a "true" professor of education because I use constructivist approaches to teaching and learning that engage preservice teachers in teaching themselves. Part of what contributes to the sense of vulnerability that self-study researchers like Schulte (2002) express is potentially this disjunct between images of our identity as professors and that of the inherent obligations, duties, and rights implicated in our identity as teacher educators.

Even more than most teachers in public schools, university faculty members are certain they taught themselves to teach (in most cases this is probably an accurate statement). They have little sense that teacher education could improve their teaching practice or that their students have much to learn from it. As a result, the university teachers who have first contact with future teachers have only a faint idea about pedagogy. They may have a disdain concerning the need for teacher education regardless of the quality of their own pedagogy. At our institution a few coherent efforts contribute to change in this regard. Through the Center for the Improvement of Teacher Education and Schooling (CITES) in connection with the BYU/Public School Partnership, faculty members across campus have participated in study groups and partnership projects that have educated them about pedagogy and connected them to teacher education. Another effort is participation with the Carnegie Foundation initiative on the scholarship of teaching. These faculty members think differently about teaching and the role, purpose and potential of teacher education.

Furthermore, the current debates in history, art, math and science around the characteristics of knowledge and the value of particular kinds of knowledge have led university faculty to think differently about their own pedagogic obligations to their students.

Finally, an increased attention to institutional assessment has educated university faculty about issues of teacher preparation. Our university assessment committee provides internal and external reviews of the quality of departments. In departments that have teaching majors or provide service courses for elementary education, the faculty review committee evaluates the quality of a department's participation in teacher education. In preparing these departmental reviews, the faculty must confront the quality of the teacher education candidates they educate and the role of their own courses in preparing teachers. Deficits in the quality of these programs require that the department address the issues. CITES, Scholarship of Teaching, and Institutional assessment educate university faculty members about teacher education and invite them to take on the identity of teacher educator as part of their faculty role. However, such increased concern about their identity as a teacher educator does not mean they see more value in my role. In fact, my sense of obligation, duty and rights and their own sense of these things may collide. Since as they become more invested in an identity as both professor in a subject matter area and as a teacher educator, they may see my role as a teacher educator as peripheral and superfluous. Again, I am confronted with decisions about how to negotiate my identity position: how do I fulfill my obligations, enact my duties and embrace my rights as teacher educator in ways that welcome and value other university faculty's heightened sense of their own role in educating future teachers, particularly since another part of my identity as a teacher educator is my belief that things are learned best in context. Just as I desire that preservice teachers experience with me the pedagogic and curricular practices I advocate, I would also like them to have such experiences in all of their university education.

INSTITUTIONAL STRUCTURES AND THE IDENTITY DEVELOPMENT OF PRESERVICE TEACHERS

During the time that preservice teachers' primary attention is focused on meeting the content coursework requirements for teacher certification, they begin teacher education coursework and move through it to student teaching. In our university, that can proceed in one of three ways: subject matter department control, laissez-faire control, or school of education control. Each design has implications for my identity as a teacher educator.

Subject Matter Department Control

In the first situation, the subject matter department has an active and committed teacher education faculty who feel they have and should have primary control and authority in the matter of preparing teachers for secondary schools. The timing, arrangement, and engagement of the preservice teachers who my identity requires that I assume obligations for, duties towards, and demand rights from education are in their hands. The department based teacher educators feel they have, and should have, control over meeting obligations, enacting duties, and embracing the full rights of teacher preparation in their discipline. While on occasion they interact with teacher educators in the School of Education, they live in the colleges and departments they represent, and their primary connections and alliances are there. Regardless of how I feel about my role as a teacher educator, at my institution these discipline based teacher educators seldom perceive me or other secondary teacher education faculty members located in the school of education as equivalent in status; nor do they grant that the obligations, duties, and rights of these faculty members are similar to their own. During reform efforts, while they often respect the thinking and ideas of individual faculty members, the teacher education faculty, located in the disciplines, do not grant secondary teacher educators in the school of education the right to question and shape the secondary teacher education program in their discipline.

From past reform experiences, I often have a sense that when my colleagues from other departments speak to me passionately about their secondary teacher education program that they see their own role as primary. School of education coursework is generally perceived by them as disconnected from their effort, delivered from a philosophy of pedagogy different from their own, and as hoops students must jump through but not content actually germane to the preparation of teachers in their disciplines. In this arrangement, no matter how passionately I feel about teacher education, I am likely to be considered irrelevant and not really a companion or potential ally. This perception changes somewhat as relationships and trust with these faculty members are built one person at a time and across multiple years of experience. Even then this respect does not generalize to all school of education faculty engaged in teacher education but is granted on a person-by-person and experience-by-experience basis.

Laissez Faire Control

A second organization, while rarer than when I first came to the university, is one I would characterize as laissez faire parenting or benign neglect. In this case, either the department long ago hired theoreticians to replace the teacher educators in the department and the department chair or the assistant chair is responsible for overseeing the content and quality of method preparation in the department or a single faculty member is responsible for teacher education in the department. Often this faculty member is more engaged in and committed to the subject matter and enacts the teacher educator role as jovial uncle (or aunt). In each of these cases (where administrators or a kind but disinterested single faculty member control the program), students are given a list of coursework requirements and the timing, arrangement, and engagement in preservice teacher education are primarily in the hands of the preservice teacher. The preservice teachers' educated in these departments experience teacher education as an independent negotiation of a series of courses. How can I enact the obligations and duties and establish the rights my identity as a teacher educator requires?

School of Education Control

A third organization is one where the preparation of secondary teachers is housed completely in the department of teacher education. In this case, preservice secondary teachers feel that their departments have no say in or responsibility for their preparation as secondary teachers. Usually, preservice teachers in these disciplines are further along in their coursework before they turn their attention to teacher education; or they complete their teacher education coursework early in their academic career and we have no contact with them until they appear to apply for student teaching. Within the department specific faculty members are positioned as the teacher educators of these students, while my ability to enact the moral aspects of my identity as a teacher educator is expanded, the moral commitments that undergird my identity as a teacher educator and the arena for my action on them is often as restricted.

The Role of School of Education Faculty and Conceptual Coherence

Given these three main and quite different routes through secondary teacher education certification, students' experiences of their teacher education programs vary radically. However, in almost none of these scenarios do they view teacher education faculty housed in a school of education as central to their education as teachers.

Standing in this position has been, and continues to be, morally difficult for me. In the current reform plan and climate, this will continue to be my position. Institutionally, my role is to teach a single course collaboratively designed to be interchangeably placed in each individual teacher education program, which while it agrees to attend to similar competency standards, is fueled by the dreams, beliefs, and ideology of teacher education held by others. Thus, while I feel the obligations, duties, and rights of being a teacher educator, my ability to impact on the quality of teachers educated at my own institution is problematic and places me in the position of agitator rather than participant. My analysis of my role has always filled me with deep humility concerning the impact I can make on the practice of an individual student teacher (Boote, 2003). I can hope that in such a position I can "trouble" teacher education in productive ways; but it also means that I occupy an institutionally defined and constrained oppositional role. While the agitation I produce may result in the production of a pearl, I am reminded that pearls form around the agitating agent rather than causing any change to the clam.

As self-study researchers can attest, it is often a personal Herculean task to make certain that what we say we believe, we enact in our own teaching. A corollary task over which we have even less control is whether our students interpret their experience with us according to the conceptual framework we have proposed.

But secondary teacher education, at least at my institution, involves preservice teachers in experiences with others in addition to me. We can mandate, organize, and routinize the ways in which institutions will relate to each other politically and procedurally, but we can never hope that individuals involved in teacher education will be able to completely share belief systems. Nor is it likely that such systems can be organized, managed, controlled or coordinated. Brigham Young University, a private university funded by a single religious entity (the Church of Jesus Christ of Latter-day Saints) places students in public schools where public school faculty are also likely to share the same religion (over 75% of the teachers in local schools are members of this faith). As a result, one might assume that coherence of belief is less a problem than it is at public institutions; yet, personal experience suggests that this is not always true.

MORAL AUTHORITY AND THE IDENTITY DEVELOPMENT OF PRESERVICE TEACHERS

A purpose of this book is to support teacher educators in analyzing their own programs attending to the "missing links" that result in problematic disconnects between the vision of a program and how it is experienced or the conceptual coherence. Such conceptual coherence is vital if teacher education is to impact the development of future teachers. Research in teacher education and various accreditation processes (NCATE or TEAC for example) underscore the importance of this fact.

Thus, conceptual coherence—the coherence and continuity of a students' experience in learning about teaching and learning—can seldom be uniformly maintained. Models, philosophies, and methods will never be completely coherent with either each other or the program model promoted. Each boundary a student crosses is represented by both individuals and institutions which have ideologies, belief systems, moral conceptions of schooling that are potentially at odds with each other. Each teacher educator brings an identity as a teacher educator that individually resolves these conflicts; but while it may be congruent with others is also idiosyncratic. In teacher education (as in other university programs), these issues of differences in teacher educator identity are silenced rather than resolved in reform meetings and efforts. These are foundational issues in promoting a conceptual framework for teacher preparation. Of course, even when there is some coordination, students may still personally experience the program as incoherent. This will always be true when these issues are not discussed clearly within programs, and where programs do not place teacher educators in primary positions to set the conceptual framework, where teacher educators are not involved with students as they negotiate the inevitable differences in these frameworks and where more than one other person works with the student teacher.

While I believe my identity is central in my work as a teacher educator and for the quality and impact of experiences students have with me, I also know that in my current position as a teacher educator my identity will not be systemically visible nor uniformly supported during students experience in teacher education. I have little institutional authority for uniformly controlling the experience preservice teachers have in developing as teachers; and therefore, there is great difficulty in enacting my beliefs as a teacher educator throughout their experience. In order to have an impact on preservice teachers development, I must look for other sources of authority that can influence my students as they negotiate the institutional, philosophic, and conceptual boundaries of secondary teacher education. Also, this authority must be able to travel in multiple directions so that in this moment what they experience with me has the power to lead to a reconceptualization of past experience, reevaluation of current experience and revisioning of future experience.

We know as teacher educators that who students are as teachers will emerge from who they are as people (Bullough, 1997). We know that students quite often maintain a Teflon shield as they move through teacher education coursework (Holt-Reynolds, 1992, 1994). They can demonstrate the competencies we request, but they may or may not embrace the philosophies and ideologies that undergird and give a particular coherence to those actions. As a teacher educator, I am always concerned about the moral heart of the teachers I am educating (see Hansen, 2001). Yet, I have and probably ought to have little control over the heart. More troubling to me, however, is the question of how much influence I have over educating, informing, or influencing the development of that heart. As teacher educators, we only gain influence on lived conceptual experience when we have the trust of our students and they look to us to speak with moral authority on their past and current experiences in classrooms and on their development as a teacher.

It is not so much a matter of making certain that all participants (university content teachers, teacher education curriculum, foundations, diversity, and educational psychology teachers, subject matter and teacher education departments, school district, state agencies, school level administrators, department missions and goals, and individual cooperating teachers) share the same ideology as it is to position oneself as a teacher educator so that you share preservice teachers' dilemmas in negotiating these boundaries. *Teacher educators need to develop the kinds of relationships that potentially make us a central figure in the private and personal considerations of preservice teachers concerning their beliefs about the obligations, duties, and rights of teachers.* It also requires a particular kind of personal humility which honors preservice teacher's agency in determining their own future as a teacher and an honesty rather than arrogance about the importance of one's own knowledge and power in the institution.

While teacher educators may be able to politically position themselves in such roles, they will have different levels of success in positioning themselves to have moral authority in these roles. One need only examine the literature on the impact of multicultural education, social justice, or diversity curriculum on the identity and belief systems of preservice teachers to understand the difficulty of gaining such a position (Zeichner & Hoeft, 1996; Boote, 2003).

Moral authority is based on trust, respect and support. It requires individual teachers to be trustworthy, deserving of respect, and provide appropriate support for student learning and development. Indeed most teachers think of themselves as having moral authority even if they are morally bankrupt. Lack of moral authority is not a sin we can always or easily see in ourselves. As a result positioning oneself to be accorded moral authority by students actually means positioning oneself in a role of great vulnerability. While it is necessary for garnering moral authority, acting in trustworthy and supportive ways that should elicit respect, is always open to the interpretation of students. When teacher educators speak truth to students or try to support their development, the students may not experience what is done as either truthful or supportive. Furthermore, regardless of student experience of the event, the more important point is that the preservice teacher is completely in control of whether or not moral authority is accorded to the teacher educator (Hamilton & Pinnegar, 2000). The preservice teachers own level of moral authority may be a factor as well.

Not long ago, I found myself in conversation with a preservice teacher one semester from student teaching. In every interaction, the preservice teacher blamed the teacher educator for the preservice teacher's poor performance and insisted "everyone else felt the same way." Recognizing that if the preservice teacher was so consistently blaming in our interactions, she would also be blaming in her interactions with her students, my obligation to both her development and the development of her future students required that I point out her defensiveness and refusal to accept responsibility for her learning. I struggled with the decision to take action because of the negative impact it might have on her as well as other preservice teachers in the course and because I also recognized that her critique could be accurate and fair. Finally, talking to her and other students and analyzing my own duplicity, I felt compelled to speak.

This was not a pleasant conversation. I think the preservice teacher accepted what I said and she did think seriously about her behavior and ameliorated it in her interactions with me. However, I am uncertain whether she accepted my moral authority to discuss the issue, and I doubt that she would seek me out as she faces additional difficulty in her student teaching based on this attitude and disposition. I was able to move her development forward and impact her thinking at a single moment in time, but unless she seeks me out, the end of the course signals our last interaction around issues of her development of a teaching identity. Guiding this kind of learning is a cyclic process, whereby one watches, responds, watches, responds. Deep changes where learning is repentance usually do not occur in just one cycle.

One of the ironies of secondary teacher education is that while we attempt to shape and support the development of a teaching identity in our preservice teachers; we are preparing them to teach students whose primary developmental task is identity development. Furthermore, often preservice teachers, for the most part in their early twenties (at least at my institution), are engaged at some level in the resolution of their identity.

Developmental Tasks of Adolescence

The primary developmental tasks of adolescents include developing autonomy and identity and preparing for intimacy (Steinberg, 2000). Adolescents must be able to act autonomously emotionally, socially, economically, and intellectually. They must develop an identity which realistically represents their own choice, talent and action. This is of paramount importance if they are to develop the capability of appropriately engaging in close, open, honest intimate relationships with others in their lives. In completing these three tasks successfully, students position themselves to be healthy, contributing members of society (Clausen, 1993). Their teachers may have the greatest opportunity and potential to support them in their identity development.

In our culture, adolescent development, like the identity development of a beginning teacher and that of a teacher educator, is negotiated against a fragmented and potentially disconnected social climate. A junior high or high school student routinely negotiates the boundaries of seven classrooms, lunch period, and after school activities. They move across boundaries where in some situations they are viewed as adolescents (or sometimes children) and given support or at least allowance for their development. In other situations, they are considered independent and functioning young adults and expected to act appropriately. They have the freedom, economic resources, and independence to engage in very adult activities with adult expectations. As a result, adolescents often experience their adolescence as a time of "living a double life" (Garrod, et al., 2002).

In addition, given the rise in divorce rates and the increase in diversity, they may be routinely expected to negotiate more than one family structure or culture with finesse. People and institutions that interact with adolescents hold expectations for their behavior. These expectations are seldom, if ever, clearly communicated and they are never uniform across boundaries. One teacher may expect childish, others adolescent, and still others adult behavior. Furthermore, while adolescents are working to develop an identity, they are also growing and changing in fundamental ways physically, cognitively, and socially.

Yet, achieving identity requires being able to create a coherent account of one's behavior across settings and encounters in ways that provide a uniform and rational explanation of how in each interaction the response is coherent (MacIntyre, 1997). Research increasingly shows that adolescence has been expanded in length in our society in both directions so that while young people may enter early adolescents as young as nine they may not emerge as young adults until after their mid to late twenties (and sometimes not until they reach 30) (Cotterell, 1996).

Identity Development and Teaching Practice

Goodlad (1984) argued that in our current society schools and homes provide the primary support for the development of young people and that as the stability of the home continues to erode the schools are called upon to play even more central roles. Nowhere is this more important than in the lives of secondary students.

It is into this mix that beginning secondary teachers step. They are expected to hit the ground running as autonomous human beings, with a clear sense of their identity as a person and a teacher, and with the ability to engage in and maintain appropriate intimate teacher-student relationships. Yet, in teacher education we rarely if ever attend to their development in completing the tasks of autonomy, identity, and intimacy as humans (Erikson, 1980) or even more specifically in their development of an identity as a teacher.

As we prepare teachers for today's schools, teacher educators usually focus more on preservice teachers 'competency than their identity, even though we understand that the teachers' identity fuels their behavior and development as teachers. Those teacher education programs in the United States that seek NCATE accreditation, create assessment systems that evaluate preservice teacher performance across their experience in teacher education. This means we assess preservice teachers competence rather than teach them to be competent. Furthermore such structures attend to the behavior of teachers rather than their hearts. What we communicate to preservice teachers are increasingly complex systems of accountability and judgment, which look like performance checklists—lists of discrete and unconnected behaviors.

We may fail to realize that preservice teachers can potentially meet with excellence each item on the checklist, without the belief and philosophy on which the checklist item was based ever becoming part of their teaching personna. Many may argue that as long as we get good performance (they can display and do display the competencies requested) does it matter whether or not our work with them supports or connects to their identity development as a person or a teacher? Such a stance marks differences between my identity as a teacher educator and that of many others, since a commitment of my identity is to teachers' stance, habit and manner and not just their classroom performance.

AWARENESS OF THE RECIPROCITY OF IDENTITY DEVELOPMENT

In order to understand why the development of identity as a teacher matters, we must return to our earlier discussion of moral authority. Just as a teacher educator's moral authority can guide the development of preservice teachers, so a teacher who can speak with moral authority can guide and support the development of adolescent learners. In order to learn, students must trust their teachers. They must respect them and feel confident that if they do as the teacher asks they will progress in their learning and in their lives (Pinnegar & Carter, 1990; Pinnegar, 1989). This trust can be limited or broad in scope. The following statements represent a potential range of such judgments: "I trust this teacher implicitly." "I trust this teacher knows history." "I trust this teacher likes people and tries hard."

A teacher develops relationships where students can trust both in terms of what is required to learn the content and what is required to develop as human being to the degree that the teacher is capable of having appropriate open, honest intimate relationships. What this statement argues is the preservice teachers must have content knowledge and pedagogic skill that students can have confidence in [note such accountability pertains to the teacher educator as well]. However, to truly support the learning and development of students, preservice teachers must be capable of intimacy. As Erikson's (1980) model demonstrates, the ability to engage in and develop appropriate intimate relationships emerges after identity is established. Just as this is true for general human development, it is also true for development of identity as a teacher.

My own reading of the literature on teacher development (e.g., Munby, Russell, & Martin, 2001; Richardson & Palcier, 2001; Richardson, 1996; Sprinthall, Reiman, & Theis-Sprinthall, 1996) leads me to conclude that we know little about either how our students are positioned in their identity as teachers when they join our programs or how they are positioned when they leave. We know they have unrealistic optimism about their ability at every turn in their development (Woolfolk & Hoy, 1990). We know they are generally more altruistic than other students (Brookhart & Freeman, 1992) and thus, usually, have appropriately caring dispositions. We know that they enter teaching with metaphors that will guide their development (Bullough, 1992). Our programs may indeed on occasion elicit commentary or assignments that reveal some of these issues; but engaging directly in identity development with our students may sound more like therapy than education for a profession (Boote, 2003). Yet, the development of a teaching identity is vital to action in teaching.

As teacher educators, we must be clean in our own action if we expect to have moral authority over our students and promote their development. We must be humble and trustworthy in our interactions with not only the preservice teachers but also our colleagues who are part of the process of teacher education (Boote, 2003). What strikes my heart as I write are deep questions about my own development. I wonder at my ability to have open honest intimate relationships with my students. I wonder about the power and coherence of my own identity as a person and as a teacher educator. I wonder about my autonomy to act appropriately as a teacher educator in spite of the institutional constraints I experience.

When our focus in preparing teachers is that they meet competency standards, the very processes of evaluation and assessment we engage them in may lead preservice teachers to distance themselves (their identity) from the process. When such preservice teachers enter classrooms having distanced themselves from teaching and as teachers, they give up their potential to have moral authority over their students. Learners, at any level, recognize that emotional distance and it reduces the learners' ability to trust a teacher and the potential for a teacher (or teacher educator) to have maximum impact on the learning and development of the student.

As Bullough's chapter in this book clearly demonstrates, identity development as a teacher educator and in the role of teaching and teacher is not a once and for all issue. It involves a fluid positioning and the assigning of roles to others. As we engage young adults in preparing as teachers, their identity development as a human, as well as a teacher, may be in flux, and how they position us as their teacher educators matters. For it is in their positioning of us in relationship to their preparation as a teacher that holds the most promise for our ability to improve the quality of teaching. Davies and Harre (1999) are instructive on this point:

> Accordingly who one is, that is, what sort of person one is, is always an open question with a shifting answer depending upon the positions made available within one's own and others' discursive practices and within those practices the stories through which we make sense of our own and other's lives" (p. 35).

What this quote suggests is that we as teacher educators may not concern ourselves sufficiently with questions about what positions we allow preservice teachers to take up or how we communicate, through the discursive practices of teacher education, the obligations, rights, and duties of teachers and how we attend to our own.

We know that just offering preservice teachers the opportunity to take up positions that enable them to develop identity as a teacher may not be sufficient for them to take up those positions. We must consider carefully and analytically first our own identity formation and then our attention to the "missing links" articulated in this book. We must ask whether our experiences with preservice teachers continually reposition them in the ways that are most likely to support them in developing autonomy and identity and as a result make them capable of developing and engaging in appropriate intimate relationships with others in their identity as a teacher.

We might consider whether their university coursework makes them autonomous in terms of their ability to both display and help others develop knowledge of the content they will teach. We might consider whether they know how to act autonomously in a classroom (or are they forever feeling positioned as adjunct to a teacher rather than as an actor as a teacher). We might question whether they are prepared to interact autonomously in the obligations teachers have for student development and interaction with parents. We might concern ourselves with whether or not the things they learn about student learning and development transfer into the designs they make for schools, for assignments, for their professional responsibilities as teachers. As preservice teachers develop autonomy in these areas and become confident in their ability to enact these roles, they also develop the ability to position themselves as teachers and assume an appropriate teaching identity. However, if in the process of teacher education, this positioning is only procedural display rather than action connected to their beliefs and dispositions—their commitment to righteous interaction with their students. We must continually be concerned about the discursive practices of teacher education and wonder not only whether we provide opportunity for preservice teachers to develop autonomy as a teacher, but whether we engage them in discursive practices that allow them to explore, question, and enact such positions in their identity as teacher.

We have evidence that preservice teachers have granted us moral authority when they embrace and enact the practice and theories we have taught them in other settings. We have evidence when we get phone calls from student teachers struggling in student teaching. They ask us to come watch their worst class and help them solve their difficulties. We get notes from former students that say, "Teaching in rural Idaho is hard. When my students are unkind, I remember how you were with us and I try to act the same way. Your example has helped me be a good teacher when I just wanted to give up." In that moment of seeing evidence of our moral authority, we are humbled and made vulnerable and we recommit to teacher education.

CONCLUSION

When a preservice teacher grants either an individual teacher educator or the institution preparing them moral authority for guiding their development as a teacher, then teacher educators have the greatest potential for impacting the belief, behavior, thinking, and development of teaching prowess. What this means is that teachers educators must be present as well as care about the critical events and learning of the preservice teacher's autonomy, identity, and intimacy development. Yet, few teacher education programs consistently use discursive practices that allow for such positioning. We seldom have consistent assignments, interactions, or experiences that have the power to reveal or provide opportunity to attend to such issues.

Indeed, we may be preparing teachers who can display competent teaching behaviors but who have faulty and immature conceptions concerning their obligations, duties, and rights as a teacher. Our programs practices and field experiences may not allow preservice teachers to successfully position themselves in appropriate teaching roles. Insecure in their own identity as a teacher, these beginning teachers may not develop discursive practices that support students in positioning themselves to successfully complete their identity development.

Furthermore, we as teacher educators need to examine our own beliefs and values as well as the way in which we enact them with our students. We must wonder if we present in our interaction with them the loving, open, honest communication we want them to engage in with their students. We must wonder if we take seriously our obligation to prepare and present the best knowledge for teaching. We must consider deeply with a willingness to change our practice (both action and belief) our own interactions in teacher education those with preservice teachers, public school teachers and administrators, teacher educators located elsewhere on our campuses, and faculty in the arts and sciences. We must also be as active as possible in construction and alteration of the systems and programs that educate perservice teachers. We must seriously and continuously attend to function and dysfunction in our teacher education programs and in our own action as teacher educators. All of this is part of serious attention to our own identity as a teacher educator which can be achieved through ongoing engagement in self-study as a teacher educator (Hamilton & Pinnegar, 2000). This professional approach to the role of a teacher educator holds the greatest potential for supporting preservice teachers in their own identity development.

At the end of this chapter, I wonder what positions I allow my preservice teachers to take up? How do I position them and how am I positioned by them? Most importantly, is my quest to understand my identity as a teacher educator both healthy and sufficiently robust to permit me to respond appropriately to their positioning attempts and allow me to speak with moral authority to them?

REFERENCES

Arizona Group: Guilfoyle, K., Hamilton, M.L., & Pinnegar, S. (1997). Obligations to unseen children. In J. Loughran and T. Russell (Eds.). *Teaching about teaching: Purpose, passion, and pedagogy in teacher education* (pp. 183–209). London: Falmer Press.

Arizona Group: Pinnegar, S., Guilfoyle, K., Hamilton, M.L., Placier, P. (1995). Becoming teachers of teachers: Alternative paths expressed in beginners' voices. In F. Korthagen and T. Russell (Eds.). Teachers *Who Teach Teachers: Reflections on teacher education* (pp. 35–55). London: Falmer Press.

Boote, D.N. (2003). Teacher educators as belief-and-attitude therapists: Exploring psychodynamic implications of an emerging role. *Teachers and teaching: Theory and practice, 9*(3), 257–277.

Bullough, R.V., Jr. (1992). Beginning teachers curriculum decision making, personal teaching metaphors, and teacher education. *Teaching and Teacher Education, 9*, 385–396.

Bullough, R.V., Jr. (1997). Becoming a teacher: Self and the social location of teacher education In B.J. Biddle, T.L. Good, & I.F. Goodson (Eds.), *International handbook of teachers and teaching* (pp. 79–134). Boston: Kluwer Academic Publishers.

Bullough, R.V., Jr., Knowles, G., & Crow, N.A. (1991). *Emerging as a teacher.* London: Routledge.

Clausen, J.A. (1993). *American lives: Looking back at the children of the depression.* New York: Free Press.

Cotterell, J. (1996). *Social networks and social influences in adolescence.* London: Routledge.

Davies, B., & Harre, R. (1999). Positioning and personhood, In R. Harre & L. van Langenhoven (Eds.). *Positioning theory*, (pp. 32–51). Malden, MA: Blackwell Publishers Inc.

Erikson, E. (1980). *Identity and the life cycle.* New York: Norton.

Garrod, A., Smulyan, L., Powers, S.I., & Kilkenny, R. (2002). *Adolescent portraits: Identity, relationships, challenges.* Boston: Allyn & Bacon.

Goodlad, J.I. (1984). *A place called school: Prospects for the future.* New York: McGraw-Hill Book Co.

Hansen, D. (2001). *Exploring the moral heart of teaching: Toward a teacher's creed. The moral heart of teaching.* New York: Teachers College Press.

Harre, R., & van Langenhoven, L. (1999) *Positioning theory* Malden MA: Blackwell Publishers, Inc.

Hamilton, M.L., & Pinnegar, S. (2000). On the threshold of a new century: Trustworthiness, integrity, and self-study in teacher education. *Journal of Teacher Education, 51*, 234–40.

Holt-Reynolds, D. (1992). Personal history-based beliefs as relevant prior knowledge in course work. *American Educational Research Journal, 29*, 325–49.

Holt-Reynolds, D. (1994). When agreeing with the professor is bad news for preservice teacher educators: Jeanneane, her personal history, and coursework. *Teacher Education Quarterly, 21*, 13–35.

Loughran, J.J. (1996). *Developing reflective practice: Learning about teaching and learning through modeling.* London: Falmer

MacIntyre, A. (1997). The virtues, the unity of a human life, and the concept of a tradition. In L.P Hinchman and S.K. Hinchman (Eds.). *Memory, identity, community: The idea of narrative in the human sciences* (pp. 241–263). New York: SUNY Press.

Munby, H., Russell, T., & Martin, A.K. (2001). Teachers' knowledge and how it develops. In V. Richardson (Ed.). *Handbook of research on teaching, (4th ed)* (pp. 877–905). Washington, DC: American Educational Research Association.

Oda, L.K. (1998). Harmony, conflict and respect: An Asian-American educator's self-study. In M.L. Hamilton (Ed.). *Reconceptualizing teaching practice* (pp. 113–123). London: Falmer Press.

Pinnegar, S.E. (1989). *Teachers' knowledge of students and classrooms.* Unpublished dissertation, University of Arizona, Tucson, AZ.

Pinnegar, S., & Carter, K. (1990). Comparing theories from textbooks and practicing teachers. *Journal of Teacher Education, 41*(1), 20–27.

Richards, J.C. (1998). Turning to the artistic: Developing an enlightened eye by creating teaching self-portraits. In M.L. Hamilton (Ed.), *Reconceptualizing teaching practice* (pp. 34–44). London: Falmer.

Richardson, V. (1996). The role of attitudes and beliefs in learning to teach. In J. Sikula (Ed.). *Handbook of research on teacher education* (pp. 102–119). New York: Macmillan LIBRARY Reference USA.

Richardson, V. & Placier, P. (2001). Teacher change. In V. Richardson (Ed.), *Handbook of research on teaching, (4th ed)* (pp. 905–950). Washington, DC: American Educational Research Association.

Russell, T. (1995). Returning to the physics classroom to re-think how one learns to teach physics In Russell, T. & Korthagen, F. (Eds.). *Teachers who teach teachers: Reflections on teacher education* (pp. 95–112). London: Falmer Press.

Schulte, A. (2002). Do as I say: A teacher educator reflects on her practice. In C. Kosnik, A. Freese, & A. Samaras (Eds.). *Making a difference in teacher education through self-study* (pp. 101–105): Herstmonceux IV, the fourth international conference on self-study of teacher education practices. Sussex, England. Toronto: OISE, University of Toronto.

Sprinthall, N.A., Reiman, A.J., & Thies-Sprinthall, L. (1996). Teacher professional development. In J. Sikula (Ed.). *Handbook of research on teacher education*, (pp. 666–703). New York: Macmillan LIBRARY Reference USA.

Steinberg, L. (2002). *Adolescence, (6th ed).* Dubuque IA: McGraw-Hill

Tidwell, D., & Fitzgerald, L. (2004). Self-study as teaching. In J.J. Loughran, M.L. Hamilton, V.K. LaBoskey and T.L. Russell (Eds.). *International Handbook of Self-Study of Teaching and Teacher Education Practice, Vol. 1.* (pp. 69–102). Dordrecht: Kluwer Academic Publishers.

Woolfolk, A.E., & Hoy, W.K. (1990). Prospective teachers' sense of efficacy and beliefs about control. *Journal of Educational Psychology, 82*, 81–91.

Zeichner, K., & Hoeft, K. (1996). Teacher socialization for cultural diversity. In J. Sikula (Ed.).*Handbook of research on teacher education* (pp. 525–547). New York: Macmillan LIBRARY Reference USA.

Chapter 15

Using a Multi-Linked Conceptual Framework to Promote Quality Learning in a Teacher Education Program

Garry F. Hoban
University of Wollongong, Australia

> Deliberation about worthwhile goals and appropriate means must be an ongoing activity in the teacher education community. These deliberations would be aided by a conceptual framework that identifies central tasks of teacher preparation, those core activities that logically and practically belong to the preservice phase of learning to teach.
>
> (Feiman-Nemser, 1990, p. 227)

The purpose of this final chapter is to bring together ideas from the previous four parts of this book into a complete multi-linked conceptual framework to guide teacher education design. As explained in Chapter 1, a conceptual framework is a vision or plan to guide the content of courses, approaches to teaching and learning, and relationships between schools and universities. It may also describe the type of teacher that the program is trying to develop.

When considering the quality of a teacher education program, a key question to ask is, "Does it have a conceptual framework and, if so, what is the basis of its structure?" In a conventional teacher education design, it is likely that different knowledge bases determine its structure with the intention that students apply these ideas on practicum during their school experiences. This step-by-step approach selects courses to promote different knowledge bases, allocates them in an order, places the practicum, and last of all allocates instructors to the courses. Such mechanistic thinking often produces an incoherent teacher education program with many elements acting in isolation to one other. Moreover, this fragmentation between courses and between university and school experiences inhibits sustained engagement by students and hence the quality of learning. Such an approach is underpinned by an assumption (more fully discussed in Chapter 1) that the nature of teaching is simplistic and that teachers can learn about the profession or be "trained" using a bit-by-bit mechanistic approach. This is like trying to build a fire by putting one stick on at a time; but there is a lack of critical mass to get it started and keep it going.

G. Hoban (ed.), The Missing Links in Teacher Education Design, 281–291.

There are now increasing numbers of different conceptual frameworks to guide teacher education design. A "google search" on the World Wide Web using the term "conceptual framework" identifies over 200 different examples. Many have a clear conceptual framework and are underpinned by current research into teacher education. The components of these frameworks are described using terms such as "themes," "competencies," "outcomes," and "accomplished practices" usually in the form of a list of desirable principles or characteristics of teachers. Some of the principles include terms like "diversity', "developing in-depth knowledge", "developing content or pedagogical content knowledge", "reflective practitioners," "community of learners", "cultural diversity", "nurturing leadership", "educational leaders", "competent researchers", "constructivist", "culturally sensitive", "lifelong learners", "values history", "collaboration", "authentic inquiry", "technology literate", "knowledgeable", "nature of knowledge", "think critically", "make ethical decisions", "change agents", "pedagogy", "coherence", "caring", "communication" and "professionalism". Many of the explanations of these conceptual frameworks also highlight the importance of "coherence" inferring that the components of the conceptual framework should relate to each other to be synergistic and create a dynamic interplay between them.

The principles or themes used in these conceptual frameworks displayed on the World Wide Web have educational merit, however, most relate to the *goals* of teacher education in terms of the type of teacher they would like to produce. Although this does provide a guide for teacher education design, it often lacks details about *how* such a teacher is to be developed. Also, listing these goals of teacher education as independent elements may not be the best way to ensure coherence in the design of a teacher education program. For instance, it is possible that courses are designed to address these principles independently which does not promote coherence and connectedness between them. In some cases, there is even a trap of falling back into conventional mechanistic ways of thinking, particularly if the themes or principles are still treated as a "list" to be addressed one by one.

The conceptual framework promoted in this book is different. In addition to identifying the *goals* of teacher education in terms of desirable principles or characteristics of a teacher, the multi-linked conceptual framework also identifies *structures* to develop such a teacher which are the nominated links. These links with ideas distilled from relevant chapters is shown in the complete multi-linked conceptual framework in Figure 15.1.

The conceptual framework in Figure 15.1 includes the desirable characteristics of a beginning teacher and refers to the necessary structures that are likely to develop such characteristics. These structures are embedded in the university courses, the relationship with schools and the identity of teacher

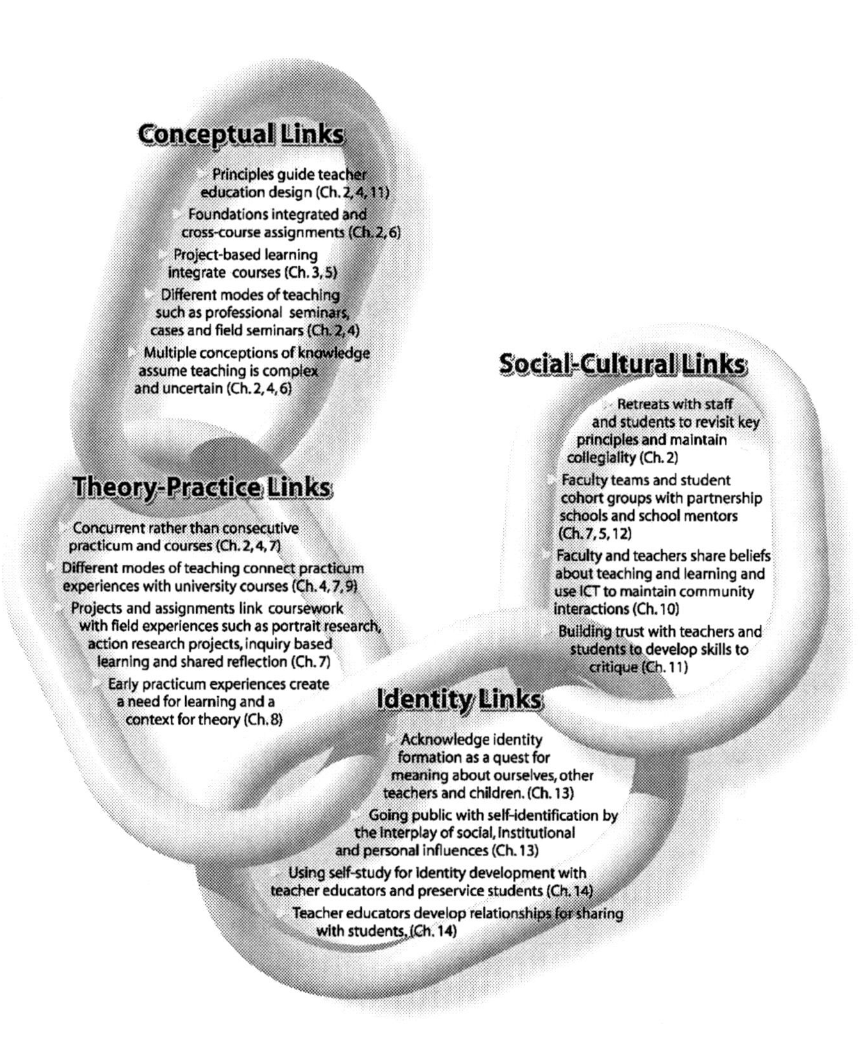

Figure 15.1. A multi-linked conceptual framework for teacher education design.

educators that are needed to develop such characteristics. For example, having strong conceptual links across the university curriculum such as courses that are related via common themes, common assignments or project-based learning increases the likelihood that students will develop appropriate characteristics or principles such as "content knowledge" and "think critically".

Moreover, if there is a reciprocal relationship between school and university settings that encourages mutual research suggests that student teachers are more likely to develop skills for the principles of "authentic inquiry" and become "lifelong learners" of teaching. Importantly, if there is agreement by instructors that there are multiple conceptions of knowledge and that teaching is by nature complex and uncertain implies that student teachers are more likely to become "reflective practitioners". If teacher educators use and model self-study (Loughran, Hamilton, LaBoskey, & Russell, 2004) to promote identity formation within a collaborative community implies that student teachers are more likely to understand the importance of building trust and working as a "community of practice". Also, the likelihood of having the components or elements of a teacher education program complement each other to develop coherence is increased because the framework begins with the links, not independent elements. Focusing on links across the program design and not independent elements means that the design features of the program are considered concurrently, not consecutively.

In this book the ideas to address the four nominated links in teacher education design—conceptual links, social-cultural links, personal links and theory-practice links—have been distilled from existing innovative programs. These links attempt to collectively address the problems or issues of conventional teacher education designs identified by Tom (1997) and Korthagen (2003). Addressing these issues not only identifies important goals and structures of a teacher education program but should also ensure a coherent teacher education program to portray the interrelated nature of teaching and encourage learning that is sustainable and dynamic.

Using the multi-linked conceptual framework means taking into consideration how courses relate to each other *and* how the practicum relates to the courses *and* who the best people are to teach the subjects *and* how to keep them all socially connected. This last point is very important because a teacher education program is not a static entity. Even after it has been designed and implemented, its structure still changes because teacher education faculties and schools are constantly evolving. Hence, it is especially important for those involved in teacher education (teachers, teacher educators and students) to "keep the conversation going" and manage the design of the program in light of ongoing change.

There are many ways to implement a multi-linked conceptual framework. However, what is key is to develop coherence in the design such that the components or elements relate to each other. Program designers can use the existing identified key features or deduce their own to suit their particular context. Importantly, decisions made early in the planning process have implications for the type of program that results. The main message of this book, therefore, is that these decisions need to be based on multiple considerations or "links" to increase the likelihood that teacher education programming is internally coherent amongst the courses and externally coherent to other settings. Coherence is important because it promotes quality learning by preservice teachers as well as creating possibilities for developing a conception of teaching as a complex profession.

"DYNAMIC LEARNING" vs. "DISCONNECTED LEARNING" IN A TEACHER EDUCATION PROGRAM

The two main purposes of a teacher education design should be to promote quality learning by students and to prepare them for coping with the complex nature of the profession. A brief discussion of the nature of knowledge will assist in understanding these goals. From an epistemological viewpoint, knowledge is a "justified true belief" (Gettier, 1963) such that the process of generating knowledge requires individuals to examine their beliefs in light of evidence to "justify" or confirm beliefs to knowledge. It is the justification of beliefs to knowledge involving others within a community that makes this knowledge "true" for a particular context (Longino, 1993). Alternatively, evidence can be used to disconfirm beliefs to seek better explanations for phenomena in a particular context.

Not surprisingly, most preservice students have beliefs about teaching before they start their program. These initial beliefs have been called students' "apprenticeship-of-observation" (Lortie, 1975, p. 61) and have been generated from their own experiences as students in school. Although these beliefs are strongly held, they are often at an emotional level and are not analytical about the quality of teaching:

> The student's learning about teaching, gained from a limited vantage point and relying heavily on imagination, is not like that of an apprentice and does not represent acquisition of the occupation's technical knowledge. It is more a matter of imitation, which, being generalized across individuals, becomes tradition. It is a potentially powerful influence which transcends generations, but the conditions of transfer do not favour informed criticism, attention to specifics, or explicit rules of assessment. (Lortie, 1975, p. 63)

Hopefully, these beliefs are acknowledged, built upon and modified in a teacher education program. A key focus of a program, therefore, should be to help students make explicit their beliefs and to confirm and disconfirm them with educational theory and experiences in schools. Korthagen (2001) has argued for a similar process in which students' beliefs should be made clear (their episteme) and then confirmed or disconfirmed using educational theory (their phronesis). Learning about teaching in this way is consistent with a constructivist approach to learning (von Glasersfeld, 1989) that values the prior knowledge or beliefs of individuals. When beliefs are confirmed with evidence, then knowledge is generated. If this knowledge is local and relevant to a particular school setting, then the outcome is practical knowledge. If, however, this knowledge is generalisable to other school settings, then the outcome is formal knowledge (Fenstermacher, 1994). In order for preservice students to engage in a process of sustained knowledge-building (Bereiter & Scardamalia, 1993), the elements of a program need to have some relevance to each other so that the students can compare and contrast ideas generated in different settings.

When university courses complement one another and there is a relationship between university and school settings, students are able to *learn dynamically* through an iterative knowledge-building process. This means using multiple sources for learning by reflecting upon personal beliefs, confirming or disconfirming beliefs to knowledge using evidence generated in different settings and shared within a community. When university courses have a common link as well as a relationship between university and school settings, students can learn dynamically and generate a much deeper understanding of concepts. However, possibilities for this type of dynamic learning are only encouraged if preservice teachers experience a coherent program structure and are assisted in making their own connections to build their own knowledge about key concepts from course to course and from setting to setting.

Importantly, there should be a reciprocal relationship between university and school settings. Students can confirm and disconfirm theory promoted by university courses in the action setting of a school. Similarly, beliefs generated in school settings can be confirmed or disconfirmed in university courses as long as there is a flexible curriculum as explained in Chapter 8. As such, insights generated in a school setting can be used as part of the curriculum in university courses which uses educational theory as evidence to confirm or disconfirm beliefs generated in school settings. This is not to say that insights from a university course must equate with what preservice teachers learn in a school setting. However, if there is some congruency between the school and university settings, it will promote students reflecting upon their experiences to confirm or disconfirm beliefs. The consequence is that insights generated from experiences in either a school or university setting establish a dynamic relationship and is more likely to lead to the generation of knowledge. In short, preservice teachers will generate knowledge from a particular belief about education because it has been justified as "true" or "untrue" for them a particular setting.

For example, preservice teachers may discuss their own beliefs about literacy learned in an English course that has been generated from their own schooling. A formal theory of literacy teaching may then be presented to students in university courses to compare and contrast with their own beliefs. The same theories may also be discussed in an English method class as well as strategies for teaching which may lead to the confirmation or disconfirmation of the original beliefs. It is then important to compare these beliefs/knowledge with those views from practicing teachers in school and to "try out" the theories in a classroom (or preferably different classrooms). Preservice teachers may even reflect upon why particular theories do not work in all settings. As such, reflection upon school and university experiences becomes iterative with one source informing or disconfirming the other.

But sometimes personal reflection alone is not enough. Fendler (2003) recently critiqued the notion of reflection stating that both Dewey's scientifically rational approach to reflection and Schön's intuitive approach are limited by a person's existing ways of thinking. For example, it is common to encourage preservice teachers to write reflective journals or autobiographical narratives, however; these are often "confessional" and can reinforce existing practices:

> When the device of autobiographical narrative is considered together with the technique of self-disclosure in journal writing, the combination functions to construct the idea of teachers as a people who repeatedly confess and affirm their identity in terms of categories that reflect existing popular assumptions. This construction is a technology of the self tends to perpetuate the status quo because the autobiographical markers are based on stereotypes and the conventions of what constitutes an autobiography are historically constructed. (Fendler, 2003, p. 23)

She concluded that reflection may sometimes be an undesirable practice on its own because it involves "circular ways of thinking" to reinforce existing views on pedagogy, race, gender or class. Hence, reflection is sometimes a conundrum because it is "disciplined by the very social practices and relations that the reflective process is suppose to critique" (Fendler, 2003, p. 21).

This is why multiple perspectives about teaching, which may result in conflict or disagreement, are welcomed as explained in Chapter 5. Moreover, insights about teaching can be gained from using different modes of teaching such as using case studies, action research in schools, professional inquiry seminars and lectures as explained in Chapters 3 and 4. When this injection of new ideas occurs, the "valid information makes dilemmas recognizable, which creates tension to resolve them" (Argyris & Schön, 1974, p. 97). Huberman (1995) called these new ideas, which are introduced into community discussions, "conceptual inputs". If these ideas are also shared with other preservice students in a group it brings more validity to the process as ideas are openly presented, critiqued, tested and made public. The eventual outcome of justifying beliefs that are true for certain contexts is knowledge about literacy teaching that has been generated from an iterative process of making personal beliefs explicit, comparing these to educational theory, making them public within a group, testing them out in different school settings, discussing them with teachers and bringing these results back for discussion in university classes. Dynamic learning is not unlike Argyris & Schön's (1974) notion of "double-loop learning" which occurs in workplace settings where learning is sustained, iterative, and involves new ideas to challenge the "status quo" of conventional practice.

Importantly, educational theory plays a key role to provide new ideas that may not be evident in a particular school setting and to confirm and/or disconfirm personal beliefs. When preservice students learn "dynamically" it means that there is a sustained iterative process established amongst the elements of a teacher education program. Importantly, the learning is often nonlinear and messy because of the interplay among the multiple elements of a teacher education program. A learning environment, therefore, is created from more than just the sum of the elements; the connections between them are essential. For the elements to interrelate there needs to be a 'congruence' or 'fit' such that elements coalesce and reinforce one another. The basis of the knowledge-building process comes from the reciprocity amongst the elements such that the more reflective preservice teachers are, the more they contribute to course discussions, the more likely they are to compare their school experiences with insights from their university courses which will further enhance their reflection. The result is quality learning as they are building knowledge that is cumulative and continuous. It also means that preservice students use theory to test out in schools rather than accepting (or rejecting) it without question. Also, students may need to modify theories and work out what is missing or unique to particular settings. The outcome of such an approach is a deeper understanding of educational issues; equating to high quality learning for preservice teachers.

This type of sustained and dynamic learning, however, is difficult to establish in a "conventional" teacher education program. In such programs, students study teaching "bit-by-bit" in independent courses and there is often little chance to confirm or disconfirm theories in schools. Because there is often little relationship between courses at university and school settings, students cannot transfer their beliefs from course to course and are unlikely to build their own knowledge by comparing their insights with school experiences. Learning still occurs, but it is *disconnected learning* most likely resulting in a shallow understanding of the concepts being studied.

Often this is as a result of the many and varied assignments that students "have to" complete. For example, in a semester with four different university courses which have little connection, students may have three assignments for each course, resulting in up to 12 assignments/semester, each bearing little relationship to the other. Preservice students try to "deal with this" by attempting one assignment at a time creating a view that such programming is akin to "participating in a hurdles race". Students jump one hurdle (or assignment) at a time and then move onto the next. Unfortunately, by the time they get to the end of the one semester race, they have usually forgotten all about the initial assignments they attempted. This type of disconnected learning is exacerbated when students go on practicum with little relationship to the university courses that precede or follow it. As such the disconnected learning promoted by an incoherent teacher education program inevitably results in shallow or surface understanding of the particular concepts being studied. This is not to suggest that learning does not occur, rather, that it is shallow because it does not build upon what was learned before or is not encouraged to be continuous by revisiting key educational issues in different settings.

DEVELOPING A CONCEPTION OF TEACHING AS A COMPLEX PROFESSION

Engaging preservice students in dynamic learning using both university and school settings as contexts for knowledge-building shows students that teaching is not simplistic. Moreover, knowledge is rarely generalisable for all contexts. It shows that educational ideas are not set in concrete but are fluid according to the type of children, school, resources and curriculum. One of the most important ideas for preservice teachers to understand is that there are no simple prescriptions for teaching children in schools. Although lesson plans are important to develop, it is naive to assume that they will be implemented exactly as planned because preservice teachers (like all teachers) need to be flexible to the moment and the type of children. Importantly, preservice teachers need to understand is that what may be "true" for one setting may not be "true" for another. For example, any teacher who has taught the same lesson to two different classes knows that the lesson has unfolded in different ways because of the different contexts. Hence, lesson planning, although important, should not be viewed as a preordained formula for completion or success. The planning is what matters, not a dogged adherence to it.

For preservice teachers to develop an understanding of the complex nature of their profession necessitates a more comprehensive approach to designing teacher education programs than the simplistic "application of knowledge" approach. Wideen, Mayer-Smith, and Moon (1998) emphasized that there needs to be many perspectives involved in teacher education design to bring out this complexity, "we believe that only when all players and landscapes that comprise the learning-to-teach environment are considered in concert will we gain a full appreciation of the inseparable web of relationships that constitutes the learning-to-teach ecosystem" (p. 170).

Developing an understanding of the complex nature of teaching is *why* a teacher education program needs to be coherent. If it is reasonable to assert that teaching is a complex profession, then we need an approach to designing teacher education programs that "educates" preservice teachers in the complexity of teaching as well as taking into account the different social-cultural contexts of university and the schools. This does not mean that there is a "one-size-fits-all" best model of teacher education—this does not exist. In fact, there are many different kinds of teacher education models that evolve in light of contextual influences such as the resources, types of students, schools and needs. However, using a multi-linked conceptual framework to guide teacher education design, I would argue, will help preservice teachers "learn dynamically" and embrace teaching as a complex profession. Having such a conception means that preservice students will likely perceive teaching as an "ongoing inquiry" that cannot be "mastered" but can always be improved. As is continually demonstrated in the literature such a mindset sustains teachers through the highs and lows of their career and helps them to engage and enjoy their pursuit (Hoban, 2002).

CONCLUSION

In this book I have promoted the use of four links—conceptual links, social-cultural links, personal links and theory-practice links—as lenses for proposing a conceptual framework to guide teacher education design. There are, however, other influences such as government policies, resources and pressures from interest groups that are beyond what is possible to fully incorporate in the scope of this book. These other influences may well establish other "missing links". But the key point is that coherence counts to improve the quality of teacher education. However, it is a rare occasion that a program is designed from scratch as the large majority of programs have been in existence for many years and are adapted over time. If a program cannot have a complete redesign, it is important for instructors to make their subjects as coherent as possible. Loughran's Chapter 11 shows how a fundamental aspect of good teaching—learning to accept and provide critique can be accomplished within one subject is one way of establishing coherence within existing programs.

It is fitting that the two chapters in Part 4 focus on identity formation of teacher educators and preservice teachers. These two chapters delve into the deep philosophies underpinning teaching and highlight the often unspoken aspect of the identity of who teaches teachers. It seems reasonable to assert that unless teacher educators consider their own moral commitment to teaching as part of their identity formation, there is little hope that the quality of teacher education will be at the forefront of their thinking. Moreover, commencing a process of identity formation for teacher educators may well be the catalyst to create a need to redesign an existing teacher education program.

Finally, of the four main links described in detail in this book, I do not suggest that each has the same influence on program coherence. I see social-cultural links as most important because these have such a strong influence on the other three. It is the social and cultural connections amongst teacher educators, student teachers and teachers that impact on their own identity formation. It also determines how well key ideas or themes are shared between university and school participants and how teacher educators might work creatively as a team in program design. Furthermore, it is the social interaction between the participants that enables a program design to be dynamic and change according to relevant cultural or political needs. I have little doubt that relationships and communication amongst all participants are the heart and mind of a coherent teacher education program.

REFERENCES

Argyris, C., & Schön, D. A. (1974). *Theory in practice: Increasing professional effectiveness.* San Francisco: Jossey-Bass.

Bereiter, C., & Scardamalia, M. (1993). *Surpassing ourselves: An inquiry into the nature and implications of expertise*. Chicago, IL: Open Court.

Feiman-Nemser, S. (1990). Teacher preparation: Structural and conceptual alternatives. In W. R. Houston (Ed.), *Handbook of Research on Teacher Education* (pp. 212–233). New York: Macmillan.

Fendler, L. (2003). Teacher reflection in a hall of mirrors: Historical influences and political reverberations. *Educational Researcher, 32*(3), 16–25.

Fenstermacher, G. D. (1994). The knower and the known: The nature of knowledge in research on teaching. In L. Darling-Hammond (Ed.), *Review of Research in Education* (pp. 3–56). Washington, DC: American Educational Research Association.

Gettier, E. J. (1963). Is justified true belief knowledge? *Analysis, 23*, 121–123.

Huberman, M. (1995). Networks that alter teaching. *Teaching and Teaching; Theory and Practice, 1*(2), 193–221.

Korthagen, F. (2003, April). *Professional Development for Teacher Educators.* Paper presented at the Annual Meeting of the American Educational Research Association, Chicago.

Korthagen, F. A. (2001). *Linking practice and theory: The pedagogy of realistic teacher education.* Mahway, NJ: Lawrence Erlbaum Associates.

Longino, H. E. (1993). Subjects, power, and knowledge: Description and prescription in feminist philosophies of science. In L. Alcoff & E. Potter (Eds.), *Feminist Epistemologies* (pp. 101–121). New York: Routledge.

Loughran, J.J., Hamilton, M.L, Kubler LaBoskey, V., & Russell, T. (Eds.) (2004). *International handbook of self-study of teaching and teacher education practices.* Dordrecht: Kluwer Academic Publishers.

Lortie, D. (1975). *Schoolteacher: A sociological study.* Chicago, IL: University of Chicago Press.

Tom, A. R. (1997). *Redesigning teacher education.* Albany, NY: State University of New York.

von Glasersfeld, E. (1989). Constructivism. In T. Husen & T. N. Postlewaite (Eds.), *The International Encyclopedia of Education* (pp. 162–173). Oxford: Pergamon.

Wideen, M., Mayer-Smith, J., & Moon, B. (1998). A critical analysis of the research on learning to teach: Making the case for an ecological perspective on inquiry. *Review of Educational Research, 68*(2), 130–178.

Index

Printed in the United States
50930LVS00001BA/96